Praise for *Good Comes First*

"*Good Comes First* is an essential tool for building organizations where trust and transparency are constant, and teamwork and respect are contagious. Firsthand, I saw the *Good Comes First* approach create a powerful cultural transformation when I was President at World Kitchen. In my CEO, Home Solutions role at Newell Brands, I continue to use these principles to drive employee engagement, satisfaction, and business growth. If you lead a team, you must read this book!"
  —Kris Malkoski, CEO, Home Solutions, Newell Brands

"A foundational element of the WD-40 Company tribal culture was formalizing our values. The most impactful element, though, is holding everyone accountable for modeling our values and behaviors daily. *Good Comes First* maps out a path to success for both elements."
  —Garry Ridge, Chairman & CEO WD-40 Company

"Culture has almost become a buzzword. And yet, for business leaders, Chris and Mark have created a practical field guide for creating a meaningful, deeply human company culture. *Good Comes First* is a must-read!"
  —Tamara McCleary, CEO, Thulium

"I have always led with the belief that People with Passion drive Performance. Too many companies believe 'performance' is the input when the real input is 'people' within a great culture. Chris and Mark's *Good Comes First* outlines detailed steps on how to bring a contagious culture to your company and truly create a differentiating model where respect is valued as high as results."
  —Joel D. Anderson, President/CEO of Five Below, Inc.

GOOD
COMES
FIRST

GOOD
COMES
FIRST

HOW TODAY'S LEADERS CREATE AN UNCOMPROMISING COMPANY CULTURE THAT DOESN'T SUCK

S. Chris Edmonds and **Mark S. Babbitt**

Foreword by Venus Williams

Matt Holt Books
An Imprint of BenBella Books, Inc.
Dallas, TX

BenBella Books, Inc.
10440 N. Central Expressway
Suite 800
Dallas, TX 75231
benbellabooks.com
Send feedback to feedback@benbellabooks.com

BenBella and *Matt Holt* are federally registered trademarks.

Printed in the United States of America
10 9 8 7 6 5 4 3 2 1

Library of Congress Control Number: 2021938098
ISBN 9781953295651
eISBN 9781953295996

Editing by Rachel Phares, Alyn Wallace, David Ellis, and Ellen M. Babbitt
Copyediting by Michael Fedison
Proofreading by Jenny Bridges and Sarah Vostok
Indexing by Amy Murphy
Text design and composition by PerfecType, Nashville, TN
Cover design by Paul McCarthy
Cover image © Shutterstock/Blan-k
Printed by Lake Book Manufacturing

S. Chris Edmonds

I'm indebted to my wife, Diane, and my family for keeping
me on track with coaching, humor, and love.

My mother, Mary Jaene Edmonds, was the first author in the
family. I believe she's smiling upon my efforts from above.

I'm grateful for the partnership and friendship of my
colleague and coauthor, Mark Babbitt. Mark's insight, clarity,
and passion have made my life and business richer.

I'm thankful for my clients, who accept my coaching (and prodding
and pushing) with grace and enthusiasm as we work together to
create uncompromising work cultures where good comes first.

Mark S. Babbitt

To my wife, Deb: I know I'm lucky to have you—your love
keeps the lights on. Thank you for tolerating my attempt
to make a difference while still trying to grow up.

To my kids—TJ, Ryan, Katlin, Lindsay, and JW: We may not be
together as much as I once imagined, but you're in my heart. And
to my grandchildren—AJ, Posey, Kaiden, Bodie, and Kinsley:
My only hope is that you'll always think Grandpa is funny.

To my mother, Ellen: You always believed in my ability to
put words to paper—and I'm forever in your debt.

And to my coauthor, Chris: You brought a sense of
balance first to my life, then my work—and now my
words. I'm forever grateful for your friendship.

Finally, to those leaders and coaches who inspired this book: From
the great mentors to those who helped mold my thoughts and work
in their own ways, my experiences with you helped me realize that
good must come first—especially now. And to those who have worked
with me and for me all these years—from the baseball fields to the
start-up incubators to the corporate boardrooms—I thank you.

CONTENTS

SECTION I:

PURPOSE AND PRINCIPLES: WHY A GOOD COMES FIRST CULTURE?

SECTION II:

TACTICAL & PRACTICAL: HOW TO DEFINE, ALIGN, AND REFINE YOUR CULTURE

SECTION III:
ACTIONABLE INSPIRATION: BUILDING YOUR CULTURE FROM THE INSIDE OUT

FOREWORD

by Venus Williams

People know me as a tennis player—four Olympic gold medals, twenty-three Grand Slam titles, and a world No. 1 ranking. But I'm more than just a tennis player. My world is bigger than that.

I'm also an aunt who loves her niece very much, a *New York Times* best-selling author, an owner of the NFL's Miami Dolphins, and a vocal advocate for equality and diversity. For nearly twenty years, I've also been an entrepreneur. As a business owner, I'm ultimately responsible for results. I also feel responsible, at least in part, for the livelihoods and happiness of the people who work with me and for me.

That deep feeling of responsibility—the same one you feel as a business leader—is how I came to know the authors of the book you have in your hands now, *Good Comes First*.

In 2018, I read *The Culture Engine* by S. Chris Edmonds. I immediately understood that the cultures of my two companies—as successful as we had been—weren't created intentionally. Just as important, I learned those cultures weren't always positive or productive—and they weren't always purposeful. After reading Chris's book, what really struck me was that my company and my team didn't fully understand our company's values—and perhaps mine.

As the CEO of both companies, I realized I was solely responsible for building the company cultures I had imagined as an entrepreneur. I also realized I didn't know everything about building a values-driven company culture. The fact was, I didn't know how to articulate our values so every member of my teams would understand, and *believe*, so much that they would embrace and model those values. Not only when I was physically in the office, but always.

Knowing my organizations needed more polish, and everyone needed to know what we were aiming for, and what we should rally around, I took a big step with V Starr, my interior design firm. I brought Chris in to help me create a positive and purposeful company culture where good consistently comes first—and respect is expected as much as results. I wanted to give my team that greater purpose—to be that company where you know why you're there and what you're working toward.

Precisely as outlined so well here in *Good Comes First*, we jumped right in. Chris helped our senior leaders immediately begin creating our Organizational Constitution for V Starr by formalizing our company's servant purpose, then brainstorming and defining our values. My team, including some of the smartest people I've ever met, signed on. They completely embraced the process you're about to begin—to them, it was a complete no-brainer. They knew this change would make a better workplace for them. Soon, instead of asking, "What does this mean?" they were excitedly asking, "What's next?"

Within a few days, after seeing the clarity of our values and the benefits for my V Starr team members, I asked Chris to do the same work for my second company, activewear by EleVen. Again, the process was straightforward, starting with defining our company's servant purpose and the team's values and behaviors. Soon, we had built the foundation for an intentional, purposeful company culture. Our work, at first a sprint as we completed our Organizational Constitution and then more of a marathon as we began living our values, continues.

And the benefits to our team members continue to become more apparent. Now we model, coach, monitor, and celebrate our defined values daily. Not only has this impacted our businesses considerably, but I also credit the good work we've done for helping us weather the economic downturn caused by the pandemic.

As I write this foreword, I don't want to give you the impression that everything went perfectly for everyone. Change is hard. Initiating change is hard work. It took about a year for some players to realize they weren't a solid fit for our new culture and the increased level of accountability. For others, this culture refinement represented too much change. And some realized they weren't aligned well with our defined values.

Of course, we want to see every team member do well. But it's my philosophy that sometimes we need to let people do well elsewhere. That's the kindness of this culture system; it allows people to know that even if they can't succeed here, we still want them to find success.

As you engage in this culture change process, some people will leave. Heartache and hard feelings are often part of people leaving. But those who remain at our companies are wholly aligned with our desired culture. They are better leaders and contributors. They ensure good comes first. So, in that way, it wasn't like we lost anyone. As a team, we are all now driven by the same purpose—making us much more productive.

Even better, when we bring on a new team member, it's exciting! We sit them down and say, "Hey, we are a culture-driven company. That uncompromising culture comes first. Good comes first! So here is our servant purpose. Here are the values we expect you to model." From orientation on, we talk about who we are, our culture, and how we behave while supporting that culture.

It's important to note that the people we hire, in large part, have personal values that align with our company values. Our culture appeals to them; our collective servant purpose inspires them. That's exciting for people! People want to know what we as leaders and employers expect of them, how they can contribute, and how they can serve others. They want to know what they're working for, besides a paycheck. Even as we diversify our team and product lines, this singular focus inspires us to be a better team—and a better company.

Look, this is a scary time for many businesses. And not just because of the once-a-century pandemic. While political leaders too often draw self-serving lines in the sand, many of us business leaders deal with in-your-face issues like social unrest, blatant inequalities, climate change, and—yes—business failure amid economic upheaval. So many of us, for so long, have wondered how we will survive.

But there is light. There is a way out of these scary times. At my companies, that light—and some needed reassurance—came in the form of defining and living our values. Even during the scariest times, we leaned into the culture we created together. Now, we're off and running. And we know we're going in the right direction.

As a fellow business leader, I encourage you to take in every word Chris and Mark have written here in *Good Comes First*. More importantly, I challenge you to take on the role of change champion as you begin redefining your company culture and make the demonstration of respect as important as achieving results. The task before you isn't easy. You'll occasionally grow weary of being a perpetual role model. Along the way, you'll lose people you always considered loyal; you might even consider them friends.

But in the end, the journey is so worth the effort. Because what you gain are leaders and team members—fully engaged, fully contributing, and fully serving within your intentional workplace every day.

You've taken a bold step by picking up this book. Now, you must do what's best for yourself, your fellow leaders, your employees, and your company.

You must put good first.

INTRODUCTION

Welcome to a Working World
Where Good Comes First

We thank you for picking up this book!

By reading and applying the concepts found within these pages, you soon will be ready to build a Good Comes First work culture—in other words, a work culture that is purposeful, positive, and productive.

But before we dive in, there is something you should know: We did not write *Good Comes First* to tell you "why" your company should consider creating a workplace that doesn't suck. We did not write the book only to help you learn "how" to build an uncompromising work culture.

As authors, our servant purpose—our reason for being within these pages—is to take you, our reader, beyond a simple understanding of the elements that lead to an effective work culture. Instead, we wrote this book to present proven and actionable strategies that—when implemented in collaboration with your work teams—create a work culture that ensures good comes first for employees, customers, leaders, and stakeholders.

In other words, this book—based on your authors' fifty combined years of experience in driving sustainable and impactful organizational change—will help you actually *do* it.

Our greatest satisfaction will come when you, in your organization, apply the concepts in this book to make *respect* as important as *results*.

Because you have opened this book, chances are—even though your organization may excel in many other areas—your work culture is not always one that makes people feel valued or respected. Chances are your work environment is not inspiring, or driven by purpose, or compassionate or fun or productive. Your culture may not be as competitive as you would like. Or perhaps you would like to see more business wins, or would like your leadership team to be more purpose-driven.

You see these cultural shortcomings firsthand—and you know your company can do, and be, better. You want your company to become a better place to work, and one that produces better results. But you do not know where to start. Without tearing apart existing operations, you do not know how to change your work culture.

Not knowing how is okay—for now.

The fact is that no one taught us how to proactively manage a work culture that values respect and results equally—in other words, a work culture that puts good first. We did not learn that skill in business school. Our bosses did not know how to do it, nor did our mentors or predecessors. Until recently, chances are no one ever asked you to manage company culture actively—and perhaps you never thought it necessary. But today, that approach to company culture is decidedly outdated. Since Social Age thinking replaced Industrial Age "best" practices, how we think about company culture has changed significantly.

Because now, as we are all learning, culture change is often needed before our company can realize its full potential. Before we start to see the business-focused results we expect and perhaps promised stakeholders and shareholders, it is required. And culture change is undoubtedly needed before we can attract, retain, and celebrate talented, engaged players—the top-tier players necessary to help your company excel.

That is where this book comes in. Step-by-step, we give you the tools needed to build and sustain a Good Comes First work culture—a purposeful, positive, and productive culture for every team leader and team member, in every interaction, every day.

As we go through these steps, you will benefit from the been-there-done-that experience of leaders who have already built uncompromising company cultures. We will show you where potential barriers to success hide—and how to push through them. We will point out which areas are most likely to cause frustration. And we will illuminate those moments when you will feel the most satisfaction and gain the most traction.

As a leader, you already know most change efforts stall or fail, so you are aware that culture change is not easy. But after reading this book, you will see that, done right, change is not just possible . . . change is practical, powerful, and well worth the effort. And you will be the right person, at the right time, to make that change happen.

HOW THIS BOOK IS ORGANIZED

The three sections of *Good Comes First* are a proven pathway for senior leaders to create and sustain a healthy, vibrant, productive work culture. You will learn why a Good Comes First culture is an essential part of a successful company, and how to implement a cultural change—no matter how intimidating a change process may seem. We will share our hard-won tools and advice—which come from decades of personal experience with our own companies and working closely with others. Soon, you will feel well equipped for the journey.

Section I outlines the steps required to lay the foundation for a solid culture change initiative. These first five chapters introduce the Good Comes First model (as well as, notably, defining what "good" means). We present insightful research that supports the model. And we outline the vital role senior leaders play in modeling and coaching their Good Comes First culture daily. By closely examining the precedent set by companies that place good first—and those that do not—you will come to understand exactly how a culture that puts good first benefits your employees, customers, communities—and your bottom line.

Section II guides you through the logistics of the entire change process itself, starting with step-by-step directions for creating an effective Organizational Constitution. As you will learn in these six chapters, your Organizational

Constitution is a formal statement that includes your company's servant purpose, defined values and desired behaviors, and strategies and goals. More important, it becomes the core of your defined Good Comes First culture.

By the end of this section, you will understand the importance of aligning your company's plans, decisions, and actions to your defined culture. And crucially, you will know how to collect the relevant and objective data from within your organization required to change your work culture for the better.

Section III focuses on building a Good Comes First culture from the inside out. The three chapters in this section describe the leadership qualities you will need to drive and sustain a culture change. This third section then discusses how hiring and team building must be grounded in your Organizational Constitution, so every member of your company models and expects a shared set of values. Finally, we walk you through exactly how to reboot your current working environment—no matter where it stands now—toward a Good Comes First culture, and how to get your team on board.

Before you turn the page to begin Chapter 1, get ready to take detailed notes in real time. Throughout this book, we will ask you to articulate—in writing—insights into your organization's operating model, work culture, and more. We will also ask you to craft—again, in writing—the elements that will become the foundation of your new work culture.

This is not just another business book you read, then never think about again. This book is a *call to action*. This book is part work plan and part manifesto. In the end, this book serves as a powerful guide to what is possible. You will see how creating a Good Comes First culture will improve your employees' satisfaction and your company's success—and why the two go hand in hand. You will see how this change must start with *you*, dear leader. You will also see you are not in this alone, and that we will equip you with the tools to initiate real change.

If this sounds too good to be true right now, we get it. But we are confident that by the end of this book, you will realize that a Good Comes First culture is not at all too good to be true—that these changes are well within reach, and well worth the effort.

Ready to lead a company or team that inspires good people to do good work in a good place to work?

Let's get started!

SECTION I

Purpose and Principles: Why a Good Comes First Culture?

 **CHAPTER 1**

Good Comes First:
A Business Imperative in
the Future of Work

Before the Industrial Age took many workers from farms to factories, human beings gained a sense of fulfillment by putting food on the table. Not just their own tables, but the tables of extended family, friends, neighbors, and even rivals. That was how they lived—and survived. By way of a mutually beneficial barter system, nearly everyone needed to work well with everyone else. There was a sense of community and belonging borne from those reciprocal relationships.

As the second Industrial Revolution matured in the early 1900s, a different kind of barter system evolved: Skilled laborers traded work-hours for dollars. The best companies treated their workers well, but too many organizations did not. Over time, the relationship between bosses and workers became patriarchal—perhaps even dictatorial. Managers and owners told employees what to do. Employees did what employers said. While often trying to outdo each other to earn more work, employees developed an ultra-competitive environment. The "every man for himself" era had begun, which formed the basis of the toxic, bottom-line-obsessed work-place culture we know today.

After every pay period, those workers cashed their checks and paid their bills. For many, the work itself had no other purpose except to make money—to make living possible. To keep their jobs, employees worked hard—sometimes enduring deplorable working conditions while perform-ing labor-intensive, monotonous tasks—all while tolerating one-sided rela-tionships with autocratic bosses.

The rules of this newly industrialized working world were clear: Do the work. Don't complain. Go home. Do it again tomorrow. Do that enough times over enough years and earn a little praise along the way, and the bosses would reward you with an awkward retirement party and a gold watch.

For our grandparents and parents, this was the American Dream. From the lumber mills in Oregon to the streets of Tampa, Florida, people mea-sured entire generations by the ability to get and keep a "good" job. Initially judged by the quality of the roof over their families' heads, then by the type of car in the driveway, they did their best to keep up. And always, in good times and bad, putting food on the table served as the ultimate measurement of success—as it had for their mothers and fathers before them.

To members of these older generations, the words "fulfilling," "inspir-ing," and "happy" were rarely used to describe work. Work was work. Trading work-hours for money was enough. For many, that is all there was. Many could not imagine anything more.

A SPARK OF RESISTANCE—A RAY OF HOPE

Then, just a few decades ago, a hint of resistance sparked a fire in the work-force. Baby boomers replaced members of the Greatest Generation in fac-tories, mills, and offices. After growing tired of one-sided relationships with bosses, many joined labor unions. Soon, they came to expect more from employers. While the relationship between worker and boss remained patriarchal, employees exerted more influence in their workplaces. Better working conditions followed. More people had the opportunity to excel. And especially at better companies, more voices became heard.

Starting in the 1980s, improving working conditions, better relationships with bosses, and increasing compensation made work more tolerable. But for the best employees, that still was not enough—how employers treated people also mattered. Soon, the work itself again shifted significantly. Manufacturing and manual labor gave way to knowledge workers, meaning employers started paying people to *think*. And not just about the work itself: Thoughts turned to how, and for whom, people did the work. People wanted their work to matter—really matter. In the broader sense, workers wanted to help generate profits while improving their customers' lives and supporting the communities in which they worked and lived.

The relationship between boss and employee continued to evolve. In many ways, both workers' happiness and the team's productivity depended on the quality of the manager. Words like "leadership" and "teamwork" became workplace standards. And by the late 1990s, as employee satisfaction became a key topic of conversation, people talked about the importance of "employee engagement" and "company culture." It became increasingly clear that the effectiveness of the boss (and, ultimately, the quality of the company) correlated to higher employee satisfaction. Higher employee satisfaction meant more management merit badges, more milestones hit, and higher profits. So, in short order, the mandate for leaders became simple: to ensure people were content and productive, increase employee engagement, and improve company culture.

For the next three decades, organizations spent billions of dollars attempting to fine-tune company culture and increase employee engagement. They invested in all manner of manipulative employee surveys, ineffective engagement platforms, and often inadequate leadership training to improve their companies' cultures. Yet most of our workplaces and company cultures still sucked.

The data is undeniable:

- Fifty-seven percent of workers worldwide leave their job primarily due to a lousy relationship with their direct boss.[1]
- Ninety-eight percent of the employees interviewed over the past twenty years have experienced incivility or rudeness in the workplace.[2]

- Over 65 percent of employees across the globe are not engaged or are actively disengaged at work—a number that has not shifted significantly in three decades.[3]
- The respectful treatment of employees at all organizational levels occurs in only 38 percent of the global workplace.[4]
- As of 2020, a measly 26 percent of employees feel strongly valued at work—down from 31 percent in 2016.[5]

So, despite billions of dollars spent and the best of intentions, why haven't we made a meaningful dent in employee engagement? Over the last three or four decades, why did efforts to reinvent company culture and organizational climate mostly fail? Why do those efforts continue to fail today? And why is the workplace still considered a place where innovative thinking, enthusiastic participation, and employee validation go to die?

Because despite those billions of dollars and the best intentions, most change initiatives and engagement programs *do not work*! And they have not worked for a long time.

Then along comes pure upheaval to an already broken process: the COVID-19 crisis. The pandemic forced many companies (those not forced to close their doors, of course) to reevaluate their working conditions. Remote—and more autonomous—work became the norm. From Fisher Investments to Ford to Facebook, bosses and employees worked together to keep doors open while fighting a common enemy. But instead of company cultures improving, the active management of company culture took a back seat as companies functioned in constant reactive mode. Yes, many people enjoyed their work more—and for a time, they were more productive. But without boundaries and a purposeful company culture to lean on, many found themselves in freelancer mode: working more hours to get more work done. In the absence of culture norms, casual conversations, and the camaraderie often found in a shared office, many workers lost connection to company culture.

And as areas like New Zealand, Australia, and Japan started to get an upper hand on the COVID-19 crisis—in a trend sure to continue in areas late to limit the spread of the virus—the problem only got worse. After being given tremendous autonomy around when, where, and how they worked, employees were told to reintegrate into the old normal (even though, as you might recall, most of those "normal" work environments sucked). As employees started coming back to the office, it was like nothing had happened—as if employers said, "Yes, we gave you all that freedom. But now we are taking it back." The workplace—especially in primarily results-focused organizations—became even more challenging than it was pre-crisis.

After rallying around each other and genuinely feeling like part of the solution to the massive problems caused by a global viral challenge, employees felt a genuine sense of betrayal. Perhaps their work still mattered, but the respect and trust earned during the early days of the pandemic seemed quickly discarded. Those employees, in turn, rejected any effort to restore company-first or shareholder-first objectives.

They called out manipulative stories—no matter how masterfully spun—designed to make old business practices smell new. They noted when company culture, after being ignored for months, was suddenly important again. Ultimately, attuned employees saw reintegration efforts—just as they saw previous insincere culture change efforts—as more company- and shareholder-centric public relations than employee relations.

As many old-school leaders have already learned coming out of the virus era, a new approach to designing our workplaces—and specifically to building intentional company cultures—is now required. The Industrial Age tactics leaders relied upon for so long will no longer work.

That is where Good Comes First—a proven approach to building a positive, productive, and purposeful company culture that works today and tomorrow—comes into play.

Unlike past change initiatives, which focused primarily on vague mission statements designed to increase shareholder value through a relentless focus on results, our approach to culture transformation *works*. We know this because when leaders create and sustain a Good Comes First culture, their companies enjoy increases[6] in:

- Profits by 35 percent
- Productivity by 35 percent
- Customer satisfaction by 40 percent

- Employee engagement by 40 percent
- Retention of key employees by 100 percent
- Employee referrals up to 250 percent

The benefits of adopting a Good Comes First culture are clear. But what happens should leaders decide to revert to what they know—versus what they need to know—to improve their company's culture? Or attempt reintegration of employees now accustomed to working from home—and who have settled into a lifestyle that finally allows the balance of work and life—into a rigid, company-first business model already proven to be less than ideal? What happens when that culture is driven by leaders who rhetorically or literally say to their employees, "You're lucky to have a job. Take it or leave it"?

The leadership styles of those with these Industrial Age views lie in direct contrast to the personal values and priorities of Millennials—which will be the most dominant generation in the workforce for the next several decades. Gen Z, which demonstrates similar values and priorities, is coming right behind them. What drives these generations is the desire for meaningful work, to balance work with life, and a focus more on making a difference than making money. Together, they represent the most socially engaged—and outspoken—workforce the world has ever known.

These vocal employees expect companies and their leaders, now more than ever, to do what's right: to make respect—how they treat employees daily—as important as results.

RESPECT *AND* RESULTS

When organizations and their leaders place respect and results on the same pedestal—when they are modeled, monitored, measured, and celebrated equally—the expectations of employees, customers, and stakeholders organically change. The new expectation is that these companies will proactively serve their customers and communities well. Employees expect leaders of these companies to create and sustain work cultures that embrace diversity and equality, where everyone has a voice. In the form of respectful radical candor, they expect to hear the truth. Employees and contributors carefully choose to work for and with organizations and leaders who take a stand on global issues like homelessness, community service, and climate change. When a company earns a reputation for being a good place to work by equally valuing respect and results, it attracts employees who match its values—and a virtuous cycle develops.

Respect demands truth and trust. Truth and trust drive results. Results drive respect.

After witnessing a prolonged period of self-serving leaders, alternate facts, and fake news, we can't emphasize the truth aspect of this cycle enough. Employees now expect—and deserve—to hear the truth from their employers. In times when we do not know who to trust, trust within the workplace is essential. Yes, mistruths, mistrust, and disrespect—particularly on social and digital platforms—will remain rampant. Specific segments of society will continue to accept divisive behaviors and polarizing personalities as normal. But today's best employees will expect these good behaviors—truth, trust, and respect—from their employers. And business leaders must deliver.

As we have seen, the trouble is that even before the COVID-19 lockdowns, business practices were not keeping pace with the growing demand for respect (and truth and trust). Failure to adapt has created a chasm between what people *expect* from their work environment and what most employers *deliver*.

Gone are the days where a company's primary focus is shareholders' interests. Companies—and their leaders—are no longer measured exclusively by profits and market share. To remain competitive, companies must now invest in their employees while enabling a healthy work-life balance. They must provide real value that improves their customers' lives and nurture the supply chain by consistently dealing fairly with remote contributors, contractors, vendors, and partners. And the company's best interests do not stop there: Employees demand—and deserve—more traction from their workplaces on issues such as income inequality, diversity and inclusion, caring for their local communities, and climate change.

This shift toward treating people with dignity and respect comes at an inconvenient time for many business leaders. While being tasked with rallying around a post-pandemic vision for their companies, they feel stuck between the often bottom-line-oriented demands of their boards of directors and shareholders, and their employees' and customers' cultural desires. If these leaders do not find a mutually beneficial middle ground, their employees will go work for companies better aligned with their values, and for more inspirational leaders. Customers will move their allegiance to organizations that genuinely care about their communities. Industry influencers, emboldened in part by information about the company they can gain quickly online, will back a firm that shows a high level of social awareness.

And those business leaders who fail to adapt to new realities? They may need to update their resumes or retire—because a tsunami of change is coming right at us. As many more workplace complexities come into play, that wave will only gain strength. And it will seemingly target those leaders who stand their ground—and who fail to move to higher ground.

The post-pandemic workplace already exists in a new reality, one where business as usual . . . is unusual. So, we must adapt. To be competitive in the future of work, tomorrow's best leaders must:

- Define a work culture that puts good first, valuing respect as much as results
- Create a workplace where trust is contagious, validation is pervasive, and growth—both personal and professional—is constant
- Craft a servant purpose that ensures equitable treatment of all stakeholders (not just shareholders)
- Monitor, measure, and reward alignment to agreed-upon standards for behavior
- Be proactive in helping to resolve local and global issues such as inequality, poverty, health crises, and climate change

Yes, these are lofty goals. They are also the heart and soul of a Good Comes First culture, which we will learn much more about in Chapter 2. And, more important, they are business imperatives in our new world of work.

Daunting? Perhaps.

Necessary? Absolutely.

Stick with us. As you are about to learn, *Good Comes First* presents leaders with a powerful, practical, and comprehensive model for creating an uncompromising company culture. A culture that treats stakeholders—and not just shareholders—well.

The goal of a Good Comes First culture is simple: Good people. Doing good work. In a good place to work.

THE CHALLENGE AHEAD

Since you picked up this book, chances are good you already know that you, and your organizational priorities, must change. You are also aware that what you have done in the past will stop working in the near future (if it has not already). You are probably also aware that the next decade or two will present more challenges to the next generation of leaders than any before.

After all, we are well beyond the days of admiring leaders and managers who focus on conformity and compliance (sorry, Andy Grove). We no longer offer our unconditional respect for intimidating leadership styles (we are looking at you, Roger Ailes). Today, we judge personal behaviors equally with our professional results (not good, Steve Ballmer). And leaders who rose to "God" status have been reduced to mere mortal status after further review of their relentless tactics (our apologies, Steve Jobs).

Sure, these leadership styles have led to some impressive results in the past. Despite being considered a relentless micro-manager, Grove took Intel to the top of an ultra-competitive mountain in Silicon Valley. Ailes's management style was undoubtedly terrifying (not to mention racist and sexist), yet he led Fox News to financial greatness and transformed broadcast news (and perhaps an entire political ideology) along the way. Ballmer, known for his antics and temper tantrums (and the throwing of furniture), led Microsoft into the cloud era. And Jobs? He not only launched Apple; he reigned over the company's glorious resurgence—accomplished while becoming known as a ferocious tyrant.

In each of these examples of Industrial Age–style leadership, results mattered more than showing respect. And for a long time, we judged these leaders on growth and profits—not by their lack of generosity, their failure to show empathy, or their personality flaws. So why can't leaders today— and tomorrow—take this same approach? Why would you not want to emulate Steve Jobs's demeaning ways if he achieved so much success?

Because the Industrial Age is gone.

Welcome to the Social Age—a new era in workplace culture that focuses on people as much as profits.

In the Social Age, we expect leaders to serve respectfully while driving results. In this era, the most influential leaders are exceptional relationship builders and collaborators—as opposed to efficient managers, they are engaged mentors. They know building trust and respect is vital to inspiring employees to do their best work. To attract and retain the best team members, these leaders intentionally create a sense of community—or, even better, a sense of belonging—within their companies.

The most successful Social Age leaders build their legacies by serving as stewards of individuals' potential while developing and rewarding high-performance teams. They make decisions based on doing the right thing at the right time—not on making quarterly reports look better. And rather than focusing on a that-is-the-way-we-have-always-done-it legacy, these leaders serve as architects of an uncompromising work culture—that is, a work culture that is purposeful, positive, and productive.

Simply put, today's best leaders put good first.

And they do all of this despite the failure of the business world, our higher education system, and our old-guard leaders to prepare the next generation of leaders for success. After all, there is no precedent for this new style of leadership. No one—not their business school professors, predecessors, or members of their boards—knew how important it would become to focus not just on getting our work done but on *how* we get our work done. They did not realize that the fair treatment of employees would take priority over winning at nearly all costs. Not even the mentors many Social Age business leaders turn to for guidance can help: When it comes to learning how to lead based on equally valuing respect and results, too few can provide coveted been-there-done-that advice because they have not been there. They have not done that. Not many have.

After all, at no time in the past did we task any leader with coalescing four generations of workers—each with different working models, motivators, and priorities. We did not ask leaders to integrate massive amounts of technology into the workforce. We did not require leaders to manage quickly assembled micro-teams, entrepreneurial subgroups, and remote contributors in the Industrial Age. And we certainly did not expect leaders to be active, let alone approachable, on social media (we did not even have social media!).

We also did not hold our past executives accountable for gender parity, inclusion, and unbalanced work-life integration. Focusing almost exclusively on shareholders and often motivated by self-interest, we never asked corporate leaders to join the fight against poverty. We did not ask them to fight social injustices, take a stand against politically motivated decisions, or actively work to prevent climate change.

Until now.

These are—or, in most organizations, soon will be—the demands facing today's leaders. Our best leaders already know this.

During a business roundtable in August 2019, executives from over two hundred companies as influential as Apple and JPMorgan Chase discussed this issue of leadership. Collectively, they came up with a set of commitments and imperatives for companies operating in this new era that are strikingly consistent with the Good Comes First principles we have discussed. For example, they declared companies must invest in employees and deliver value to customers and communities. They determined organizations must equally focus on protecting the environment. Finally, they concluded companies should no longer advance only the interests of their organizations and their shareholders, but should instead prioritize stakeholders.[7]

As Adam Kingl, author of *Next Generation Leadership*, discovered, the pressure toward balancing human-centered and performance-based objectives will only continue to build. Kingl asked Millennials what their primary focus would be if appointed their organization's leader. Contrary to the consensus from executives of the past, just 1 percent chose "financial worth of the business" as their top priority. Ranked higher in the survey were "renewal of personal and organizational mission," at 43 percent, and instilling "an entrepreneurial perspective," at 33 percent.

Does that mean Millennials do not care about making a profit? As Kingl writes:

Absolutely not. Business has to survive and thrive. But chasing ratio optimization is a short-term game. Before one knows it, the purpose of the business is about tacitly, implicitly pleasing analysts. Making decisions toward long-term objectives takes a back seat.

Furthermore, Kingl says:

This is a critical mass of employees demanding their organizations shift focus from shareholder to stakeholder (customers, employees, community, planet) capitalism. A vigorous focus on customers and employees first.

In other words, Millennials—who represented 50 percent of the workforce in 2020 and will be 75 percent of the workforce in 2025—have issued a clear directive for leaders guiding their companies into the Social Age: We must place respectful treatment of our stakeholders on the same pedestal as results.

No, this is not your grandfather's workplace—nor is it your mother's or father's. This is a new world of work.

Yes, sometimes it seems like we are making up the rules as we go. However, history shows we *can* find fulfillment in our work. We can build a community around a common purpose. And treating each other with respect and dignity is more than possible. In fact, especially during turbulent social times, it is a business imperative.

GOOD COMES FIRST: THE END GAME

Make no mistake, the end game of Good Comes First is not to create a kumbaya playing field. We do not design these cultures to make people feel insincerely good about their contributions, especially when they underperform. And it is not meant to devolve into an "everybody gets a trophy" atmosphere where profits perpetually sit on the sidelines, waiting for their chance to enter the game.

Good Comes First is not even a way to balance what often seems like a high-wire walk: treating people well *and* meeting expected business deliverables.

Instead, Good Comes First is a proven, practical method of exceeding the expectations placed on leaders. When good comes first, increased profits, better results, engaged employees, wowed customers, and greater retention predictably follow right along.

FIRST: WE MUST UNDERSTAND OUR SERVANT PURPOSE . . . OUR "WHY"

To build a Good Comes First organization, you must establish your servant purpose, which, as we briefly mentioned in the introduction, is essentially your reason for being; it is what your company does, for whom, and to what end. Put another way: Your servant purpose is how what you do as a company improves customers' lives. This comes down to your "why," or the core motivation for your work. The "why" discussion is not new in our society. Everyone from the famous philosopher Friedrich Nietzsche to modern influencers like Simon Sinek has tackled the importance of our "why." Sinek, whose book *Start with Why* unleashed a Social Age movement centered on this very concept, asked leaders to reevaluate our organizational operating systems based on inspiring others. As a result, many of us now consider our "why" a staple concept of Western business thinking.

Not sure you agree that the concept of "why" has reached the mainstream? Bring up the topic at your next corporate happy hour. The "why" conversation is likely to outlast the drink specials and buffalo wings.

Yet, despite understanding the importance of "why," many of us active leaders have not risen above the doctrine created by those in power fifty to one hundred years ago. Our focus remains someplace other than our personal or professional "why." Generations after the launch of the Industrial Age, we still do our work under the Industrial-era premise of "trading work-hours for money."

Still, others believe their "why"—their company's stated servant purpose or mission—is purely a marketing tool. This belief is particularly true when organizations don't practice what they preach—when they ignore foundational principles and prioritize business outcomes over values. In those cases, leaders wield the purpose sword to manipulate employees, customers, and community members. They ask them to buy into a purported greater cause when, in reality, the primary driver for those leaders and marketers is meeting the next VC-set milestone or exceeding the next quarter's business objectives. As Phil La Duke said in *Forbes*, "Hypocrisy is having two sets of values—the ones on the walls versus the ones in the halls [felt by] demoralized and disillusioned employees."

Then we have leaders and companies that steadfastly incorporate their "why" into their cultures, no matter how technology-driven that work has become. Organizations often thought of as some of the most culturally and corporately competent, such as (pre-Amazon) Whole Foods, Southwest Airlines, Warby Parker, and The Container Store have reached vaulted status as the best-run companies on the planet because of the relentless focus on their servant purpose—their "why."

That focus guides these exceptional companies to live their noble servant purpose and to lead with integrity. They make evidence-based decisions *and* human-based decisions. Through the deliberate development of a mentor-first approach, companies also build mutually beneficial relationships with employees and contractors. These leaders make the best version of values—how people treat each other at work—just as important as the achievement of traditional business outcomes. As a result of this values-oriented approach to company culture, leaders build a genuine sense of community within their teams, their departments, and throughout their organizations. Most important, they retain their decidedly human approach to work—and thrive as a result.

THERE'S *NOT* AN APP FOR THAT

As we discussed just a few pages ago, organizations have already spent tremendous amounts of money trying to improve company culture and increase employee engagement. In our consulting and coaching practice, we often hear this question:

I have an Applicant Tracking System, an employee engagement plat-form, and an entire Human Resources department that runs the best personnel software. Isn't this technology enough?

No. Or, more precisely, "No, it's not, unless you intentionally put good first."

The leadership teams at the "old" Whole Foods, Southwest Airlines, Warby Parker, and The Container Store know: Technology can dramatically improve "what" we do and "how" we do it. The "how" tech can deliver messages, manage projects, and more. And without a doubt, tech can help us provide a better product—our "what." But it will not—it *cannot*—replace a leader who genuinely believes in and cares about their organization's mission—and their people. It cannot touch that powerful and purely human driver of action: our "why."

Technology is no substitute for human beings who believe in the contributors so vital to accomplishing their missions. No matter how good technology becomes, it will not replace the mentor-first mindset the best culture leaders will possess.

In short, technology cannot *care*—not as we humans *can*, and not as great leaders *do*.

One such leader who embodies this imperative is Tamara McCleary, founder and CEO of Thulium. We recently spoke with Tamara about compassionate leadership, and she gave us her unvarnished perspective on the responsibility of a modern leader to care:

The purpose of leadership today isn't just to drive results. Today's lead-ers must engage and inspire team members to align to shared values and goals while achieving desired business outcomes within a purpose-ful company culture. Leaders can't engage and inspire if they don't love their purpose first, then their people.

In other words, an inevitable test of a Social Age leader's mettle is sure to be the humanistic integration of technology into their organization. More specifically, leveraging the best technology—without *relying* on tech to build the human-to-human relationships—is critical to a Good Comes First culture. It is the only way an organization can achieve business success without sacrificing its humanity. Social Age leaders must know when to rely on technology and when to set the phone down and just be *human*.

Please realize: We will not ask anyone to turn their back on technology—after all, some of the best emerging leaders were born digital natives. Instead, we emphasize a roll-back to a time that featured some of the better aspects of pre-industrial, barter-style workplaces: When our faces were not always in a device, and eye contact was a social norm. When people solved problems by conversing in a civil—albeit sometimes spirited—manner. When, in the best partnerships, trust and respect were natural outcomes of the mutually beneficial collaboration between people who were respected for their expertise and driven by their innate sense of community.

As you will see in Chapter 13, we call this return to humanity "Bringing Back Barn Raising"—a metaphor we hope will inspire leaders to return to a time when people selflessly gathered to perform good work for all the right reasons.

That is where our servant purpose—the "why"—comes back in. A servant purpose drives those community-driven, raise-the-barn, worthy efforts. The "why" helps us create optimistic working environments and contagious pockets of excellence. And it is our "why" that ultimately enables us to build nimble, self-managed, and strengths-driven work teams where everyone brings the best version of themselves to work.

The "why"—however we define it—inspires us to work hard, pivot when necessary, and serve others effectively. And often, our "why" helps us win the day even when those bottom-line-focused skeptics do not believe we should—and many did not think we could.

Before pushing on, and getting that much closer to understanding what it takes to become a Good Comes First leader, take a moment to reflect and write some detailed notes on the current state of your organization. Ask yourself:

Do you know your organization's servant purpose? Your "why"?

Does your leadership team? Do your employees? Your customers?

Go ahead. Take a few minutes. We'll wait . . .

THE ROLE OF LEADERS IN A GOOD COMES FIRST CULTURE

The one takeaway we have discovered after decades of helping companies build cultures that put good first?

Leaders do not clearly understand the personal impact they have on their company's culture.

Your actions and decisions deeply affect how your company operates. Align your behaviors with chosen "corporate values" and people will see you as a shepherd of all that is good. In this way, a leader's impact can be positive; Garry Ridge at WD-40 Company and Michael Arena at General Motors immediately come to mind.

But if a leader's actions run counter to their stated values, the impact can be profoundly damaging. For instance, take the president of a faith-based nonprofit who initiated a culture improvement effort after a merger event. After his followers and other stakeholders discovered his leadership style was the root cause of the company's chronic culture failures, he halted culture improvement efforts. This leader could not accept that his behavior had eroded good in their workplace. He did not understand—nor did his fellow autocrats—that *he* was the problem, not the culture. He set a negative tone for his organization but refused to take ownership of his destructive impact.

Of course, most leaders have neither a 100 percent positive nor 100 percent negative impact on their organizations—every personality comes with admirable traits and its own set of challenges. But if a leader consistently displays desirable behaviors, employees will emulate those traits. Over time, the demonstration of those positive behaviors will reinforce the desired company culture.

On the other hand, the undesirable behaviors demonstrated by a leader (perhaps unknowingly)—especially those that contradict stated corporate values—tacitly permit others to act in the same culture-killing manner. In the end, those behaviors do not just tear down trust and morale—they soon target productivity and profits. Employee experience is the next casualty, followed by employee defections to other companies—even competitors. Thus, a leader whose behavior does not align with their company's stated values creates a vicious cycle of bad behavior. A cycle that often proves lethal for employee satisfaction and terrible for the bottom line.

How do you, as a leader in the Social Age, prevent this from happening?

Perhaps for the first time since the Industrial Age began, it is absolutely critical that you show respect in every interaction. You must model the desired behaviors. You must serve as Chief Role Model.

You, every day, must put good first.

We understand this concept is both retro and revolutionary—simple but seemingly complex. So, throughout the pages that follow, we will show you exactly how to create and sustain a purposeful organizational culture. One that today's most engaged, talented, and socially aware employees covet—and even demand. And in Chapter 13 specifically, we will dive deeper into the leadership aspect of building a Good Comes First culture. Our promise is that, by the end of this book, you will fully understand the unique demands on you as a leader as you usher your employees into a new era of work.

For now, though, know this: A leader who champions a company culture based on mutual respect and trust must work diligently to be respectful and trustworthy in each interaction. From this page on, your words matter. Your actions matter. As a leader, how and why you craft decisions—from the mail room to the boardroom—*matters*. And any tolerance of undesirable behaviors matters—a lot—to your team, your division, and your entire company.

From the moment your company begins the transformation to a Good Comes First organization, *you* are the role model. Embrace it. Own it. And expect others to do the same.

This is how good—consistently, and for the benefit of all—comes first.

CHAPTER 2

Defining the "Good" in "Good Comes First"

"You can't change anything by fighting or resisting it. You change something by making it obsolete through superior methods."
—Buckminster Fuller

After reading our first chapter, you have a better understanding of how a Good Comes First company functions. You know respect must be just as high a priority as results. And you have a sense for how the best Good Comes First leaders think and must act as they serve as their organization's primary role model.

Now, let's talk about how to define the "good" in Good Comes First— and understand how "good" looks and feels within a workplace culture. And, no, it is not as easy as it might sound.

After all, "good" is a simple word, but an inherently subjective one. Even if we agree to define the word "good" in the same fundamental way, we might still interpret it differently depending on individual perspectives and in different situations. For example, one person's "That's *good*!" is another person's "Not *good* enough." Or one leader might say, "This is a *good* time for change," while another says, "But we're in a *good* position now."

Even Merriam-Webster lists over fifty possible uses for the word. Whether used as an adjective, noun, or adverb, though, "good" has a universally positive connotation. It is the one word each of us can use to describe someone, or something, worthy of our respect.

- "He showed me how good I was doing."
- "Her promise is as good as gold."
- "The good of the community."
- "We're in good company."
- "Good intentions."
- "Good quality."
- "Good effort."
- "A good person."
- "A good friend."
- "A good team."
- "A good leader."
- "A good place to work."

As it so happens, these phrases (many taken directly from Merriam-Webster's online dictionary[1]) embody many of the qualities we look for in an applicant, a coworker, and a leader. This is how many of us want to live our lives. And it is how we can choose to run our companies.

And yet, as we discussed in our first chapter, and with all due respect to Jim Collins, far too many companies do not reach the status of "good"—let alone great. Their "About Us" pages and job descriptions repeatedly tout a "fast-paced, dynamic" working environment, but everyone in HR knows what that cliché really means:

"Stress, chaos, and cover-your-ass."

As we now understand, "good" is relative. It is subject to many definitions and applications—and is a bit too open to interpretation. But it is also universal. Aspirational. Inclusive. And inspiring.

Remember our ultimate goal: *Good* people. Doing *good* work. In a *good* place to work. By this definition, "good"—and good-ness—is more than good enough.

OUR DEFINITION OF GOOD IN "GOOD COMES FIRST"

From both an observational perch and directly in our work, we have been fortunate enough to know and work with some of the world's best business leaders. Some are famous, and others, based on how they treat their people and their companies' success, *should* be famous. We have also known and worked with leaders we would not put in the "best" category. Or even "good." (Not that they didn't have the potential; if we did not think that, we wouldn't have started working with them!)

To put this in perspective, let's look at two very different companies: BambooHR and, well, The Other Company, the name of which we changed to protect the not-so-innocent.

BambooHR

Founded in Utah by Ben Peterson and Ryan Sanders in 2008, BambooHR develops software used by twenty-thousand-plus human resources organizations in more than one hundred countries. But its customer base and market penetration are not what make this young company special. Instead, what truly sets it apart is a relentless focus on its employees—specifically, their quality of life.

BambooHR—which operates in an ultra-competitive industry full of behemoths, has-beens, and would-be players entering the market annually—has managed to stand out by providing good people a place to do good work. Period.

For example, BambooHR emphasizes an "anti-workaholic" view of work that promotes a work-life balance. They also provide employees with a "paid paid" vacation. No, that *is not* a typo: employees are *paid* (up to $2,000) to take a vacation by BambooHR. As you might expect, this kind of focus on employee experience has a virtuous effect: When companies treat employees well, those employees do *good* work—which is *good* for business.

Mark was fortunate enough to be a speaker at BambooHR's own industry summit, held at Snowbird, outside Park City, Utah. After Mark's talk, he had a chance to talk with Ben Peterson.

Asked about BambooHR's focus on people, Ben reiterated why treating employees well is a no-brainer: It is not about the money or getting attention for the company (of which there is plenty). The concept is simple—treat people well. And while people toss around the phrase "work-life balance" with abandon, Ben insists treating people well is about more than that. It is about happy, loyal people doing really good work.

HOW WE SEE IT

From our experience, BambooHR does not just treat their employees right. This good-ness permeates their culture—and their interactions with clients and vendors (and even us speakers). There is no doubt BambooHR's legacy as a Good First Company will flourish in the years ahead. That kind of "good" does not just go away.

The Other Company

Alas, not every company can be BambooHR (or any of the several Good Comes First companies we will discuss in Chapter 3). Some organizations (in this case, despite an evangelical mission and an entire company full of amazing people) just cannot find their way to good.

We briefly touched on this organization in our last chapter. On the surface, and on the verge of a significant merger, this company had everything going for it. It had the right mission in the right niche and the right products for its customers at the right time. The company had vice presidents who truly believed change was necessary and good was possible. It also had employees who would walk through walls for those VPs. The employees believed their work was making a difference; they felt driven to service—in their eyes, service was not just for their customers, but also God.

Then—after fifteen months of progress toward a respectful, transparent work culture—the leader of this organization decided he no longer wanted to be involved in day-to-day operations. He shifted the authority and trust placed in him into the hands of his right-hand person. Unfortunately, this business leader's autocratic, bullying leadership style seemed fresh out of

Detroit in the 1970s. Leaders, apparently in his mind, were meant to be feared—not respected.

Shortly after this new leader's hostile takeover of operations, nearly 20 percent of the firm faced disciplinary action. Respect within the workplace disappeared. Terminations were routinely threatened—even among those with decades of proven service to the organization and ministry. And in one of our last conversations, the autocratic leader told us: *We spent the last year giving these people a voice . . . and all they did was bitch!*

HOW WE SEE IT

Any one leader, especially in what should be a wholesome workplace, has a significant impact on people, process, and productivity—good or bad. While there is no doubt the original leader of this faith-based organization entered a culture change initiative for all the right reasons, he delegated responsibility for those changes. Worse yet, he trusted someone who (ironically, given his influence in the ministry) did not believe in putting good first. In the end, this company culture truly sucked.

We don't mean to serve up the two preceding examples as a "There are two paths before you; you may only take one" parable. However, the leadership groups of each of these companies chose different paths: one of respect and validation, and one of fear and devaluation. From day one, the leaders at BambooHR wanted their people to know they mattered. The other leader chose to make it quite clear to his employees that he, and his way, mattered more than creating an inspiring company culture.

And it was not long before the behaviors of those leaders began to manifest themselves in results. BambooHR is one of the most respected companies and employers on the planet. The other guys? Well, this recent development makes it hard for them to retain, or attract, proven talent. To this day, positions—and good people—are being eliminated to accommodate this leader's need for power. The heavenly mission may inspire future team and ministry members. Still, the chances are good that the workplace—as long as that autocratic leader maintains his presence—will remain a living hell.

FOUNDATIONAL PRINCIPLE AND CORNERSTONES: CULTURE BUILDING BLOCKS OF GOOD COMES FIRST

So how does all this work? How do you start the process of creating a culture focused on doing good? We have come up with an easy-to-use framework for doing just that.

We build a Good Comes First company upon a proven foundational principle and four culture cornerstones that sit atop that foundation. After decades of practice, observation, and experiential education, we can tell you the organizations most capable of putting good first intentionally feature these culture building blocks:

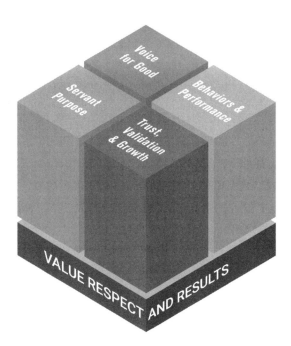

Value Respect and Results

Create and sustain a work environment
that expects respect and drives results.

Our foundational principle, upon which you will build your Good Comes First culture, can be summed up as follows:

- **Equally Value Respect and Results** | Create and sustain a working environment that expects respect and drives results simultaneously.

And the cultural cornerstones that sit upon that foundation of respect and results are:

- **Live Our Servant Purpose** | Define and activate a servant purpose that ensures a service-first leadership approach and equitable treatment of every contributor.
- **Lean on Trust, Validation, and Growth** | Provide good people with a work environment where trust is contagious, validation is pervasive, and growth is constant.
- **Understand Behavior's Impact on Performance** | Model, measure, and celebrate people and teams that wholly align with agreed-upon desired behaviors.
- **Use Our Voice for Good** | Actively look outward, working to resolve local and global issues such as inequality, poverty, health crises, and climate change.

We will get into our foundational principle and each of our cornerstones in a moment. But, if you are like many of our clients, you are already asking yourself, "How many of these do we have, or do, right now?" And that is a fair question.

We know from experience, and you will soon learn, that each of these independent yet connected elements of a Good Comes First culture is—like the word "good" itself—open to interpretation. After reading your own sets of community guidelines, shareholder reports, and social media channels, you might *think* you are okay—at least in some of these areas—and you just might be!

But we, as humans, do not get far by thinking. We reach our goals by knowing—and doing. And since you are one-and-a-half chapters into this book and still reading, we guess you would rather know and do than think.

So let's expand the five building blocks of a Good Comes First culture, one at a time, beginning with our foundational principle.

(Note: Keep in mind that while all of these concepts are imperatives in a Good Comes First organization, your job as a leader is to emulate them well enough to drive real culture change.)

OUR FOUNDATIONAL PRINCIPLE: EQUALLY VALUE RESPECT AND RESULTS

Our goal: To create and sustain a working environment that expects respect and drives results simultaneously.

We already talked a great deal about what happens when company leaders focus exclusively on results (take The Other Company, for instance). And you have probably heard about companies like Volkswagen, Wells Fargo, Uber, United Airlines, and dozens of others that earned their reputations as win-at-all-costs organizations at a steep price. Business historians have extensively chronicled their failures, so we do not need to beat any dead horses here.

Don't be a dick.

Enough said.

Instead, let's talk about the single foundational principle upon which we build everything else associated with Good Comes First: equally value respect and results.

Set this foundation in the wrong way, or at the wrong angle, or for the wrong reasons, and nothing built upon it will ever be square. Get it wrong, and no matter how well you fortify everything above this level, nothing will ever be right.

Perhaps you, as a leader, are experiencing this right now. Maybe your people are not treated with respect. Maybe they do not treat each other respectfully. Worse yet, perhaps your leadership team does not think your employees deserve respect—and maybe they don't. Just maybe, you have the wrong people—and leaders—trying to do the job right. Faced with any one of those situations, how can a company possibly drive optimum results?

That is precisely why "expects respect *and* drives results" is an AND statement—not an OR statement. Long-term results are nearly impossible to achieve without respect. And we sure cannot maintain long-term respect without sustained results.

We know what you might be thinking, or maybe thought at one time in your leadership career:

My team isn't particularly respectful, but we still get results.

We get it. In a short-term context, results without respect are momentarily possible—in sports, for example. Both of us have coached sports at several levels, from T-ball to college ball. We know that in some sports with short seasons on some teams, it is possible to generate results without showing respect. A team can occasionally sail through to the championship game with zero respect for each other, their coaches, and even their schools and communities.

In some business-world scenarios, we know the same can be true: Results can happen without respect making an appearance—for example, at start-ups, during grant-writing season for nonprofits, and during market launches for established corporations. We know, because we have lived through each of these scenarios ourselves.

In each of these results-oriented scenarios, the expectations are clear: Push yourself hard. Push each other harder. Fight over everything. Hate each other if you must. But as long as you get the funding, the endowment, the bigger market share . . . you live to see another day. Even if, as this same cycle of grueling work and animosity repeats itself over and over, you begin to hate your life.

But this is not how most leaders want to live. And it sure is not how most employees—especially Millennials and Gen Z'ers—choose to work.

As we continue to learn how to navigate our post-pandemic world, this unhappy scenario becomes an even bigger factor in how people choose to work and live. Exhausted from months of work-at-home isolation and bombarded with confrontation from every social media platform and news channel, we find ourselves drawn increasingly toward situations and people with a positive outlook. We look for people whose actions and behaviors make even the smallest communities (like work teams) more productive and pleasant. From social media to email to personal relationships, there is—and will continue to be—a deliberate disconnection from those too willing to fight over stupid stuff and for stupid things. But good people—or at least those powerfully drawn toward good—will shed themselves of the unnecessarily negative, unproductive, or emotionally unsatisfying, including work. And these good-focused individuals are the kind of people leaders will want to hire. And these good people, inspired by good leaders, will do good work.

Given this next normal, our foundational principle becomes even more important: Our job as leaders is to create a workplace where people expect respect *and* help drive tangible results. We understand this may cause a challenge for your organization. We know it is hard to rebuild from the bottom up. So we promise not to scold you and yell, "Well, stop building your dream house on quicksand!"

But we will tell you: Establishing the foundational principle of respect and results is where the hard work starts. Thankfully, this is also where the BS—the drama in your company—stops. For you, your employees, and your company, this is the proverbial tipping point.

This change in expectations—this significant change in your company culture—will not happen overnight. We will talk more about timelines in Chapter 14. For now, though, it is important to answer these questions, in this order:

1.   Who will lead this transformation?
2.   Who will serve as the primary role model?
3.   Who will make sure disrespect is monitored and mitigated?
4.   Who will ensure respect is recognized and rewarded?
5.   Who will take that first step toward a culture that expects respect?

Spoiler alert: The answer to every single question is "You!"

No one else can own this. You are the one standing at the very center of that fulcrum, that tipping point (or soon will be). And you cannot stay there forever. You must make the jump.

You must choose respect AND results.

Once you commit to that ideal, we can look at the first of our four cornerstones . . .

CULTURE CORNERSTONE 1: LIVE OUR SERVANT PURPOSE

Our goal: Define and activate a servant purpose that ensures service as a leader and equitable treatment of every contributor.

Since Robert K. Greenleaf first used the phrase "servant leadership" in 1970, entire industries have formed around the concept. And for a good reason: Greenleaf's approach represented the first significant effort to change how Industrial Age–trained leaders behaved in the workplace, gradually shifting the focus of work from purely results-oriented to also being people-oriented.

Greenleaf was not wholly successful in altering the leadership landscape at the time. Nor did he immediately change how the typical workplace is managed (the results of which we saw in Chapter 1). However, the Servant as Leader concept is even more prevalent today than it was fifty years ago. In this cornerstone of a Good Comes First culture, however, we want to take the philosophy of the Servant as Leader one step further: to servant purpose.

As you have heard from us already, your servant purpose is what your company does, for whom, and to what end. A servant purpose describes how what your company does or makes improves customers' quality of life. Essentially, your servant purpose is your reason for being—other than making a profit.

That higher purpose shifts your organization's primary focus from making money (or making truck bumpers, or circuit boards, or widgets—none of which are innately inspiring) to generating tangible benefit to both your customers and your community. When a leader lives her servant purpose, she does not just serve the purpose—she also serves her people. And by doing so in a selfless fashion, she serves both the cause and the well-being of the people *driving* that cause.

So how does this show up in a Good Comes First company? First, a leader must ensure she is not the only leader in the organization modeling its servant purpose.

Remember the data point from Chapter 1 that showed over 70 percent of people leave their job primarily due to their relationship with their boss? This "phenomenon" has been going on for so long we have to stop thinking of it as a phenomenon! Unfortunately, there is no longer anything non-standard about having a crappy boss who is more concerned about compliance and conformity than creative work—a boss who does not care about their people, only about their bottom line. In today's world of work, this has been—and still is—our global normal. It is a major reason far too many of our workplaces suck.

Good Comes First companies, on the other hand, actively work to change this. They employ and promote the leaders and team members fully capable of serving the servant purpose and their people. Those servant-first leaders genuinely care about personal and professional growth—and see each stakeholder (employee, contractor, vendor, and partner) as an integral part of that growth. Just as important, these leaders treat any sign of inequality—from responsibilities, to pay, to promotion—as the cancer it is. And they insist other leaders follow suit.

These Good Comes First leaders are more than just managers. They willingly serve as mentors to their veteran team members and new hires. They treat others with respect, earn trust, and offer their employees autonomy and authority in their roles. And at crunch time, they have the confidence to clearly state the challenge ahead, provide the necessary resources, and then get the hell out of the way.

This is how Good Comes First leaders—from the top down—live their servant purpose. It is how they contribute to a company that puts good first. But this servant purpose, while crucial, is not the whole picture. Leaders also need to create an environment of trust, validation, and growth in their organization.

CULTURE CORNERSTONE 2: LEAN ON TRUST, VALIDATION, AND GROWTH

Our goal: Provide good people with a chance to work where trust is contagious, validation is pervasive, and growth is constant.

Experienced executives often say trust is hard to come by—and in many cases and workplaces, that may be true. That is because, of all the traits of a Good Comes First company, trust is the most profoundly human: It requires vulnerability and commitment. Just as critical, it is counter to the autocratic leadership styles of old. And yet, if we leaders want to move our work teams closer to an ideal Good Comes First culture, we must work hard to defeat this norm. *Especially* as leaders, we must earn trust—or, in some cases, re-earn trust.

This earning and re-earning of trust is not an easy task, but it is more than possible. In many Good Comes First companies, leaders have already established trust. And just like engaging the "employ and promote members of the leadership team who genuinely care" concept from Cornerstone 1, earning and re-earning your employees' trust can only be done through action. (Yes, when making the transition to a culture that puts good first, a combination of attrition and rejuvenation can be our best friend.)

This is why we say, "Lean on Trust, Validation, and Growth." Because when trust is lacking, the best way to rebuild that trust is to demonstrate genuine care for others. And in the workplace, how do we best show an appropriate level of unmistakable care?

Every day, we validate the good work of others.

Through our actions, we fully support our people and our teams. We recognize and reward not just outstanding one-off performances but the daily grind—the work that helps keep the lights on. We are the biggest champions of our employees' productivity—and their potential.

At every opportunity, we also provide avenues for personal and professional growth. We help our employees get better at what they do in the office, certainly. But we must also help the entire person grow, not just the part that shows up to work every day. We help them grow as people, parents, sons and daughters, baseball coaches, homeschool teachers, den mothers, members of our community, and mentors. After all, we know good people do good work.

Just as important, as leaders we must provide our employees with the opportunity to do meaningful work—work that our employees believe, with bone-deep pride, really matters—to them personally and each other. And to each stakeholder and to the customers they serve, their boss and leaders, and the company.

If you want to build trust, show employees they matter—today and tomorrow. However, as we will see, trust is not the only important behavior on display in Good Comes First organizations.

CULTURE CORNERSTONE 3: MEASURE IMPACT OF BEHAVIORS ON CULTURE

Our goal: Monitor, evaluate, and reward alignment to agreed-upon desired behaviors and their impact on culture.

So far in this book, we have discussed placing overarching human values (respect, trust, etc.) on the same pedestal as results (performance, profits, etc.). Now, in this third cornerstone, we start to look past the theory and enter the first door of practical application. And we show how behaviors—good and bad—impact performance.

First, some context: There isn't a professional organization on the planet that does not know how to measure traditional business metrics. They know how to manage a profit and loss statement. They thoroughly understand the cost of customer acquisition and their net promoter score. They know their market value, profit margins, and either growth rates or burn rates. But they should also know their employee experience numbers, retention rates, and percentage of employee referrals. All in all, there are between twelve and eighteen business metrics every company—and every leader—should know. And they are not just the results-oriented metrics most business leaders are used to measuring.

When we discuss the need to focus on values as much as results, we are not asking you as a leader to do anything more than co-create—with your work team (or teams)—a list of the values and/or behaviors that impact performance. Specifically, those values your Good Comes First company will model, coach, measure, and—ultimately—celebrate.

Of course, you have already learned some of the behaviors on which a Good Comes First culture relies, including respect, trust, validation, growth, rewards, recognition, equity, mentorship, autonomy, and authority. The reality is, though, that we are just getting started. And we have not even asked you, the reader, which values surface most often in your organization right now. Which are most prevalent? Which are the most problematic? And which more productive behaviors would counter those problem areas?

You do not have to answer these questions just yet. Just know that at some point soon—perhaps after digesting the concept of "Define, Align, and Refine" introduced in Chapter 6—you will want to think about your company's dominant values and behaviors. You will also want to discuss how your teams will monitor, measure, and reward those carefully selected and defined behaviors.

As you anticipate this task, keep in mind this does not need to be complicated. Many of our clients, for example, generate a list of desired "leadership principles" for their organizations, complete with clear definitions so they are not open to interpretation. Each leader promises to live up to those standards in every interaction, every day.

And if leaders *do not* demonstrate those clearly defined behaviors?

At Puget Sound Energy in Bellevue, Washington, they mount a poster on every wall in every conference room that displays their leadership principles. At any time, any team member—leader or not—has permission to respectfully look those leaders in the eye, point to the poster, and say, "In this moment, it doesn't seem like you're living up to No. 3." Or, in a self-aware moment, one person can look at another respectfully and say, "I see you're making a real effort on No. 6 up there . . . and I'm not . . . but I will." The conversation, by default and precedent, gets a reboot. The dialogue becomes more productive, as do the people in the room.

This third cornerstone of a Good Comes First organization requires that leaders singularly define behaviors that impact performance. It also requires those leaders to model, coach, and measure those behaviors continuously, in real time. And, of course, it asks leaders to celebrate the wins often. That is how you put values (and behaviors) on the same level as results, simply and easily. But how do we direct those values not only inward to our organizations, but also outward to our communities?

CULTURE CORNERSTONE 4: USE OUR VOICE FOR GOOD

Our goal: Actively work to resolve local and global issues such as inequality, injustice, poverty, health crises, and climate change.

As we continue to rise out of the COVID-19 pandemic, the issues we face as a society go well beyond the virus, and well outside our front doors. Societal problems from homelessness to a lack of affordable housing plague our communities. Racial tensions too often rage in the streets and simmer in our workplaces. Minimum wage mandates and poverty levels remain significant issues, especially when compared to the average compensation for S&P 500 company CEOs—$14.8 million[2] (a CEO-to-worker pay ratio of 264-to-1). Unfair payment practices[3] penalize women and people of color even more. And given the recent rollbacks of environmental protections in the United States, our environment—our planet—is continually fighting off challenges.

At one point in time, it was okay for an organization—no matter what was happening in the world around it—to go "full ostrich." When trouble came, when society's issues knocked on the front door, many leaders just hid their corporate heads in the sand. This ambivalence is not acceptable today. To put good first, we must contribute to the well-being of not only our employees and contributors, but our communities, our regions, and our planet.

Customers, employees, influencers, and many others can see what your company stands for—and what it will not stand for—and what you, as a leader, will and will not tolerate.

You are reading this book because you care about your organization and the people who work there. You want to make your company a better place to work—or you likely would not be here, on this page, at this moment. It makes sense, then, that you also want to make the world—one little piece at a time, perhaps—a better place. It makes sense for you, and it makes good business sense, too.

In our first chapter, we talked about the pressures put on today's executives. We said that at no time in business history have we held our business leaders accountable for social injustices, taking a stand against politically motivated personalities and global climate change. We understand. These issues may not strike a chord with you. They might not spark a passion inside you, personally.

But they most likely create a spark within your customer base and your strategic and industry partners. And they must light that same spark inside a vocal segment of your employee base.

These people care. A lot. And they want their business leaders to care.

And if their employers don't?

The most committed of those employees will make their concerns and disappointments known. More and more often, in one form or another, they petition for change. The rest, after they feel unheard, will walk. They will go to a company where they feel more than just a sense of community—they feel a sense of affinity or even belonging. They will take their talent and experience where they more closely share common interests, concerns—*and values*—with leadership. They will actively look for an employer that cares.

As we move further toward a Good Comes First culture, we as leaders must be willing to create a workplace where everyone feels a deep sense of belonging—where everyone has a voice, and where each of us uses our voice for good.

LESSONS LEARNED FROM OUR TWO EXAMPLE COMPANIES

We will not beat a dead horse, just as we promised. But there is value in looking back at our previously featured companies, BambooHR and The Other Company. So please glance again through our foundational principle and the four culture cornerstones. Then, with the limited knowledge you have of them, please consider: Which company comes closest to placing respect on the same level as results? Which comes closest to living its servant purpose? Of the two companies, which leans on trust, validation, and growth?

We could go on, but the answer seems obvious. Despite all outward appearances to the contrary, BambooHR may not be the perfect company. But they are perfectly united in how they treat their people, enable growth, and develop trust.

Now, based on the descriptions provided, ask yourself: Which culture is most attractive to you? For which company—all else being equal—would *you* rather work? At which company would you prefer to invest your energy, passion, and brainpower?

Right.

That is the point. The best available employees, leaders, and mentors always have good companies from which to choose. And the Good Comes First company will be their first choice.

Every. Single. Time.

So if you want to be the best . . . you have to be *good*.

In this chapter, we talked a lot about values and behaviors. More precisely, we discussed the desired values and defined behaviors that help increase performance and productivity while creating a more purposeful culture. One of these companies, BambooHR, has done a fine job building a Good Comes First culture. Starting with respect, the leadership team created a good company full of loyal people doing good work. Each demonstration of their revered behaviors has served to strengthen their resolve; each has moved them one step closer to their organization's ideal culture. They are—without a doubt—a Good Comes First company.

The Other Company? Its culture challenges result from an organizational culture where one leader consistently fails to align with defined values. The less-than-desirable behaviors—consistently demonstrated over time, without correction—completely took the wind out of the company's post-merger sails. The behavior failures also took down some good people—and a wholesome culture went down with them. The Other Company failed to put good first. Consequently, the company may never reach its full potential. And it certainly will not be considered an employer of choice.

To learn more from organizations that have earned vaulted status as Good Comes First companies, we will next move on to Chapter 3. As we do, you will naturally start to think about how to transition your company's culture to one that puts good first. As that happens, remember this . . .

We build company culture by rewarding desired behaviors. We tear down culture by tolerating disrespectful, unproductive behaviors.

CHAPTER 3

The Good: Companies Setting the Good Comes First Standard

Why do exceptionally run organizations like the WD-40 Company, Zappos, and Ritz-Carlton thrive in an era of constant change? How do these organizations continue to operate work cultures where team members feel respected, valued, and validated every day? These companies are resilient because their leadership understands that if their employees feel respected and validated—even in times of dramatic change and socially acceptable incivility—they do their best work. Period. Full stop.

Furthermore, in Good Comes First organizations like these, those employees' beliefs are created and sustained by their daily interactions with leaders and each other. They routinely experience positive validation. Additionally, leaders grant employees the authority to apply their skills and passion for serving each other, the company, *and* their customers well. Their contributions are apparent. On a daily basis, their value is reinforced and appreciated. Company-wide, trust between bosses and employees, and among colleagues, is earned. And respect, in every interaction, is expected.

Of course, at these Good Comes First organizations, results still matter. Our goal is not to create a workplace utopia where people feel good but don't get a damn thing done (more on this later in the chapter). While a Good Comes First company drives toward optimal results, it knows that the employee helping the company achieve those results also matters. The employees know that, and they work harder—and smarter—because of it. As they feel trusted and respected, employees speak up when aspects of work—process, team, and leadership—could be better. Rather than becoming part of the problem by remaining complacent, employees are more willing to offer well-considered solutions.

In a Good Comes First culture, leaders will listen to these concerns, then act. Knowing their voices, concerns, and opinions are heard, employees work even harder. And even smarter.

As this self-fulfilling cycle continues within Good Comes First cultures, nearly every tangible business metric invariably heads in the right direction as a result. Processes improve. Milestones are hit. As the employees grow and thrive, so do profits. Retention rates soar, saving millions of dollars in recruiting, onboarding, and training. And with bone-deep pride established in their work and the company, employee referrals roll in—making it easier to attract the most talented people who thrive within these intentional, nonnegotiable cultures focused on good.

This leads to the outcome we want: good people, doing good work, in a good place to work.

Now, let's look at five organizations that have achieved this very outcome. These companies exemplify Good Comes First principles, and as a result, their cultures and profits are better than ever. Apply their hard-earned wisdom to your company—and expect the same phenomenal results.

GOOD COMES FIRST COMPANIES

Radio Flyer

Radio Flyer is a Chicago-based manufacturer of children's red wagons, tricycles, scooters, and ride-ons. You, your children—or even your parents and grandparents—may have had one of their iconic products in your garage. Founded in 1917, Radio Flyer is a family-owned and -operated organization that has been an iconic part of American life for generations.

Radio Flyer's employees, known as Flyers, rate the company as one of the top companies to work for with a perfect 5.0 score on Glassdoor, an online platform where current and former employees post anonymous reviews of their workplaces. Incredibly, 100 percent of Flyers reporting to Glassdoor approve of the CEO, and 99 percent of employees recommend Radio Flyer to others as a good place to work.[1]

Flyers' comments on Glassdoor emphasize the company's investment in employees' growth and well-being, how transparent senior leaders are with employees, how fun the work environment is, and more. One reviewer said:

Our Chief Wagon Officer [Robert Pasin, the founder's grandson; his title is a creative reference to the company's flagship product] and the senior leadership team lead by example . . . they've created a culture that is supportive, positive, and FUN.

Another reviewer said:

The thing I love most about my job is the freedom to use my creativity to solve complex problems and invent new products that delight families.

Glassdoor's platform also allows reviewers to post advice to management. About Radio Flyer's leadership, one reviewer said:

The approach you have taken in light of COVID to care for your employees has been awesome. Through transparency and increased communication, you have made me feel secure in my job and valued in the work I do. Thank you, THANK YOU!

The company's response? A note from CWO Pasin (who we'll learn much more about in Chapter 14) expressing appreciation for the thanks and closing with:

I look forward to the day we can all return to the office and see each other.

This genuine demonstration of care for employees by their workplace leaders has obviously gone over well with Flyers, and is a hallmark sign of a Good Comes First leader.

In 2020, Radio Flyer also earned high marks from the people analytics, assessment, and consulting company Great Place to Work[2] (GPTW). An astounding 100 percent of employees rated Radio Flyer a Great Place to

Work on that platform's Trust Index (compared to the 59 percent a typical US-based company receives). GPTW's Trust Index indicated that 100 percent of employees believe:

- Management keeps me informed about important issues and changes.
- Management makes expectations clear.
- Management is competent at running the business.
- Management trusts people to do an excellent job without watching over their shoulders.
- Management gives people a lot of responsibility.

It's worth noting these accolades aren't brand new for Radio Flyer. The company has earned numerous awards over the past ten years from Crain's Chicago,[3] including Best Workplace in Chicago (2018), Best Places for Minorities to Work in Chicago (2017), Best Small and Medium Workplace (2018), and Best Place to Work in Illinois (2016).

How does Radio Flyer generate this high level of respect and earn such high praise? How does the company ensure that good comes first with each employee? Radio Flyer clearly states its values and servant purpose (or mission). Sure, many organizations have defined their purpose and values. They plaster their stated mission on their walls for all to see . . . and for most to ignore. But few organizations inspire the consistent demonstration of those behaviors by senior leaders like Radio Flyer. And they do that exceptionally well. That consistently respectful treatment, where senior leaders kindly serve their team members in each interaction, creates an environment of calm, credibility, contribution, and admiration.

HOW WE SEE IT

The Good | Both the clarity of values and the servant leadership demonstrated by leaders throughout the organization are crucial elements of Radio Flyer's success. But the most important lever Radio Flyer pulls is empowerment. The company enables talented, engaged

Flyers to apply their skills, creativity, and passion for solving problems—and, ultimately, to "delighting families." The degree to which Radio Flyer validates employees—through leaders who trust employees to do the right thing and then respect the decisions made—is powerful and impactful.

Are your company's employees valued? Is their work frequently validated?

Stryker

Our second Good Comes First company is Stryker, a global medical technology company headquartered in Portage, Michigan. Stryker is a thirteen-time winner of the Exceptional Workplace Award[4] by Gallup's analytics and advisory arm. In five out of the last six years, Stryker was also a recipient of Glassdoor's "Best Places to Work" award. Stryker's Glassdoor ratings,[5] derived from over 2,700 employee reviews, include an overall 4.2 company score. In addition, an admirable 96 percent of the employees approve of the CEO, and 84 percent would recommend the organization to a friend.

Positive comments on Glassdoor include:

- *Great people, great technology, fantastic experience.*
- *Great work environment with a motivated team.*
- *Fantastic culture, very fast-paced, ambitious, driven, and the company is full of talented people. The focus is on talent over experience, understanding people's individual strengths and finding ways to develop people so they are continuously challenged and can grow.*

And as if the Gallup and Glassdoor awards and certifications weren't impressive enough, in 2019 and 2020 Stryker earned over sixty best-workplace awards for its offices and operations around the globe.

Stryker's Chairman and CEO, Kevin Lobo, believes the company's unique, inspiring work culture is due to "highly engaged people creating innovative products and services to make healthcare better." Employees believe the company's values of integrity, accountability, people, and performance—which are lived daily by all team members—are the foundation of its purposeful, positive, and productive work culture. Perhaps that explains the over one hundred uplifting, positive employee testimonials in Stryker's Culture Book.[6]

Stryker founded its company strategy[7] upon its "talent offense"—its people and culture. The company acts from the belief that leveraging employees' strengths and trusting them to solve problems creatively generates success. Performance targets are high, and the company's track record is exceptional, with thirty-eight consecutive years of financial and market growth.

But clearly, while business growth is a constant focus for Stryker, the commitment to the growth of its culture and people is just as important. And that commitment can be measured—a critical component of a Good Comes First culture. In Stryker's recent GPTW certification,[8] 90 percent of employees said the company is, indeed, a great place to work.

HOW WE SEE IT

The Good | Stryker's Good Comes First culture is driven by leveraging its people's strengths and creativity. Those assets are not only valued and validated; they are used to solve problems and increase efficiency. Yes, Stryker has great people and technology; certainly, employees are ambitious and driven—those are all contributors to the healthy culture. But the foundation of Stryker's success is good people doing good work, each focused on making healthcare better.

Does your work culture leverage people's strengths and creativity in service to your customers? In our experience, that is a rare occurrence, but Stryker has cracked the code.

ABC Supply Company

Our third Good Comes First organization is ABC Supply Company, a wholesale building supply distribution business based in Beloit, Wisconsin. ABC Supply is a fourteen-time winner of Gallup's annual Exceptional Workplace Award, and was a Glassdoor "Best Places to Work" winner in 2019 and 2020. The company's overall rating[9] on Glassdoor is 4.5. An impressive 93 percent of its employees recommend working at ABC Supply to a friend; 98 percent approve of the job CEO Keith Rozolis is doing.

On Glassdoor, ABC Supply's employees emphasize how much they appreciate the company living its values. One reviewer said:

> *This is the best company in America to work for! It does not shy away from giving back to the associates, from growth and opportunity to trust and compensation. ABC works hard to keep their core values in line with all they do.*

Another said:

> *The company truly stands behind their values, especially when it comes to family! If you want opportunities for growth, and [to] be challenged in a positive way, then this is the company for you.*

As you can probably tell, ABC's servant purpose is to be recognized as an employee-first company, producing world-class associate engagement, customer engagement, and financial results. The original company planners founded the company on seven values,[10] which team leaders and team members strive to live every day: respect, opportunity, work hard / have fun, entrepreneurial spirit, family, give back, and American pride. Employees and leaders routinely demonstrate ABC's "American Pride" value in their continuous efforts to hire, train, and retain military veterans. The company has also partnered with a reality television series, *Military Makeover*, to help with home repairs for veterans and their families—free of charge.

Growth at ABC has been entirely organic; acquisitions[11] have been a large part of ABC's growth over the years. It can be challenging to duplicate the parent company's work culture in the acquired company's environment. Still, ABC Supply learned how best to tackle that issue by leaning on their seven stated values to set the standard for these new acquisitions. Today, they excel at developing an employee-first culture in all branches and businesses they acquire.

HOW WE SEE IT

The Good | ABC Supply has built its brand and reputation on putting employees first, but it is not an "anything goes" free-for-all. The company has set exact parameters, the company's seven values, and expects all staff members to operate within them. Those values make the acquisition of complementary companies and product lines a far less painful process for employees and customers than most of us experience in typical mergers. To create their Good Comes First work culture, ABC Supply has deliberately made values—how you treat each other at work—as important as results.

Does your company?

In-N-Out Burger

Fast-food restaurants do not often show up on "great places to work" lists. One that consistently does is our fourth example of a Good Comes First organization, In-N-Out Burger.[12] Harry and Esther Snyder founded the California-based, privately owned, made-to-order hamburger chain in 1948.

Though the simple In-N-Out menu features only four items, customers, through the use of not-so-secret code words,[13] can personalize their burger's preparation, giving them a customized experience—and a sense of ownership about their food choices. In-N-Out is proud that customers will find no microwave ovens, heat lamps, or freezers in any of its restaurants. Employees make fresh burgers with fresh ingredients—and nothing else. Period.

What really helps set In-N-Out apart, though, is not its burgers (which, we admit, both of us eat at every possible opportunity!). What makes

In-N-Out a Good Comes First company is happy, enthusiastic associates who deliver exceptional customer service. The founders' granddaughter, CEO Lynsi Snyder, says the company's strong company culture—one that goes back over seventy years—is the primary driver of success. Snyder says an integral part of that culture is having fun at work while surrounded by great people. "Day to day, the work environment has to be positive, and the associates actually create that themselves by being so upbeat and enthusiastic," she said.[14] This atmosphere is maintained in part because all of its three-hundred-plus stores are company-owned, with no franchisees. This approach enables In-N-Out to maintain its established Good Comes First culture, without being subject to the many outside variables of a typical franchise-driven business model.

In-N-Out's associates seem to strongly agree that their employer provides a great place to work: Over 1,600 employees have rated the company on Glassdoor, earning it an overall rating of 4.4 out of the possible 5 points. Ninety percent of employees say they would recommend working at the company to a friend. And an impressive 97 percent approve of the job CEO Snyder is doing.[15]

Employee ratings for this upbeat burger joint on Glassdoor emphasize the distinctive company culture, fast-paced shifts, great pay, a free meal every day, room for promotion, and the family-like "all in it together" foundation.

To further create a caring culture, the chain hires from within. All store managers and assistant managers start out as associates, working the counter, the grill, and the drive-thru window, so they have experienced the hard, yet fun, work. Because of this firsthand knowledge and empathy, Snyder says store managers embrace servant leadership practices, which she and her executive team also model daily.

Clearly, the company treats associates well. And because In-N-Out puts its money where its mouth is, associates are also paid well; each starts at $13 per hour. Store managers earn $160,000 annual salaries. In-N-Out also offers benefits, including 401(k) plans, paid vacation, and dental and vision coverage for part- and full-time associates—a rare occurrence in the corporate world, particularly for part-time staff. And in the quick-service restaurant industry? Pay and benefits like these are unheard of—except at In-N-Out.

> ### HOW WE SEE IT
>
> **The Good |** The Snyder family has built and sustained a great business founded upon the concept of happy associates making fresh burgers and wowing their customers. Even in times of significant change and challenge, the foundational business model has not changed since opening their first restaurant over seventy years ago.
>
> The keys to In-N-Out's success? First, its everyday appreciation and validation of associates' efforts; even during the busiest shifts, managers and peers applaud good work. Second, compensating managers and team members exceptionally well. Of course, good pay alone does not make employees happy. Respectful, fun, validating, challenging, and inspiring leaders and peers *and* good pay, though, is a winning combination. Make our appreciation for their Good Comes First culture a double-double!

How fun is *your* workplace? How much do your employees enjoy their work?

St. Jude Children's Research Hospital

Founded in Memphis, Tennessee, in 1962, St. Jude's official mission is to advance cures, means of prevention, and treatment for catastrophic pediatric diseases. The organization's bumper sticker reference to this critical mission is more to the point: "Finding Cures. Saving Children."

St. Jude's, our fifth Good Comes First organization, has been recognized for six consecutive years by *Fortune* magazine as one of the "100 Best Companies to Work For" and was also recognized as a Great Place to Work in 2018. It was awarded Glassdoor's Best Places to Work in 2018, 2019, and 2020. On the 5-point scale, employee ratings earned St. Jude's a pride-worthy 4.6 overall rating. Ninety-three percent of the employees would recommend working at St. Jude's to a friend. An impressive 98 percent approve of the job CEO James Downing is doing.[16]

St. Jude's employees, in reviews on Glassdoor, praise the mission-focused work, great benefits, great teams, and regular recognition and validation. They also appreciate the positive and inclusive work environment. Noteworthy quotes among those reviews include:

"I've never felt so valued as an employee as I do at St. Jude," and "St. Jude truly puts the care of our patients first. Employees are treated like they matter and are shown appreciation."

One postdoctoral research fellow described St. Jude's as "totally dedicated to the health and safety of their patients. The resources available to patients and families are incredible. Everyone works together to achieve the goal of making catastrophic childhood diseases a thing of the past."[17]

HOW WE SEE IT

The Good | St. Jude's has created a purposeful, positive, productive work culture by keeping every employee deeply connected to its servant purpose, every day. It attracts topflight talent and provides the support needed for leaders and team members to solve difficult problems. Just as important, St. Jude's brings its mission home by delivering that same level of care to patients and families.

The foundation of St. Jude's Good Comes First culture is cooperation, respect, and teamwork. Ultimately, though, the most unique characteristic is the unwavering dedication to the noble mission of saving children's lives.

How noble is *your* mission? How well do you serve that mission?

WHAT DOES "GOOD" MEAN TO YOU? TO EMPLOYEES?

We defined our version of "good" in Chapter 2. And so far in Chapter 3, we've recognized a few companies that have absolutely earned their place as "Good Comes First" organizations.

Now, we ask you to look inward a bit—maybe grab your pen and paper or another note-taking device to record your thoughts. Specifically, we want to give you a chance to think about what "good" means to you—perhaps compared to Radio Flyer, Stryker, ABC Supply, In-N-Out, and St. Jude's, what does good look like to your leadership team? Your organization?

As you give these pivotal thoughts a few moments, ask yourself the most crucial question:

How do my employees define "good"?

This question is vital because we cannot depend on the definition of "good" based on the carefully chosen language for your company's "About Us" page. Good is not what a manager says while handing out slices of pizza at a Friday "All Hands." Nor is it the rosy picture a senior leader paints from a podium during a shareholder meeting.

Instead, the single most valid assessment of whether your company or its leaders create genuine good-ness comes from employees. Do those employees feel your company creates good in daily decisions? Do they see good in interactions with leaders, managers, and each other? With customers and stakeholders? Do they believe leaders model the stated company values and desired behaviors?

Do employees feel trusted? Respected? Valued?

The only way you'll know . . . is to ask.

To ask these questions of existing employees takes courage, open-mindedness, and a willingness to listen—really listen—even when the news delivered is not positive. As many Good Comes First leaders have already learned, the messages they receive from employees, when carefully heard, may sting a bit. Some will be downright painful. And all of them will most certainly present challenges that require our full attention.

To get to a place where leaders can actually hear these critical insights, companies must create safe and efficient channels for employees to share their perspectives. Otherwise, you will get the same answer you receive when you ask your partner, "What's wrong, honey?"

"I'm fine."

But as you have hopefully already learned from your personal relationships, the worst possible time to walk away from a conversation is when you hear any form of "I'm fine"!

The unfortunate reality is that most leaders, when we emphasize the need to actively listen to their employees' feedback, are in denial that problems exist in their organizations at all. They often respond with some form of: "That isn't a problem here. We have a company-wide open-door policy." Then, once they reach out to employees and receive less than glowing feedback, these leaders get stuck in a loop of defensive, unproductive thoughts, such as:

- *We were totally blindsided by the feedback.*
- *We had no idea people were so unhappy.*
- *I can't believe no one came to me with this.*

Bottom line: If you have an open-door policy and people rarely walk through that door? That is on you, and your leadership team. After all, in a Good Comes First culture, the onus to create psychologically safe (and career-safe) feedback mechanisms falls solely on the shoulders of the leadership team. It is absolutely *not* up to the employee—or customer, influencer, or stakeholder—to start the tough conversations!

We leaders are the conversation starters, the data collectors, and the active listeners. *We* are solely responsible for facilitating the kind of communications that will give us a clear picture of exactly how our employees define good—and whether they feel good in almost every interaction, every day.

GOOD COMES FIRST COMMUNICATIONS: BUILDING TRUST ONE HUMAN AT A TIME

Of course, the best way—especially at smaller organizations—to collect data from employees is through one-on-one, human-to-human conversations.

However, we are not naïve; we know it is impossible, for example, for every person at General Motors to sit down with CEO Mary Barra. Besides, in many companies, an invitation to sit down with the CEO would create less-than-comfortable "What-did-I-do-wrong?" reactions.

This limitation of scale means it is up to you and your leadership team to determine which data collection channels might work best within your culture. You must also consider the precedent for communication you want to set for your ideal culture . . . or what will become your Good Comes First culture.

Such channels can include values surveys (which we highly recommend), pulse surveys (one question a week to all company members), and digital suggestion mailboxes (which also work well for communicating concerns). One of our favorite, almost-never-fail, communication channels: small-group meetups with senior leaders (think: "Lunch with Louise"—where Louise is the CXO). These informal meetings are feedback gold mines for confident leaders who have proven themselves to be active listeners!

Not ready to survey employees? Or, just as important, don't want to risk poorly setting expectations that organizational change is coming? Use the same resources we employ in our practice—and this book—to discreetly gauge the current culture of almost any organization: Look at Glassdoor,[18] Gallup,[19] and Great Place to Work[20] to obtain a snapshot of how employees—past and present—view your company culture, and how employees feel about working for your company.

Read more about these three verified platforms and partners and their respected workplace rating systems:

Glassdoor | On Glassdoor, employees can rate their employers on five criteria, each on a 5-point scale: culture and values, work-life balance, senior management, compensation and benefits, and career opportunities.

Glassdoor features two additional important data points: the percentage of employees who would recommend the company to a friend and the percentage of employees who approve of the job the CEO is doing. This combination of data provides an accurate picture of the quality of the company's current work culture as perceived by current and former employees.

Gallup | Gallup's Exceptional Workplace Award has top-tier criteria and a rigorous selection process; for example, Gallup requires survey responses from *every* employee within an organization rather than a small sample of responses. Scores on Gallup's Q12 employee engagement survey must place the applicant in the upper echelon of applicants. Finally, a panel of Gallup workplace scientists and experts assess detailed evidence about strategy and leadership, performance and accountability, communication and knowledge management, and development and ongoing learning.

Only applicants recognized as having the highest engagement, productivity, and profits receive the Exceptional Workplace Award we mentioned earlier.

Great Place to Work | Great Place to Work is considered a global authority on workplace culture and employee experience. It helps companies worldwide survey their employees, benchmark their results, identify gaps, and improve their workplace culture. Great Place to Work's program is based on a rigorous methodology and validated employee feedback.

The company uses its "For All Model and Methodology"—a method of ensuring diversity, equality, and inclusion throughout the organization—to evaluate the pool of Great Place to Work–certified companies. Top-performing companies are recognized as Best Workplaces by their respective geographic areas, company size, and more.

Whether through quantitative or qualitative surveys, online research, or all of the above, collecting thoughts on how employees view good-ness—and your company culture as a whole—is just the beginning. Now you must also objectively analyze the feedback in a careful, balanced way. This unbiased analysis helps leaders understand how well they are creating a Good Comes First work culture. Perhaps even more important, leaders will learn the exact steps necessary to create a more ideal Good Comes First culture in the near future.

The work for you and your leadership team does not stop there, however. Next, you must share the feedback you obtained through surveys and research with managers and employees. And after you have shared this feedback, you must implement changes based on that feedback—which usually generates a "Hey, they really listened!" reaction from employees. This, in turn, helps create a circle of goodwill and trust—because people now know that leadership cares.

And they have good reason to care back.

GOOD-NESS IS PERSONAL

As mentioned in Chapter 2, when considering and sharing feedback with our leaders and employees, we must remember that we all have a different interpretation of good-ness. These differences are nuanced, yes, but they are important to address as you "scratch" each unique itch—and deliver good effectively for different types of people each day.

The key to considering and sharing this feedback is to start with one of the elements of our Good Comes First model: respect and validation.

As we covered in Chapter 1—and as you might have learned firsthand as your career progressed—employees have been treated poorly by organizations (and leaders) for generations. Building a foundation of civil relationships based on mutual respect and frequent and public validation has a substantial positive impact on employee good-ness. In every company, regardless of industry or niche, respect and validation generate confidence, creativity, results—and, with sustained good-ness, joy.

Of course, reaching "joy" status is not easy. (After all, has anyone ever used the word "joy" to describe your company? Your workplace?)

Creating individual relationships and an overarching work culture based on the Good Comes First model requires leaders to evolve beyond a pure focus on results. In fact, becoming a Good Comes First leader often requires entirely new beliefs, new behaviors, and new degrees of engagement. As you can imagine, that overhaul leads to two personal challenges every Good Comes First leader must overcome: change and growth.

PERSONAL CHALLENGE 1: CHANGE

We humans do not like change. Oh, we might *say* we welcome change. But then our comfort zones slap us right in the face.

Sure, we leaders might learn new skills and behaviors well outside our comfort zones throughout our careers, but we rarely practice them. That is because demonstrating new skills requires intention *and* attention, time and effort, and a certain amount of vulnerability. So, in the end, too few business leaders invest time in proactively growing and mastering the skills required to serve others better. Instead, leaders spend far too much time reacting to problems that arise. And while we are firefighting—saving old storage buildings full of "the way we've always done it"—we are not building new structures, new processes, or new ways to create good.

We are just hanging on to what we know.

We have lived those exact circumstances over the course of our careers—both as team members for reactive bosses and, truth be told, as reactive bosses ourselves. Along the way, we have learned that leaders cannot be both firefighters *and* culture architects. We must not only decide where to invest our time, but we must also seek the highest possible return on that investment. Otherwise, all that will remain is the charred ruins of a poor company culture—one that perhaps was not worth saving in the first place.

In other words, before we can ask our fellow leaders and employees to embrace change—to become change champions—we must first be willing to change ourselves. We are the role models. Every day, we lead by example. Neglecting this truth means we are launching just another insincere change effort, doomed to fail.

PERSONAL CHALLENGE 2: GROWTH

As intimated above, once leaders are in executive positions, they are not typically expected to learn and grow. They got where they are because they already learned and grew a lot, sometimes the hard way.

And yet, to move past our first challenge—resistance to change—leaders must be willing to grow. To learn. Because without demonstrating a commitment to learning and developing ourselves, we cannot expect others to learn and grow. Or change. There is no way around this. No Plan B.

You, dear reader, are actively engaged in growing right now. Your decision to read this book is a decision to learn. To be a more effective leader. A mentor. A change champion. And by consistently serving as an ambassador for growth—and good—you will set a new pace. And a new precedent.

As we have learned from the companies mentioned in this chapter, the good news is that organizations have already set this precedent. There *are* leaders who have already transformed their organizations into Good Comes First cultures. They already put values on the same pedestal as results. And through their personal growth—and the growth in those they lead—they already see significant improvements in process, productivity, profits, and retention of their best people. Growth is not just possible.

For leaders, personal growth—the very heart of a Good Comes First culture—is required.

Right about now, you may be ready to meet this personal challenge. Ready to change—and grow. We hope so!

You now know what a Good Comes First company looks—and acts—like; that is an excellent start. You may be ready to jump ahead, but before moving on to the next chapter, take a moment to ask yourself these important questions:

- What does "good" look like to you?
- What does "good" look like to your leadership team and organization?
- What does "good" look like to your employees?

Write down your answers. Refine them as necessary. Make sure they make sense.

While you are at it, take another moment to reflect upon how your organization compares to the Good Comes First companies in this chapter. What is working well? What is not? Most important, take a few minutes to think about the challenges you will face along the way and how you, as a role model and change champion, can make a difference as you move your organization to a Good Comes First culture. Think about—and write down—answers to the following questions:

- How can you help your employees, managers, and fellow leaders change? How can you help them grow?
- How can you help team members, vendors, and customers feel more respected? How can you make them feel more validated?
- How can you personally help members of your team develop a Good Comes First mindset?

Once you have these answers, let's move forward. Because in our next chapter, we will look at some less-than-good companies: the bad and the ugly. As you'll see, there are valuable lessons to be learned from the leaders and companies that suck, that put greed before good, and results before reinvention.

 **CHAPTER 4**

The Bad and the Ugly: Organizations That Failed to Put Good First

For decades, senior leaders have been taught to focus on, and have been measured almost exclusively by, results.

That is just the way it was—and for many organizations, it still is. However, based on a century of Industrial Age experience, we now know that we de-emphasize the human experience when we are hyper-focused on traditional business metrics. Even worse, as leaders almost deliberately disconnected from human-centered workplace issues, employees—by default—came to feel less important: less important than process, less than meeting deadlines, and certainly less than profits.

Within these "less than" workplaces, employees' beliefs were—and are—molded, perpetuated, and maybe even exaggerated by their daily experiences and interactions with disassociated leaders. Employees have learned to see through the "rah-rah" messaging and manipulative attempts to increase engagement. When employees realize they are simply resources to be managed, even the most inspiring work-related moments quickly lose their power to motivate. Eventually, not even the most charismatic leader can help people rise above challenges that seem to come too fast and too often, because the natural by-products of this endless cycle of drama are exhaustion, disengagement, burnout, and attrition. And, as we will learn in Chapter 5, even worse than attrition? The scores of exhausted, disengaged players still on the payroll.

In the worst organizational cultures, the problems cut even deeper. Employees' ideas, efforts, and accomplishments are demeaned, discounted, and dismissed every day. In those companies, employers seem to intentionally create policies to undermine dignity and respect. In these demotivating and demoralizing workplace environments, processes inevitably fail, teams miss critical milestones, and profits suffer. So do market share, key employee retention, and—eventually—the ability to attract top talent. When that happens, a company's culture can turn bad—and maybe even ugly.

THE DIFFERENCE BETWEEN BAD AND UGLY

We have all been part of a "bad" situation at work: Bad bosses. Bad communication. Less than desirable working conditions. Nepotism, cronyism, racism, sexism—all the isms. So we will not spend a lot of time defining "bad." Besides, based on your experiences, your definition may be quite different from ours. Or you might not know how to define a bad employer. For you, maybe bad is similar to what the United States Supreme Court said about pornography in a landmark 1964 decision: "I know it when I see it . . . and this is not that."

Ugliness, on the other hand—at least for our purposes—needs further defining. So, for this book, let's stick with a classic definition, again from Merriam-Webster:[1] "morally offensive or objectionable." Under the wide "morally offensive" and "objectionable" umbrellas, organizations in the Social Age are increasingly familiar with how easy it is to become "ugly" in the public eye. Specifically, they become outed for what employees, customers, and stakeholders perceive as leadership's immoral or intolerable acts.

In today's business climate, whistleblowers, activists, and influencers can swiftly alter a company's public image with one mouse click. When that happens, a "bad" situation (which might be considered a mostly internal issue) quickly turns "ugly" (where the bad hits an irreversible—and very public—tipping point).

In the following pages, we call out five companies that are both "bad" and "ugly." Specifically, we uncover leadership voids—where necessary aspects like strategic clarity, clear direction, and authentic validation were absent. These examples are not meant to shock (you are not reading the *National Enquirer*, after all), but rather to illustrate the impact—the logical consequences—of the type of "we only care about results" philosophy still in place in far too many organizations.

Before we dive into these five examples, though, some context: It is not our intention to paint these leaders as evil or selfish—they are not. Mostly, they are just unaware. In our practice, we have worked with senior leaders whose behaviors absolutely led to unhealthy work cultures. Some of those senior leaders were pleasant people who meant well. Driven to succeed to a fault, some did not see the negative impact their behaviors had on employee spirit, creativity, and sanity (that is "bad"). Or—they saw it and did not care (which can undeniably turn "ugly").

Ultimately, whether senior leaders *intend* to demean employees in the course of getting product out the door does not matter. In a Good Comes First culture, *intention does not matter.* Influence and impact, though, *does* matter—a great deal.

Employees demonstrate far less proactive problem solving, confidence, teamwork, cooperation, productivity, and service when faced with a negative influence or impact from the leadership team. Positive influences and impacts—throughout the organization—have the exact opposite effect: They *increase* how often employees demonstrate desirable characteristics like active listening, relevant radical candor, empathy, and accountability.

With all that in mind, let's first take a look at those "bad" and "ugly" companies—real companies doing a consistently poor job of ensuring Good Comes First. Then, let's look at global workplace trends that—despite being accepted as "the way it has always been"—must change in order for any company to transition to a Good Comes First culture.

NOT-SO-GOOD COMPANY CULTURES

Cathay Pacific

In 2019, anti-government activists in Hong Kong took to the streets in protest of a law they felt would undermine judicial independence and endanger people that the Chinese government thought to be dissidents. As these protests grew in intensity and scope, many companies in Hong Kong—especially those subject to mainland China's rules—were forced to make hard choices, including Cathay Pacific, one of Hong Kong's flagship airlines.

In response to the protests and to appease the Chinese government's Civil Aviation Administration of China (CAAC), which banned employees from working flights in China if they supported these protests, executives at Cathay Pacific implemented stringent new rules. These rules prohibited any staff member from attending what the mainland Chinese government termed "illegal" protests. Controversial? Yes. Restrictive from a free speech perspective? Absolutely. Still, while not ideal from an employee perspective, the airline's new rules did align with the CAAC's directives and were seen as "in the best interests of the company."

But Cathay Pacific did not stop there. The company revised its employee code of conduct, encouraging employees to speak up should they become aware that a fellow employee was breaking the new rules against supporting the protests. If they reported breaches of the code, employees were rewarded for what management perceived as loyalty. As a logical consequence of this new (and, in hindsight, misguided) "whistleblowing" policy, first came finger-pointing, then firings. Employees stopped trusting each other. As one Cathay Pacific pilot said, "We now live in a culture of fear."[2]

Undoubtedly, Cathay Pacific was in a difficult position. The government's policies forced the company to choose between appeasing the mainland Chinese government and supporting its employees. Pitting employees against each other, however, encouraging betrayal, and eroding trust are not how you create good-ness.

HOW WE SEE IT

The Bad | To conform to China's restrictions on anti-government protests, Cathay Pacific introduced policies that reduced or eliminated trust (of both management and peers) and dramatically increased the workplace's level of fear. In the process, they perhaps violated their employees' civil rights, effectively turning team members into the very "dissidents" the protestors rallied to protect.

The Ugly | Showing a complete lack of social intelligence, the company did not imagine anyone would broadcast its new policies to every corner of the world. It did not seem to understand the new rules would only embolden the protestors—and the airline's Hong Kong employees. Within days, the world became aware of Cathay Pacific's morally offensive decisions.

Focused on short-term results, the airline failed to adhere to an overarching servant purpose. In the process, they demonstrated a highly objectionable disregard for fundamental human values and rights. Perhaps even worse: Even today, the company still does not seem to have formalized a set of values that would ensure respectful treatment of employees or customers, especially in times of crisis or change.

Have you ever been in a situation where you let short-term goals or pressures get in the way of protecting your employees? Or your company culture? What was the fallout?

The Boeing Company

As you are likely aware, the Boeing Company has been making airplanes for over a century. It has done this with great success over the years by abiding by several stated values, including "engineering excellence" and "being accountable."

In 2011, Boeing turned its focus to its newest flagship: the 737 MAX, which promised to be a state-of-the-art aircraft. However, very early on in the development process, employees and test pilots warned company leadership that the 737 MAX exhibited systemic safety concerns. Rather than listening to these concerns and taking action, Boeing carried on with business as usual, doing nothing to address the safety issues. The aircraft was ultimately sold as is—without notifying the buyers of any safety concerns.

Two major crashes and 347 tragically avoidable deaths later, the 737 MAX was grounded. Customers canceled existing orders for the aircraft. Future sales were nonexistent. In the end, Boeing had no choice but to halt production of the former flagship indefinitely. Altogether, Boeing shelled out almost $5 billion to cover the 737 MAX disaster. However, what may have been even more costly was the blow to the Boeing Company's reputation as a manufacturer devoted to safety.

Though official reports state the cause of these crashes was a loss of communication between human pilots and the digital-dependent aircraft, the root cause was Boeing leadership's complete failure to listen to employees and pilots. When we examine the information that was available to Boeing's senior leaders and the decisions they made, it is clear that selling airplanes (even flawed airplanes) was more important than everything else, including saving lives.

HOW WE SEE IT

The Bad | Senior leaders, discounting reports by internal experts that the 737 MAX demonstrated unsafe conditions in flight, were only concerned with delivering the airplanes on time and on budget. Clearly, Boeing did not live up to the company's first two values:[3] "engineering excellence" and "being accountable." In hindsight, management entirely ignored these values while working on the 737 MAX project.

The Ugly | Had Boeing executives listened—really listened—to their employees, the problems surrounding the 737 MAX aircraft would have been handled internally as a quality control issue. Instead, Boeing—deservedly so—found itself featured regularly in the news cycles for months after the public learned of internal memos revealing company leaders had advanced warning about the safety issues of the 737 MAX. In some eyes, Boeing's brand—and reputation—may never recover.

Stopping production to address unsafe flight systems would have saved the company billions of dollars and saved the lives of 347 people.

While the stakes may not be as high for your company as they were for Boeing, have you ever failed to listen to concerns from your team and ultimately been forced to deal with the consequences? What processes can be put in place to ensure every voice is heard and respected within your company?

Liberty University

Liberty University, founded in 1971, promises to deliver "an education that is both academically challenging and rooted in a biblical worldview." Despite this lofty goal, for years, the culture at Liberty University was steeped in controversy. Both on and off campus, rumors of authoritarian leaders who disrespected faculty and staff and oppressed students' and teachers' First Amendment rights flourished, until finally, a former editor of the university's student-published weekly newspaper wrote a *Washington Post* article in 2019 titled "Inside Liberty University's 'culture of fear.'"[4]

The article described how CEO Jerry Falwell Jr. systematically limited free expression by faculty, students, and employees. In particular, the article alleged that any public disagreement with Falwell Jr.'s conservative views was dealt with harshly, and dissent was "ruthlessly neutralized."

Falwell also failed to put good first at Liberty University by not offering tenure. While tenure for educators—an elite post and career milestone—is a staple in the academic world, Liberty hires many faculty members on year-to-year contracts. If a faculty member did not toe the line (based on evaluations that leaders made by carefully monitoring campus email servers and social media posts), their contracts were allowed to expire. Often, Liberty failed to renew contracts so late in the academic hiring year that finding another teaching job became virtually impossible for instructors.

Even worse, terminated and otherwise removed faculty are forced to sign nondisclosure agreements in perpetuity. Former employees cannot disparage the university, its leaders, or its policies at any time. Such NDAs are unusual in the university setting—and are difficult to enforce in any setting. And yet, Liberty's nondisclosure agreements serve the university's self-protecting purpose by intimidating those who sign them, essentially acting as self-imposed gag orders. To save their current jobs, or to avoid negatively impacting the chance of securing another job outside Liberty, many former Liberty staff members feel compelled to quell damaging information about the university—even years later.

Despite this toxic culture, it was not until Falwell Jr. posted a risqué photo on social media that the board at Liberty University took action. (Apparently, the posted pic was counter to the university's code of conduct . . . but a soul-crushing, career-canceling culture was okay.) A short time later, after it was revealed Falwell and his wife engaged in an extramarital affair, Liberty University fully parted ways with Falwell.

HOW WE SEE IT

The Bad | For at least five years (if not longer), the university's administration and its board tolerated Falwell's quashing of free expression. His aggressive tactics created a "culture of fear" among faculty, students, and employees, who learned—sometimes the hard way—not to get on the wrong side of CEO Falwell.

The Ugly | As if a blatant display of disrespect were not enough, it is evident through its actions that this university and its stated values—from the top down—did not live up to its biblical promise. In addition, the organization appears to have little or no social intelligence: Even without the questionable pic being shared online and despite an abundance of NDAs, it was only a matter of time before this toxic culture came to light publicly. And eventually, so did that controversial affair.

At Liberty University, everything that makes for a Good Comes First environment was utterly absent. A contradiction between the organization's stated and demonstrated servant purpose and values? Definitely. Leaders failed to trust their employees (evidenced in the way they monitored social media) or validate them (seen in the lack of tenure positions they offered faculty) and stymied any growth opportunities. And they certainly did not use their voice for good. Of all our examples of companies that failed to put good first, Liberty stands out as a company whose unintentional culture too closely followed a troubled leader's tragic flaws.

Have you experienced a situation where a bad leader whose undesirable and unproductive behaviors go unchecked has negatively impacted company culture? What systems does your organization have in place to ensure the alignment of leaders to desired behaviors?

The Ellen DeGeneres Show

The Ellen DeGeneres Show first aired in 2003, and quickly gained a reputation as the epitome of fun, compassionate, feel-good entertainment. So many were surprised to learn that from 2018 to 2020, multiple current and former employees reported experiencing racism, bullying, harassment, and intimidation by executive producers and other senior staff.

As a result of what many believed to be credible insight into how the show's culture failed to live up to its on-air reputation, parent company WarnerMedia conducted an internal investigation.[5] The investigation revealed Ellen herself was not the cause of the toxic environment (and possibly did not know it was occurring, as from all outside appearances, it seemed she remained insulated from day-to-day employee experiences). However, WarnerMedia found enough "deficiencies" in the work culture that it committed to taking swift action, including making changes to the executive production staff.

In response to the report and the criticism generated, Ellen wrote a letter to her staff expressing her disappointment:

> *"On day one of our show, I told everyone in our first meeting that 'The Ellen DeGeneres Show' would be a place of happiness—no one would ever raise their voice, and everyone would be treated with respect," she wrote. "Obviously, something changed, and I am disappointed to learn that this has not been the case. And for that, I am sorry. Anyone who knows me knows it's the opposite of what I believe and what I hoped for our show."*[6]

A heartfelt message, to be sure—accountable and remorseful. But at the core of this scenario, DeGeneres proved herself to be a disconnected senior leader; she was not aware of the daily employee experience. Though it was her responsibility, she did not keep her "fingers on the pulse" of whether employees were happy while working for the show. She did not make an effort to understand whether they were treated respectfully in every interaction, every day.

DeGeneres is not alone in this; she is not the first leader to make this culture mistake. To this day, despite a growing awareness that company cultures must change, and that leaders are solely responsible for being change-makers, far too many business leaders have no understanding of their employees' daily experiences.

HOW WE SEE IT

The Bad | Despite an outward appearance that fun and happiness were at the core of the show's culture, a toxic environment created fear, anxiety, and distrust among employees. Compounding this failure of culture, Ellen was not in tune with her employees' work experience.

The Ugly | There is no evidence the show's values were ever formalized or defined—especially in terms of appropriate, measurable behaviors. There is also no evidence that DeGeneres, as a leader, made a deliberate attempt to understand the level of toxicity before the negative reports surfaced on social media and in mainstream news. Contrary to her personal brand, the court of public opinion ruled Ellen did not really care, at least for a time, about the treatment of the very employees she seemed to love so much.

Ellen's apology and accountability were timely and thorough. Her apology is only the first step, though—and there are many steps to go to rebuild, monitor, and ensure respect on the set. The second step? To understand the quality of her show's work culture and gain firsthand knowledge of whether her leadership team is putting good first, Ellen must commit to regularly and actively engage with the show's employees. Leaders who model the show's desired culture must be validated; leaders who do not must be coached and held accountable. Only then will the show's work culture evolve to reach the lofty standard of kindness promised by Ellen's on-air persona.

As a leader, have you ever fallen out of touch with your employees' experience at work? How do you ensure your leadership team is constantly aware of how employees perceive your company as an employer?

Facebook

In the United States, Facebook steadfastly commands the second-largest share of the digital ad market—only Google generates more ad revenue. In 2020, however, Facebook took what appeared to be a severe hit. Over two hundred major advertisers, many using the #StopHateforProfit hashtag, boycotted the company due to the hate speech Facebook allowed to flourish on its platform. Specifically, advertisers such as Coca-Cola, Ben & Jerry's, Microsoft, and Ford[7] drew the line when Facebook refused to take down hate speech seemingly used for political reasons.

For Facebook and its CEO Mark Zuckerberg, that "line" was the real problem. After all, under Zuckerberg's leadership, Facebook has never drawn its own line around values and ethics and was incentivized not to do so: Facebook, in fact, bases its business model on engagement and time on-site. The more controversial the content—the more outrage generated and passionate arguments started—the longer users spend their time on the site, and the more Facebook exposes them to highly profitable ads.

Without definitive boundaries, Zuckerberg and his leadership team were—and, as of press time, still are—motivated to play hard for both teams. Even in their response to the advertiser boycott, Facebook played both sides. Consider these two competing statements:

- Facebook's corporate statement to the press: "We deeply respect any brand's decision and remain focused on the important work of removing hate speech and providing critical voting information. Our conversations with marketers and civil rights organizations are about how, together, we can be a force for good."

- At the exact same time, Mark Zuckerberg's personal statement to Facebook employees:[8] "[I won't] change our policies or our approach on anything because of a threat to a small percent of our revenue, or to any percent of our revenue."

The result of Facebook and Zuckerberg's two-faced attitude was an approximate loss of $7.5 billion in advertising dollars. To counter the barrage of bad press, Facebook ultimately did an about-face and began to remove some political posts for spreading misinformation, including those of President Donald Trump and the Trump campaign.

The boycott ended in July 2020, but the repercussions lingered. While some advertisers praised the change in Facebook's policy around fact-checking and hate speech, others were more cautious. Coca-Cola, for instance, stated, "Any return to buying ads on both Facebook and Instagram will be based on Facebook's efforts to suppress hate speech." Premium spirit maker Beam Suntory took a firmer stand, saying, "We have yet to see sufficient progress to change our approach and continue to hope this collective action helps catalyze positive change and accountability."

To save face—and win back the confidence, trust, and budgets of some of America's biggest advertisers—Facebook still has some work to do.

HOW WE SEE IT

The Bad | In the eyes of many, Facebook's failure to establish and enforce a set of corporate values and ethics removed the company from its exalted status as one of Silicon Valley's best success stories. From users to industry experts, many people now see Facebook as it probably should have been seen some time ago: a greedy, multinational force driven exclusively by results.

The Ugly | In both mainstream media and online, Facebook's failures have been—and undoubtedly will continue to be—fodder for many unflattering conversations. Advertisers, users, and Facebook employees themselves rallied around the #StopHateforProfit movement, forcing Zuckerberg—however coyly—to take a stand.

But, as of press time, Facebook still cannot win. They still suck!

People on both sides of the political spectrum continue to rally against the social media platform: In the United States, progressives accuse Facebook of not doing enough to reduce hate speech and halt misinformation. Meanwhile, conservatives maintain that Facebook (and social media platforms in general) deliberately mutes their voices. In addition, refinement or repeal of Section 230 of the Communications Decency Act, which protects social media companies like Facebook from lawsuits if a user posts something unfactual or illegal, seems imminent.

In the end, we have to ask: Did the boycott work? Was the company actually hurt by advertisers' efforts to force Facebook to change its objectional, perhaps even immoral, policies?

Most experts agree that, given the $70 billion in advertising taken in by Facebook each year, this boycott—from a dollars and cents perspective—was nothing more than a proverbial drop in the bucket. Still, most analysts believe the severe public relations hit for Facebook forced it to finally take action, to leave situational ethics behind, and at least begin *some* effort to put good first.

What systems does your organization have in place to ensure leaders' behavior is consistent with your company's stated values? How can companies demonstrate that, within the company culture, values are just as important as results?

A CLOSER LOOK AT WHY

Why would executives of the organizations mentioned in this chapter create and sustain unhealthy work cultures? When presented with the fact that employees do not trust or respect them and do not feel valued, why might senior leaders ignore that input?

Our experiences and research point to a common root cause: We have never asked senior leaders to create and sustain a purposeful, positive, productive work culture. Furthermore, we never taught those leaders how to build and embed a work culture that delivers respect *and* results.

First, throughout the Industrial Age, business leaders were not recognized or incentivized to improve the quality of their organization's work cultures. Senior leaders measured, monitored, and rewarded three things: results, results, and more results. Hitting sales and profit targets or boosting market share was simply a matter of monitoring traction on performance expectations. Results were easy to measure, because results were *all* that was measured.

Second, senior leaders' role models—the people they spent a career observing and emulating—suffered from the same skill deficit. These mentors also focused (and perhaps still focus) on results. They did not typically demonstrate competency at refining their work culture, nor were they known for clarifying a servant purpose, values, or behaviors. As a result, they did not model and coach those behaviors in their protégés or people. Nor did they hold all company leaders—especially those who looked up to them—accountable for those behaviors.

Third, even the most self-aware, forward-thinking senior leaders do not know how to change their work cultures. Most senior leaders have never experienced a successful culture change, much less led one. It makes sense that few senior leaders have the skills to create a Good Comes First work culture without help. They need a push in the right direction and a clear sense of urgency—because, for them, rather than a deliberate desire to put good first, insurmountable market pressure most often sparks the need for change.

So, by following yesterday's standards for leadership, even the most successful leaders:

- Are not motivated to create a company culture that deliberately puts good first
- Like their predecessors, emulate their role models perfectly (perfectly poorly—but perfectly)
- Are not ready to reinvent—and are perhaps not capable of leading a reinvention of—their company culture

This cycle is not only vicious but is also, in a negative way, self-sustaining. For publicly traded organizations, Wall Street measures and celebrates results; the stock markets do not reflect the degree to which an organization creates and sustains enthused, creative employees. Even for non–publicly traded organizations, Wall Street's emphasis on what is good and valuable (results!) influences leaders' behaviors.

A TYPICAL BOARDROOM

For a closer look at how Wall Street–vindicated behaviors influence autocratic, results-focused leaders now faced with the need to demonstrably change their company cultures, let's take a peek inside an ordinary boardroom as recently shared by a colleague.

An executive leadership team was discussing increased turnover. The company was losing talented leaders and team members by the handful because, as recent exit interviews revealed, these players did not feel appreciated. Too many employees felt more like "cogs in a wheel" than valued contributors. One VP suggested doing an engagement survey of the current workforce to gauge perceptions; and specifically, to see if they felt aligned with the employees who chose to leave the company.

The CEO boldly replied, "I don't care about happy employees! I just want people to produce!"

(Awkward silence.)

Despite his leadership team's baffled reaction, this CEO acted precisely as trained: He focused exclusively on results. In his world, people did not matter. To him, employee good-ness did not matter—at least compared to results. Of course, there is no question that results are an essential component of an organization's effectiveness; ultimately, revenue generation outpacing expenses is the only way a business can exist and grow.

So, even in the best Good Comes First companies, leaders closely monitor traditional business results. However, in today's best workplaces—where values are viewed just as favorably as conventional business metrics—getting results is exactly *half* the leader's job. The other half is generating respect—specifically, treating others with reverence and positive regard, inside and outside the workplace. And ensuring all leaders and team members do the same.

MEASURING RESULTS *AND* RESPECT

Senior leaders already know how to measure results, but they do not yet know how to measure respect. In fact, many leaders do not believe respect— or any other value—*is* measurable. But values *can* be measured, just not as typically defined. For example, if integrity is one of your organization's values, how do you know if leaders and team members demonstrate integrity in daily interactions? If you ask twenty people in your organization what integrity means, how many different answers will you get?

As you will learn in Chapter 8, to create clarity and consistency, a Good Comes First leader must define values in observable, tangible, measurable terms. By creating and modeling valued behaviors, you explicitly validate the specific behaviors you want members of your organization—leaders and team members alike—to demonstrate daily.

Making values as measurable as results enables leaders to define their company's desired culture—and model it, coach it, and celebrate it daily. What if Cathay Pacific, Boeing, Liberty University, *The Ellen DeGeneres Show*, and Facebook demonstrated the values that help a company move toward a Good Comes First culture? They each would have avoided disappointing employees and customers, major dents in their reputations, significant revenue loss, and—in Boeing's case—tragic loss of life.

You now know how we define good. You have read examples of companies and leaders that deliberately put good first, and you have learned from the mistakes of those organizations that did not. At this point, you may even know how you—personally—define good.

You also understand exactly why—in Good Comes First companies, and some of the world's best organizations—values are placed on the same pedestal as results.

In our next chapter, we will bring the concept of Good Comes First back to the results side of this process. We will discuss why creating a Good Comes First work culture requires an investment of time, energy, and money, and how it will lead to tangible results for your bottom line. We will introduce exactly where those work-hours, passion points, and dollars will come from—so you may invest in proactively leading your organization toward a culture that puts good first.

When done right, this is a powerful, self-perpetuating cycle that generates more good—and more profits—every day!

 **CHAPTER 5**

The Business Case for
Good Comes First

In this book, we offer a different way to conduct business. We ask you to consider changing the way you operate your business by thinking about stakeholders—from team members to customers to vendors and partners—through the lens of a servant purpose. In addition, we ask you to personally lead this noble change effort. As you have already learned, executives must be the face of the transition to a Good Comes First culture; you cannot delegate the responsibility for change. *You* must be the change champion, the head coach, and the head cheerleader.

You might be thinking, "Damn, that is a lot of work. What exactly will this company gain from my effort?" In other words: What's in it for you? You know there must be a reason why your company would make this transition—this investment—even if you do not know what that reason is yet. Regardless of your why, though, the business case for deliberately creating a Good Comes First workplace comes down to precisely one issue: ROI.

What return on investment can you expect in your organization for devoting the necessary time, energy, and resources to ensuring that respect is valued as much as results? For measuring values and behaviors with the same sense of urgency as business metrics? For making sure leaders and peers treat employees with dignity—by trusting them, validating them, and giving them the opportunity for growth—in daily interactions?

If you have read many business books—especially those based on theories rather than practical application and actionable advice—it may surprise you to learn we have an answer to these questions:

The ROI of creating a Good Comes First workplace averages a significant boost of 35 percent to our "Big Three": customer service, engagement, and results.

These improvements are remarkable, and they are proven. However, those gains do not happen first. Or fast.

As you can imagine, getting these kinds of results requires more than just time, energy, and resources. It requires intention and attention, equal measures of patience and diligence, and generous amounts of consistency and resiliency. Think of this process like a commitment to a healthier, fitter you: You must exercise consistently and follow the proper diet to improve your health, right?

The same applies to a culture transformation. The result—a purposeful, positive, productive work culture—only transforms after you put in all the work over a significant period of time. But as you will see in the next few pages, the result—and the ROI—is well worth the effort!

First, let's talk about what a purposeful, positive, productive culture is worth to your company.

WHAT IS CULTURE WORTH?

In 2020, Glassdoor's economic research division released a study on "What's Culture Worth?"[1] The study examined this vital question: "Do companies with high employee satisfaction on Glassdoor outperform their peers financially?" Researchers examined the 134 publicly traded Best Places to Work winners (over the twelve years of the award's existence) and, in critical findings that align with our research and experience, Glassdoor found their awardees earned significantly higher stock returns.

- The eighty-one winners listed on the New York Stock Exchange earned an average annual stock return of 16.9 percent from 2009 to 2019.
- The fifty-three winners on the NASDAQ exchange averaged stock returns of 24.9 percent—nearly twice those of the S&P 500 index during that same time frame.

A similar 2015 study[2] by Glassdoor found companies named to their Best Places to Work list outperformed the overall S&P 500 from 2009 to 2014 by 122.3 percent. Being designated as a Best Place to Work, as we saw in Chapter 3, comes in large part from how employees feel about working at that company—also known as employee satisfaction. The greatest impact on employee satisfaction, another 2015 study[3] found, is derived from none other than culture and values.

It's true! Respondents stated culture and values meant more to them as employees than every other statistically significant predictor of workplace satisfaction: more than senior leadership, career opportunities, work-life balance—and even compensation and benefits. A 2020 Achievers survey[4] reported similar results in Europe: Employees there are less driven by salary considerations. Not a big surprise: Appreciation, work-life balance, and career opportunities are more vital contributors to increased engagement and reduced attrition than pay.

We have regarded "employee engagement" wrong for too many years. Clearly, there is something powerful and positive in this employee experience/employee satisfaction data. As you consider building your own Good Comes First culture, your employees' experiences will be a significant factor.

A REASON TO TAKE THE HILL

Throughout Chapter 3, we recognized organizations that have undoubtedly built their own versions of a Good Comes First culture. Each clearly understands the employees' experience is critical to success—which is why their impeccable reputations as employers are well earned. However, *their* healthy cultures alone do not justify a change of *your* company culture. For business leaders still measured by results, reinvention—change for the sake of change—is not helpful, nor is it enough. Similarly, being known as "good" just to be good is not good enough. As we have already said, results matter. We get it. To invest the time, energy, and resources necessary to initiate the kind of culture change suggested within these pages, there must be a definitive reason to take the hill, for both you as a reader and leader—and your leadership team and your employees.

Many leaders choose to lead this charge—especially during a post-pandemic recovery cycle—for a simple reason: to build a stronger company, one capable of meeting the most significant challenges, fending off competitors, and effectively surviving any economic downturn. They want happier customers, lower overhead, and higher profits.

To make all that happen, leaders must put good first.

By this point in the book—and likely from your own experience and reflections—it should be clear that employees who feel valued and validated generate better results with less drama. They not only welcome challenges, but also create new solutions to old problems. Remember the Glassdoor comment made by a (Radio) Flyer, quoted in Chapter 3? The one who said, "The thing I love most about my job is the freedom to use my creativity to solve complex problems and invent new products that delight families"?

Well, that is not an isolated idea. In purposeful, positive, productive work cultures, employees cooperate to share lessons learned and to leverage new knowledge. Together, they find new strengths and form new alliances. They recognize and celebrate the successes of their peers and their teams— small steps, tremendous accomplishments, and everything in between. They build trust organically.

In Good Comes First cultures, the entire organizational population reinforces and amplifies the good each person does—and the good the organization does for its customers and communities. Everyone in the organization treats leaders, peers, team members, vendors, and customers with dignity and respect. The benefit is impressive. Employees who operate in a vibrant, respectful, focused, and fun work environment prove themselves to out-produce employees who operate in a lethargic or toxic work environment by 35 percent and more.

And we can prove it.[5]

REAL COMPANIES—REAL RESULTS

Senior leaders get excited at the prospect of a considerable bump in results and profits. They are enthused about gains in engagement and customer service ratings, as well—but they are, not surprisingly, most enthused about increases in results. As we have said, in a Good Comes First culture, focusing on results is exactly half of the leader's job. Creating and sustaining the level of demonstrated respect that leads to a purposeful, positive, productive work culture—which in turn leads to better results—is the other half.

Over the years, we have had opportunities to work with a variety of organizations where leaders realized their work cultures were not healthy. They knew their cultures impeded teamwork, eroded respect, inhibited productivity, and generated dissatisfaction. While we worked with them, we had the best seat in the house as we helped those leaders create and sustain purposeful, positive, productive work cultures. From among those leaders and companies we have worked with, let's look at three bona fide success stories. Specifically, so you can use their success stories to inform your culture change journey, let's examine their "reason to take the hill," how they became Good Comes First companies, and their self-reported results.

Banta Catalog Group

Banta Catalog Group, out of Maple Grove, Minnesota, was a catalog printing company. At the time of our engagement, they had six hundred employees. President Mark Deterding brought us in to help improve their low engagement scores (which placed them at the lowest of five market groups owned by their parent company).

We helped the executive team define their desired Good Comes First culture in the form of an Organizational Constitution—a formal statement of the company's servant purpose, values and behaviors, strategies, and goals (we will cover this culture-defining tool in much more detail in Chapter 6). That statement of servant purpose helped all leaders and team members realize their purpose was not to print catalogs. Their far more inspiring purpose was to *help their customers' businesses succeed.*

Their Organizational Constitution also specified how employees were to treat each other and customers in daily interactions: with honesty, integrity, and respect. They identified observable, measurable behaviors that modeled their defined values. Leadership coached people to model those behaviors. They then measured, through surveys, how well each leader demonstrated their valued behaviors.

As a result, alignment to the desired behaviors became the norm, and measuring those values became just as important as measuring results. When the data showed people and teams had excelled at demonstrating the values and behaviors, the company celebrated those people and teams. Soon, sustained change was the norm. People treated others with dignity and respect. Leaders and employees routinely embodied greater trust, teamwork, and cooperation.

Within six months of implementing our proven process, employees of all levels were visibly aligning to Banta Catalog's desired culture. Customers noticed the increased enthusiasm for their projects. Teamwork improved quickly, both across shifts in single departments and among different divisions. Organization-wide, respect grew. At the one-year mark, with the increased commitment of all staff members, employee retention improved by 17 percent, recruiting costs and training costs for new employees greatly decreased, and employees were actively looking for ways to cut costs and improve the environment. In addition, Banta saw:

- Customer service scores jump by 40 percent
- Engagement scores climb by 20 percent
- Results and profits increase by 36 percent

World Kitchen

World Kitchen, of Rosemont, Illinois, is a manufacturer and marketer of some of the world's most iconic brands, including Pyrex, Corelle, and CorningWare. The company had over three thousand global employees at the time our work with them began. CEO Carl Warschausky and CHRO Ed Flowers brought us in to help align the culture across multiple product lines, divisions, and operations in multiple countries.

The senior leadership team members immersed themselves in their new Organizational Constitution. Leaders at World Kitchen understood their personal growth would lead to culture change throughout the organization. Over a two-year period, every leader engaged in culture leadership training that helped them learn new skills while building their confidence in the change philosophy. During and after our work together, those leaders came to fully understand how to make respect as important as results. Most important, World Kitchen leaders modeled their new valued behaviors in daily interactions, which began shifting their culture expectations and practices. By the end of year three of our work together:

- Employee engagement improved by 45 percent
- Customer service ratings improved by significant percentages
- Results and profits increased by significant percentages

The "World's Largest Retailer"

After noting their region's low engagement scores on the company's annual employee opinion survey, Joel Anderson, vice president of a three-state region of the world's largest retailer, reached out to us.

The region's senior leaders, assisted by a cross-functional, cross-level, culture-steering committee, created their region's Organizational Constitution—the backbone of their Good Comes First culture—with behaviorally defined values. Rather than reinventing the retail wheel, the founder's original principles for the company (service to the customer, respect for the individual, and striving for excellence) served as the basis for the culture change initiative.

Driven by daily interactive "mission meetings" in every location, store leadership and associates reached new engagement levels. Leaders and mentors enabled associates to discuss *why* it was important to model the region's valued behaviors in daily interactions. When the next associate opinion survey results were released, engagement had jumped by 50 percent from the previous year's ratings. Within months, Joel's responsibilities grew to include 7 states with over 400 retail locations and 85,000 associates.

Under Joel's leadership, and within eighteen months of using the Good Comes First culture model, the larger region enjoyed:

- Engagement gains of 40 percent
- Customer service ratings improvement of 40 percent
- Results growth of 30 percent

WHAT CAN WE LEARN FROM THESE CLIENT SUCCESS STORIES?

For these organizations, despite having very different initial leadership styles and widely varying operating practices, three factors helped ensure both initial traction and long-term sustainment of Good Comes First cultures:

Active Leadership | Senior leaders drove, modeled, and coached the change. Leaders cannot delegate the task of "fixing our culture." Senior leaders have both the authority and the responsibility to create and sustain their desired culture.

The Organizational Constitution | This formal statement of the company's desired culture provided clear expectations from everyone in the company. Those Organizational Constitutions stated the company's servant purpose (how the company's products and services improve customers' quality of life), values and behaviors, and strategies and goals.

Accountability | Everyone is held accountable to demonstrate the company's defined values and behaviors in every interaction. A twice-a-year employee survey gathers team members' perceptions of how well their bosses and senior leaders model and coach the organization's valued behaviors. From the front line to the C-suite, these Values and Behaviors Surveys provide a reliable, valid measurement of the degree to which values align across entire organizations. The surveys also prove the organization is just as committed to measuring values as results.

Ultimately, these companies worked hard to not suck. They intentionally led a successful transition to a Good Comes First culture. And you and your leadership team will, too. Each and every day, all formal leaders must leverage the Good Comes First Accountability Model (which we will talk about much more in Chapter 10), meaning they:

- *Model* desired behaviors and performance
- *Coach* desired behaviors and performance
- *Measure* desired behaviors and performance
- *Celebrate* desired behaviors and performance
- *Mentor* misaligned behaviors and performance

BEYOND RESULTS: COMPETITIVE ADVANTAGES OF A GOOD COMES FIRST CULTURE

With the implementation of a Good Comes First culture, you can expect your organization to enjoy a number of measurable competitive advantages, including civility, respect, confidence, teamwork, and more. With this chapter's primary goal—to build a business case for a Good Comes First culture—in mind, let's look at three of the most powerful competitive advantages organizations attain once a Good Comes First culture starts to gain traction: employee experience, talent matching, and discretionary effort.

Employee Engagement (Reimagined to "Employee Experience")

When we speak to business leaders about the powerful positive impact of a Good Comes First work culture, "employee engagement" almost always comes up, and for good reason. After all, we have taught an entire generation of business leaders that one of the keys to business success is an engaged workforce.

In the United States, there have been recent flashes of good news around engagement. Gallup research[6] found that active workplace engagement reached a new high in May 2020, hitting 38 percent. Undoubtedly, the dramatic rise in the number of people working from home during the COVID-19 crisis—many of whom, despite the challenges, experienced greater autonomy and flexibility while working remotely—contributed to these record numbers.

Of course, engagement is not just an issue in the US. To measure engagement levels and assess the main factors that impact engagement and retention, Achievers,[7] an employee engagement platform—also in May 2020—conducted surveys of employees in the UK, Ireland, Belgium, and the Netherlands. Their findings were consistent with Gallup's data:

- Thirty-three percent of employees in Ireland and the Netherlands described themselves as "very engaged."
- Thirty-five percent of British workers chose "very engaged" from the available options.
- Thirty-nine percent of Belgian workers reported themselves at the highest engagement level.

These quick rises and the global good news were short-lived, though. Within one month of these results being published, employee engagement dropped to 31 percent in the US, driven down 7 percentage points by pandemic-related unemployment from late April through May and coinciding with massive social unrest after George Floyd's killing in late May. This was the largest month-to-month drop in employee engagement (7 percent between May to June 2020) Gallup had ever measured.

Even with these recent blips of hope, we face this hard fact: Despite, as discussed in Chapter 1, more than thirty years of companies' efforts and billions of dollars spent across the globe, employee engagement has remained stagnant. In fact, in the twenty years since Gallup first measured employee engagement, active engagement has remained stagnant at roughly 33 percent of US employees.

This discouraging news does not mean we should wholeheartedly discount the impact of employee engagement; however, we should start viewing the concept differently. We need to see it not as a management manipulation tool under the ineffective label of "employee engagement," as we have done since 1990. Instead, we must see it as a way to build sincere, mutually beneficial relationships with team members through a lens of "employee experience."

A genuine focus on the employee experience is not just a random theory. It is neither new frosting on an old cake nor a clever attempt to rebrand a real issue plaguing today's workplaces. As we saw with Banta Catalog, World Kitchen, and a major region of the world's largest retail store, organizations that approach "engagement" with an "experience" mindset see consistent and sustained gains in the Big Three outcomes: customer service, engagement, and results.

So, yes, "employee engagement" is a tired and failed cliché. And for 99 percent of companies that have made an attempt, the ROI of increasing employee engagement has been—and continues to be—crap.

Treating people well, though—in addition to the inevitable bump in ROI—will never grow old. And in a Good Comes First culture, there is nothing more important than treating people well. Which brings us to the next competitive advantage your organization will enjoy once it embraces a Good Comes First culture: hiring and retaining top-tier talent.

Talent Match: Culture's Impact on Retention and Attraction

Many of the leaders and team members in your organization now—some of whom have been with the company a long time—will be a good match for your new culture. The best of them will continue to bring their skills, contributions, and the best of themselves to work every day. Moving forward, they will routinely show respect for their peers and enthusiasm for the new culture. They will put good first.

And some will not.

Of course, you will work hard to ensure a successful transition to a Good Comes First company. You will want to bring everyone along on this culture transformation with the same level of interest, or at least acceptance. But despite your best efforts, some people in your organization will be a poor match for your new culture. To ensure your desired culture takes hold and becomes self-sustaining, senior leaders must make sure that everyone—leaders and team members alike—embraces and demonstrates your desired values and behaviors. There can be no exceptions. No holdouts. No "oh, but he means well" types. Otherwise, your organization will feel perpetually stuck between what was—and what can be.

This means that in the early months of the refinement process, you must be attentive and observant. You must note which leaders, teams, and individuals fully embrace the new culture—and which do not. As you look on objectively, you will notice most players fall into one of three different groups:

Early Adopters | The early adopters are aligned players across your organization who respond positively and emphatically to the change—and the specifics of your new rules. They will promptly embrace and demonstrate—and perhaps even help co-create—the values and behaviors specified in your Organizational Constitution.

Through their enthusiastic alignment to the new culture, members of this group say, "You've clarified what a good citizen looks like, speaks like, and acts like around here! I'm all in!" Their talents are a match for the new culture; their hearts and minds are in the right place.

Opt-Out-and-Leavers | The second group are players who know in their hearts this change process is not for them, then protest using their feet. They do not see the benefit of treating others according to your company's new set of values and behaviors. Or they think values are fluff—irrelevant to the dog-eat-dog world of work.

Let them go. Sure, it will be tough to see longtime contributors, friends, and colleagues leave. But tolerating players who do not believe in the new culture—and who will not model your desired behaviors—is not an option.

When these folks self-select out of your organization, they smooth the path toward a Good Comes First culture for others by removing themselves as speed bumps and detours. They are not a talent match, and they know it. So, gracefully and lovingly, set them free. Or, as WD-40 Company CEO Garry Ridge says, "Share those employees with the competition!"

Opt-Out-and-Stayers | This third group, made up of those who mentally quit but physically stay, can be a change champion's worst nightmare.

Actively pushing against the new values and behaviors, these players will challenge you. Then they will carefully watch how well, and how consistently, you enforce the new direction. The folks in this group are counting on nothing changing—so they figure their comfort zones need not change, either. They hope that, despite all the talk, the same work will be done—the same way—with the same dysfunction.

This group most likely knows working the old way is inefficient, but for them, keeping that existing system in place is easier; it's more comfortable. Just as important for many of the members of this group, working the old way maintains the existing—typically unfair—informal workplace power structures. Typically, these few have power or influence over the many—and wield those advantages in often unkind ways. Obviously, that is not an environment where Good Comes First thrives. Just as obvious, those people will not thrive in a Good Comes First environment.

What is the best way to address this "opt-out-and-stay" group? Those people who are not a talent match but do not seem to know it yet? Model and coach your newly defined values and behaviors, and serve as a mentor while redirecting misaligned behaviors. Once the opt-out-and-stay types see leaders will not tolerate undesirable behavior by anyone across the organization, they will have two choices: 1) Catch up to the early adopters, or 2) Join those who chose to opt out and leave.

In the interest of full disclosure, there is a fourth group that evolves as this change process matures. This "in the middle" group of players represents those who are not opposed to the new way, but do not quite know how to fit in. Their more introverted nature may prevent them from going all in. Perhaps they are optimistic that the culture will shift but do not want to be disappointed if change does not happen. Or maybe they have known disappointment before when change programs were announced but never took hold. For these and many other reasons, members of this group might initially seem disengaged. In our experience, however, they are just looking for a reason to believe. They want a sign they should commit, personally, to the change.

To help those in this group, do the accountability work. At every opportunity, model, coach, measure, celebrate, and redirect their behaviors through mentoring. This steadfast work will help those stuck in the middle quickly understand this change effort is not a Band-Aid. It is the real deal—a new human operating system, starting now. When leaders—along with the early adopters—hold themselves accountable, most of this fourth group will wholeheartedly embrace the Good Comes First culture. They will eventually see themselves as a talent match, and so will their managers, mentors, and leaders.

Across the organization, this talent match process requires diligent retention and attraction efforts. As you begin your culture transformation, retain skilled players who embrace and model your valued behaviors. And as you move further toward a Good Comes First culture, attract and hire people who demonstrate the needed skills *and* model your valued behaviors.

By proactively seeking a talent match—in other words, by matching the talent to your culture and the culture to your talent—you leverage the brains, skills, and hearts of your employees. As we'll cover extensively in Chapter 13, "Team Building and Hiring While Putting Good First," the more good people you keep, the more good people want to be there. This is a mutually beneficial, self-fulfilling cycle—and a critical component of a Good Comes First culture.

Want to build a company culture that values respect and results six months from now? Two years from now? Five years down the road?

Hire the right people *now*.

Once your Good Comes First culture has attracted (and kept) the best people, you'll find that it's much easier for them to do their best work, which brings us to our third competitive advantage of making this culture change: discretionary effort.

Discretionary Effort: When Culture Stars Are Aligned

According to BusinessDictionary.com, the definition of discretionary effort is:

> *The difference in the level of effort one is capable of bringing to an activity or a task and the effort required only to get by.*

The benefits of discretionary effort include continuous improvement in all areas of the business and new product or service ideas that gain traction in the marketplace, as well as higher levels of collaboration to get a big project done or to solve problems quickly.

Discretionary effort happens when three "culture stars" align:

1. The employee feels strongly committed to the organization and its customers.
2. The employee feels confident their efforts will be beneficial and valued.
3. The company provides the employee with the latitude required to try new ways of working within their role.

If any of those three stars are not evident, however, discretionary effort is quashed.

For example, we have all seen hard workers reined in by a peer with the words, "Don't work so fast. You're making the rest of us look bad!" We have seen a confident player get their hand slapped when their enthusiasm for a project eclipsed that of their coworkers. Unfortunately, many organizations have well-entrenched practices that overwhelm any desire to leverage discretionary effort and, in doing so, do not put good first.

So how do we help the three culture stars align? How do we inspire team members to bring their best effort to every activity or task? As you will see, the answer brings us back to modeling, coaching, measuring, and—whenever possible—celebrating behaviors and performance.

Cornell University professor Dr. Tony Simons's powerful article "The High Cost of Lost Trust"[8] first appeared in the *Harvard Business Review* in 2002. In that piece, he described his team's efforts to examine a specific hypothesis ("Employee commitment drives customer service") in the US operations of a major hotel chain.

They interviewed over seven thousand employees at nearly eighty properties. Not only did the study confirm employee commitment *does* drive customer service, but they also found that a leader's behavioral integrity—which Simons defined as "managers keeping their promises and demonstrating espoused values"—is the primary driver of employee commitment.

Their research found:

- When employees believe their bosses demonstrate behavioral integrity, their commitment goes up.
- As employee commitment goes up, employees willingly demonstrate discretionary effort.
- Employees are more proactive, more present, and more productive with the application of their discretionary energy.
- Employee discretionary effort is visible to and highly valued by customers (customers respond by staying more frequently, staying longer, eating on the property, etc.).
- Those customer behaviors generate significantly higher profits.

Dr. Simons's team created an assessment that measured behavioral integrity on a five-point scale. Their analysis found that a ⅛-point gain (0.125 points) on this scale generated a profit gain of 2.5 percent of annual revenues—an average increase of $250K for each hotel! This study made an important and previously unproven link: Manager behavior, specifically keeping promises and demonstrating company values, *generates hard dollar profits*.

Not only does this landmark data prove that measuring and quantifying behaviors is possible, but it also indicates that desired behaviors—when monitored, coached, measured, and celebrated (and sometimes redirected)—have a substantial impact on both culture and results.

The moral of the story? Treat people with respect and act from within a servant purpose and with behavioral integrity. Then insist others do the same—and results will come.

Throughout this chapter, we hope the answer to the "What's in it for you?" question—your reason to take the hill—has become apparent. By now, we hope the business case for the development of a Good Comes First Culture is clear. Most important, we hope you now see Good Comes First *is* a different way to conduct business—one that will change how you think about employees, customers, and yourself.

In our next chapter, we will introduce the tactical and practical steps required to implement and sustain a Good Comes First culture. And we do a deeper dive into your most powerful tool: the Organizational Constitution.

For now, take a well-earned break. When you are ready, turn the page.

SECTION II

Tactical & Practical: How to Define, Align, and Refine Your Culture

The Organizational Constitution: An Origin Story

Throughout Section I of this book, we talked about how Good Comes First organizations equally and proactively value respect and results daily. We shared insights into exceptional organizations that have built Good Comes First work cultures. And we discussed how a Good Comes First culture is a business imperative.

Here in Section II, we will focus exclusively on how to "Define, Align, and Refine" your Good Comes First culture transformation. In Chapter 6, we provide context on the Organizational Constitution—the bedrock tool we use to help you *define* your Good Comes First work culture. In Chapters 7 through 9, we walk through how to answer the four questions every Organizational Constitution must answer (more on this soon).

Before we dive in, a bit of context.

We have been using our Define, Align, and Refine approach to culture change and the Organizational Constitution successfully with clients since 2001. After thirteen years of practical application, Chris presented these concepts in his book *The Culture Engine* (John Wiley & Sons, 2014). Of course, like our clients, we have learned a lot in the seven years since *The Culture Engine* became the go-to guide for culture change. So what follows—based on two decades of systemic success—is the latest and greatest methodology for creating and sustaining a Good Comes First work culture.

Move forward with confidence—and with the knowledge that leaders before you have set a precedent. Their experience now serves as your guide.

EVERY SUPERHERO HAS AN ORIGIN STORY

We have all had bad bosses. We all have our workplace horror stories. But we have all also had really good bosses—and coaches, and mentors. Perhaps one of those good bosses even changed the trajectory of your career. And life. We've been lucky—and maybe so have you—because we've had bosses just like that: People who cared about more than the work; they cared about us as individuals—as human beings.

Chris had a boss—Jerry Nutter—who opened Chris's eyes to the power of organizational culture. Jerry was a rare breed of Industrial Age leader who was well ahead of his time; before the Social Age began, he focused on treating his employees well. Chris met Jerry while helping him lead operations at a metropolitan YMCA with multiple locations. Before Jerry hired Chris, he had already created a team of high performers who exceeded his performance standards and demonstrated excellent team citizenship. Jerry did this by setting clear, high values standards for his team, and then made sure the team modeled those values. Just as important, he outlined how the team members were to behave—and modeled those behaviors himself.

Jerry paid attention to more than the team's performance traction and accomplishments—he paid attention to how the individuals treated each other and customers. As a Good Comes First mentor does, he promptly yet discreetly called out team members for bad behavior. He cheered aligned behaviors loudly.

Eventually, Jerry handed Chris the project of a lifetime: He asked Chris to take the ideas he used to build the culture and team at their local YMCA to YMCAs in the country's roughest neighborhoods. So off Chris went to Ys in South Central Los Angeles, San Diego, and San Francisco. At the time, each of these cities had a heavy teen gang presence. Many members of these gangs were drug users or sellers; others were into prostitution, robbery, or even murder.

Chris's job was to make the local YMCAs so compelling that teens would choose to leave their lives of crime and violence—and come to the Y instead. Chris and his team created a strategy built upon what teenagers want: a sense of belonging, cool activities, and meaningful contribution—the very same reasons teens had been turning to gangs.

Slowly, their ideas to create a more inviting culture—that sense of belonging—took hold. Increasing numbers of teenagers engaged with the YMCA's programs. Over time, some of them became Y-camp counselors, bus drivers, and camp directors. Others became YMCA program directors; a few went on to become YMCA executives. One young man, who had been a street gang member, joined the Y's California Youth & Government program. There, he learned parliamentary procedure, wrote bills, and served as a legislator in the California State Capitol facilities. All his hard work even brought him to the floor of the Assembly in a borrowed suit, passionately presenting the bill to his Assembly peers. He was inspiring, confident—and immensely proud when his bill passed the House.

Jerry taught Chris that aligned behaviors are the pathway to workplace inspiration—and that misaligned behaviors lead to workplace frustration. His experiences with Jerry so transformed Chris that he wanted to expand those ideas as far as possible. Based on the successes he saw at the YMCA, Chris became convinced that focusing equally on values *and* results could work in other areas—especially in a business world constantly seeking purpose.

So, over thirty years ago, Chris started teaching these same principles to leaders of organizations, divisions, departments, and teams. He began helping them define their values and behaviors, helped bosses become great mentors, and helped build engaging, inspiring workplaces. Once written and codified, those principles become an Organizational Constitution—where leaders define their values and the behaviors that embody them. With an Organizational Constitution, bosses become great mentors who build engaging, inspiring workplaces. And, once your authors began working together several years ago, an Organizational Constitution became the basis of a Good Comes First culture.

WHAT IS AN ORGANIZATIONAL CONSTITUTION (AND WHY DO YOU NEED ONE)?

You sense it the moment you step onto the Southwest Airlines plane. Or walk into a Trader Joe's store. Or place that first order from Zappos. These companies hire people with a service mindset and a servant heart. You know those employees serve a purpose other than making money. You know they care. They engage willingly, pleasantly, and enthusiastically with customers because *they love serving people.*

And, this far into *Good Comes First*, you are savvy enough to realize these successful, service-driven companies are intentional about creating an inspirational workplace. They do not leave their company culture—or the treatment of employees and customers—to chance. You know without us telling you that these companies measure both respect and results. You know they place values and performance on the same pedestal.

Does yours?

If it does not, what is the first step in the journey to a Good Comes First culture?

An Organizational Constitution.

Without this document in hand, it is impossible to create or maintain an intentional culture or seek purpose-driven performers aligned with your defined values and desired behaviors, because you have not defined your values and you have not chosen your desired behaviors. And you have not deliberately designed a work environment where trust is contagious, validation is pervasive, and growth is constant. The Organizational Constitution is "disruptive technology"—a powerful tool that introduces new processes and new demands into organizations that have become too comfortable with "the way we've always done it."

Shifting your team or company culture from "what is" to "what can be" will disrupt routines, alter power structures, and make ineffective policies obsolete. It will have unintended consequences, which some people—those benefiting most from "the way we've always done it"—may not like. So yes, the Organizational Constitution is a disruption. But the shift to a Good Comes First work environment is worth the short-term discomfort. And as many of us learned most recently while navigating the massive disruption caused by the COVID-19 crisis, "doing what we've always done" is not a great option.

So what is an Organizational Constitution, exactly?

An Organizational Constitution is like the Magna Carta or the United States Constitution in that it outlines specific expectations and rights of organizational members (leaders and employees). Unlike the Magna Carta or the US Constitution, though, it does *not* outline the *governance* of the organization (employee ownership and such). However, it does describe the proven elements that, when embraced, make an organization's work environment consistently productive, positive, and purposeful. As we'll discuss in much more detail soon, these elements include your organization's servant purpose, values and measurable behaviors, and your strategies and goals.

An Organizational Constitution is a living, breathing document that outlines clear agreements about your team's or company's servant purpose. It details the values and behaviors all team leaders and members believe in and commit to model. When you manage by an Organizational Constitution, your team or company culture changes for the better, driven by liberating rules that leaders and employees buy into and demonstrate daily. These rules help everyone cut through ambiguity, set high standards of excellent team citizenship, and enable outstanding team performance.

You can think of your Organizational Constitution like the rules of the road. For example: As you are driving along a road, you come to an intersection with a four-way stop. As you slow to a stop, you notice a car already stopped on your left. Do you go first? Or do they?

US traffic rules say the car arriving first has the "right of way," so you give the universal signal for "you go first." They wave a "thank you" and enter the intersection. If you had both arrived at the intersection at the same time, though, both drivers would honor the US traffic rule that says cars to the right have the right of way. This time, the other driver would signal for you to go first. In both situations, everyone would get where they need to go, efficiently, happily, and safely.

Traffic rules like these provide drivers with specific rights (for example, the right of way). They also give drivers strict guidelines to follow in situations that might otherwise range from ambiguous to dangerous. There is no drama, no road rage, and no need to exchange insurance information. As they say in Texas, everyone "drives friendly"—and everyone safely gets where they need to go.

As you transition to a Good Comes First culture, your team or division or company will need a similar set of rules—in the form of your Organizational Constitution. They will need to understand how to be great corporate citizens. Otherwise, it is challenging to get where you, as a company, need to go.

THE BEDROCK OF THE ORGANIZATIONAL CONSTITUTION: THE PERFORMANCE-VALUES MATRIX

As we have already discussed, in most organizations, performance metrics are closely scrutinized. Sales numbers are sometimes updated hourly. Productivity dashboards are updated at least daily and often at the end of each shift. In the background, performance management systems constantly focus on goal planning, goal accomplishment, exceeding performance expectations, missing performance expectations, and so on. Managers hold endless meetings to review results. For many people, tracking business metrics seems to have become a never-ending job.

As we also said, the same is not true for the human-centered elements of the workplace. Values, behaviors, and employee experience are seldom monitored—and even more rarely measured.

Of course, if you measure, monitor, and reward only production, that is where people will focus. They will achieve the desired results any way they can—even through aggressive, self-centered "I win, you lose" tactics. Depending on the personalities and working relationships between team members, they may or may not be respectful of each other and customers—and you cannot create a Good Comes First culture without requiring and expecting respect.

This brings us to a critical tool for creating a Good Comes First culture: the *Performance-Values Matrix.*

Jack Welch first used a form of this matrix while he was president/CEO of General Electric. Despite Welch's faults as an autocratic leader, he was the first corporate executive to formally hold leaders and managers in an organization accountable for both performance *and* values. Welch seemed to know instinctively that leaders and employees who exceeded performance standards, and aligned well with the values he deemed essential to success, would thrive at GE. Those who could not—or did not—were better off working elsewhere.

Our Performance-Values Matrix—which we have used in various formats for over three decades now—will be the starting point of your journey to crafting your Organizational Constitution. Through this matrix, you will learn to answer the fundamental question every Good Comes First leader must ask themselves: "How do I want people across our organization to operate and behave?"

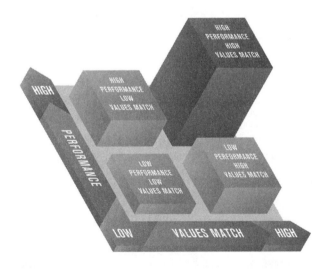

As you can see, the matrix is an X-Y graph with the vertical axis representing PERFORMANCE and the horizontal axis representing VALUES MATCH. The quadrants represent the four possible combinations of high or low performance and high or low values match.

It seems simple, right? And yet there is a significant caveat:

Before analyzing an organization using this matrix, we must first ensure expectations (for both performance and values) are clearly defined and agreed to by all parties.

That means team leaders and team members understand, and perhaps have co-created, their formal performance plans, which outline project, goal, and task expectations. Once those leaders finalize the plans, each team member agrees to be held accountable for meeting expectations and deadlines.

Of course, we must define those expected values in tangible, behavioral terms. They must be agreed to by each team leader and team member. Employees must understand that managers and mentors will measure their ability to meet those value-based expectations.

Again, only once both performance expectations *and* values expectations have been formalized and accepted can we analyze team leaders and team members using this matrix.

With that in mind, let's take a look at each of the four quadrants in the Performance-Values Matrix.

High Performance and High Values Match

The best place for staff (leaders, managers, supervisors, team members—everybody) to operate from on this matrix is the upper right quadrant: High Performance and High Values Match. Contributors consistently working within this quadrant meet or exceed performance standards and continuously demonstrate desired valued behaviors. They model the defined values and desired behaviors and expect others—leaders and fellow employees—to do the same.

Ultimately, these are the team members and leaders who will most help create and maintain a Good Comes First culture. In the process, they will not only do their jobs and lead their teams well, but many of them will also serve as mentors and perhaps change champions. As we will talk much more about in Chapter 10, leaders should recognize and reward the high-performing, values-aligned players who operate here.

Low Performance and Low Values Match

Of course, the not-so-good (read: worst) place for staff to operate from is the lower left quadrant: Low Performance and Low Values Match. Players here often fall short of performance expectations and do not demonstrate often enough the agreed-upon defined values and desired behaviors. What should you do with the Low Performance, Low Values Match player? Once you are certain expectations (for performance and values) are clear, coach them on how they may better align to the upper right quadrant mix—High Performance and High Values. Mentor them and measure their improvement.

And if they remain in the lower left? If coaching, measuring, and mentoring does not realign these players' contributions or interpersonal style? Experience shows us it is unlikely that any more time and energy spent to raise skills (to improve performance) and modify behavior (to increase the values match) will pay off as the culture change effort matures. So, as we said in Chapter 5 (and we will detail more in Chapters 10 and 11), you must lovingly set them free.

Low Performance but High Values Match

The bottom-right quadrant—Low Performance but High Values Match— offers an interesting opportunity. What do you do with the players you respect for their values and behaviors (dare we say "attitude"?), but who have not yet shown the ability to perform consistently? Of course, you do not want to lose the values match. So you must give them another chance. Coach them. Show them exactly where they are coming up short, then help close their performance gap with actionable, constructive input.

Where necessary, invest in skill building. Where possible, shift their responsibilities—perhaps including finding a role that leverages their skills, strengths, and passions.

However, if after training and/or reassignment, that team member is unable to consistently perform respectfully in any role, lovingly—and perhaps regretfully—set them free. These are the good guys. Be respectful. Be kind. But also, be firm. Because to show this person professional mercy—to allow them to remain on the team even though they do not meet minimum standards—is to show that you, as a leader, are willing to tolerate unproductive behaviors. By default, that means you are willing to compromise on agreed-upon standards—and your desired culture.

High Performance but Low Values Match

The upper left quadrant is where the most damaging players—in any company and any culture—operate. Period. The High Performance but Low Values Match players are poison in your organization. They exceed performance expectations (that is good) while demonstrating a very different set of values and behaviors from those you formalized (that is *really* bad).

What must you do with these upper-lefters? Give them a chance to align. Enable them to embrace the values and behaviors now required, without exception, of every leader and team member. Close their values gap by investing in skill-building for respectful interactions. Pair them with those who consistently model the behaviors they do not yet demonstrate. Again, coach them.

Even more critical, monitor them—after all, they have already demonstrated a low values match. You do not want them to spread these poor values like a virus when you are not looking. When the individual shows progress, praise and appropriately celebrate aligned behavior. With any repeat of unproductive actions, redirect the misaligned behavior—every day.

It is possible your coaching will flip the "citizenship switch" in these employees' brains—that they will become legitimate upper-righters. Your time and energy might result in them embracing the company's values and behaviors while exceeding performance expectations. To those upper-lefters, you and your fellow change champions *can* make a difference.

Granted, this type of personal and professional transformation is rare, but it does occur. More important: Except in the most glaring cases of toxicity, your best performers deserve every opportunity to put good first. If they do make that shift, celebrate! But continue—as with every one of your team leaders and team members—your coaching, measuring, and mentoring.

And if they do not shift to the desired upper right quadrant, set them free.

As fast as you can.

Their existence in your organization not only erodes leader integrity, but their very presence is proof your organization does not equally value respect and results. In a short time, trust—and momentum toward a Good Comes First culture—will be lost.

Ultimately, the Performance-Values Matrix is a visual representation of our foundational principle: equally value respect and results. Embrace the simplicity of this matrix. Work toward objectively seeing your most productive and values-aligned team members—leaders and employees—in the High Performance and High Values Match quadrant. Only then will you be ready to work on your company's Organizational Constitution (which we cover in detail in this Section II of *Good Comes First*).

One Senior Leader's Perspective

To help you understand the importance of formalizing your company's Organizational Constitution, we sought insights from David Mollitor Jr., President and CEO of Consolidated Electrical Contractors, in Lansing, Michigan.

The company started in 1924 as the Lansing Electric Company. Dave purchased the company in 1995 from the sons of the founders. At that time, there were fifteen employees. By 2001, the organization had expanded across Michigan and rebranded itself as Consolidated Electrical Contractors. They currently have two hundred employees, the largest staff in the company's history.

A Culture Challenge

Dave explained, "Like any small business, CEC faced challenges with good times and not-so-good times. Departments were siloed. Results were the only thing we rewarded. The 2008–2010 recession hit our customers and our business hard. We lost 80 percent of the company virtually overnight. I promised myself that if I could rebuild the business, I'd do it differently."

"It was clear to me that people (customers and staff) came to CEC because of the relationship they had with me; they appreciated how I treated them and the values I lived. Yet I'd trained our managers to drive for performance—which sometimes caused those managers to behave disrespectfully with team members. I wanted to be sure that we treated every employee respectfully, which meant changing the heads and hearts of everyone in the company," Dave said.

CEC started working with Chris in February 2018. The two-day executive team "culture process kickoff" session helped senior leaders realize they had not been intentional about the quality of their work culture. Dave explained, "The most impactful part was how your process helped expose dumb practices and, literally, to unify the executive team to be champions of CEC's culture refinement. The session helped us learn more about one another and, with your help, to design a culture that is WAY bigger than any one of us. The kickoff session was a TON of fun for us all—and, as an executive team, we were ready to drive this change." Announcing their servant purpose, values and behaviors, and strategies and goals was the easy part. The hard part was living it.

Dave found that "when people started calling each other out on values misses, challenging decisions that seemed to be purely results oriented, and more, we had to buck up—we had to hold everyone accountable, including ourselves."

Momentum began to shift. Dave explained, "We had to coach people who were high performers but who were very difficult to deal with. The coaching worked for some, but not for all. We lost several strong performers who did not live our values." Everyone in the company was watching the senior leaders very closely. "When we held our ground and stuck to our desired culture, and lovingly set free some of our High Performance but Low Values Match players, that's when things started to gain traction," Dave said.

Dave is proud of the work his executive team has done. "CEC's culture is one hundred times better today than it was three years ago. After the initial pandemic lockdowns in Michigan, every customer is back building and partnering with CEC on their new projects," Dave shared. "We've got good people doing good work for a really good company. In fact, I'm amazed at how well this process has worked for us. We're a construction company, very blue collar. It's not an industry where people pay attention to feelings! However, people are all the same—when treated with respect, they'll give their all to help customers and that, in turn, helps the business."

Dave tells senior leaders to be patient with the change process. "Culture refinement takes time. It takes energy. It takes a mind-shift from 'results are the only important thing' to 'results are HALF my job; a respectful culture is the other half!' It's worth it. And it's incredibly gratifying to see how far we've come.

THE ULTIMATE GOAL OF AN ORGANIZATIONAL CONSTITUTION

A Good Comes First culture does not often happen organically—it must be intentional. It requires clear standards, modeling, constant tending, alignment efforts, and celebration of traction toward a high-performing, values-aligned culture.

To be effective and actionable, an Organizational Constitution must include formal statements of your organizational servant purpose, values and behaviors, and strategy and goals. In short, the ultimate goal of an

Organizational Constitution is to answer the four critical questions mentioned at the start of this chapter:

- **What are we trying to accomplish?** (Your organization's *present-day servant purpose.*)
- **How are we expected to treat each other?** (Your organization's *values and behaviors.*)
- **What is our blueprint for going to market during this performance period?** (Your organization's *strategy.*)
- **What performance targets will keep us on track, delivering what we have promised to our customers and stakeholders?** (Your organization's *goals.*)

As our Good Comes First journey continues, we will dedicate the next few chapters to helping you—the real superhero* in this story—answer these questions. By the end of Section II, you will be well on your way to crafting your Organizational Constitution and your company's new origin story.

Cape not included.

CHAPTER 7

The Organizational Constitution: Servant Purpose

The first formalized and published mission statement was written for Nature Publishing Group[1] in 1869, though mission statements, in general, did not come into vogue until almost one hundred years later. In the 1960s, many businesses began to consider a mission, vision, or purpose statement critical to business success—which they are. Research[2] indicates that mission or purpose statements are consistently beneficial to a company's long-term survival.

Please note: Throughout the remainder of this book, we use the terms "mission statements," "purpose statements," and "servant purpose statements" interchangeably. Our emphasis on servant purpose remains steadfast through all the examples in this book. After all, serving others—improving others' lives—creates intrinsic motivation for those doing the work.

Also, note these terms refer to a business's *raison d'être*—its "reason for being"—*today*, as opposed to a vision statement, which is a description of the organization's desired future state. Our experience and research lead us to believe the present-day description is a stronger foundation for teams or companies. This is especially true for those embarking on a culture transformation journey toward a High Performance and a High Values Match.

What is *your* team's or company's present-day reason for being? Why does it exist? Who does it serve? Why should customers—or even employees—care about your team or company? We encourage you to keep these questions in mind throughout the rest of this chapter. First, though, we want you to ask ten people in your company or on your team:

What is the purpose of our company (or team)?

As they answer, take notes. (Alternatively, you might video your would-be research assistants as they answer this question.) Unless your team or company has been intentional about its reason for being, you will likely hear very tactical ideas about your team's purpose. Respondents will typically say things like:

- We print catalogs (or sell cars, make sandwiches, etc.)
- We make money

When you pose this question, listen beyond *the words* they say; look for signs of exasperation in the respondents' voices. Watch their body language. You might notice they feel uncomfortable—or as if they think you may be looking for a specific answer. Or that they should know the "real" answer. Perhaps they will feel like they should know a better answer than the one they are giving. You might even get the "that's-a-dumb-question" look because "everybody knows *what we do (or make)* here."

Ultimately, we should not be surprised by the responses to this crucial question; we should expect many different types of answers, both verbal and nonverbal. Because, in the absence of clarity, with no formal declaration of purpose or mission, the practical reality of day-to-day activity becomes the accepted focus—the norm.

"What we do or make" becomes employees' complete understanding of the business. Intentionally or not, it becomes their—and your—reason for being. "We make money" becomes the entire reason for any team's or company's activities.

The problem with this practical view is that it fails to inspire most players in your organization—nor is it particularly relevant to them in their daily roles.

Printing catalogs, selling cars, or making sandwiches, for example, are very tactical activities. Within those industries, the work is never "done."

Tomorrow, there will be many more catalogs to print, cars to sell, and sandwiches to make. *Activities* are never-ending. And those repetitive business activities are usually not, by themselves, inspiring to humans.

You know making money is vital for organizations; we started this book by stipulating that results matter. If companies are profitable, they can hire more people. They can impact more lives. They can reach more customers, pay more taxes, improve more communities, and so on. However, suppose employees see making money as the *primary* reason the business exists and do not directly share any profits generated. In that case, they will not be personally motivated to help achieve profit-related goals. Employees are not typically shareholders or owners of the company. So someone besides the employees has a far more vested interest in the profits generated when product goes out the door at a decent margin.

With that in mind, let's look more closely at Good Comes First servant purpose statements.

CRAFTING AN EFFECTIVE SERVANT PURPOSE STATEMENT

For members of your team or company, a clear servant purpose statement is actionable, tangible, and relevant. In its most perfect form, a present-day purpose statement is also a compelling and inspiring description of what your team or company accomplishes on a daily basis. The statement should also clearly describe why you and your team members are so passionate about the work you do.

In short, a servant purpose statement is a succinct declaration that explains:

- What your company does
- For whom
- And "to what end"

Unfortunately, most organizations do not have a clearly defined servant purpose with these three elements. A few do not have a formal statement of mission or purpose at all. Even if they do, it rarely shows why customers should care about their company and what it stands for.

As promised, in this section, we look at a few mission and purpose statements from real companies. Specifically, we will examine what elements these statements include and which they are missing. (We copied these mission or purpose statements from companies' websites and footnoted the links.)

Servant Purpose Statement #1:

Creating superior value for our customers, employees, partners and shareholders.[3]

- **Is it clear what the company does?** No—there is no reference to the company's products or services. (This is a tire company.) The statement does reference "superior value" but does not define what that value is. Is it profits? Is it a good value purchase for consumers? It could mean any and all of these "values," but it is not clear.
- **Is it clear who they do it for?** Yes—they aim to create superior value for customers, employees, partners, and shareholders.
- **Is it clear why employees put forth extraordinary effort—or why customers should care?** No—there is no "desired end state" described beyond the hard-to-nail-down "superior value."

We give this purpose statement 1 out of 5 stars.

Servant Purpose Statement #2:

To nourish and delight everyone we serve.[4]

- **Is it clear what the company does?** They aspire to nourish, which gives us a hint about their business (a restaurant). We like this reference—but would like it better if it was a bit more descriptive. For example, are they nourishing the body, the soul, the heart? More detail is required.
- **Is it clear who they do it for?** "Everyone we serve" is a big target market. That can include customers, employees, and all other stakeholders. The broad reference would benefit from more specificity.
- **Is it clear why employees put forth extraordinary effort—or why customers should care?** They aspire to delight, not just nourish. Yes, they do cover this element nicely—and succinctly.

Just 2 out of 5 stars here. Lots of work to do on this statement.

Servant Purpose Statement #3:

To build a sustainable mining business that delivers top quartile share-holder returns while leading in safety, environmental stewardship, and social responsibility.[5]

- **Is it clear what the company does?** Yes—it is a mining business that delivers top quartile shareholder returns.
- **Is it clear who they do it for?** Yes—they do it for shareholders. (Notice that the company does not reference customers or employees in this statement.)
- **Is it clear why employees put forth extraordinary effort—or why customers should care?** The primary output is the benefit to investors and their shareholders. The emphasis on safety *might* inspire employees. The aspiration of environmental stewardship and social responsibility might inspire customers. In the end, however, it seems this company views its primary "reason for being" as making money.

We give this statement 3 out of 5 stars (if we don't take away a half-star for the blatant suck-up to shareholders).

Servant Purpose Statement #4:

To inspire and nurture the human spirit—one person, one cup and one neighborhood at a time.[6]

- **Is it clear what the company does?** Yes—they aspire to inspire and nurture the human spirit. Exactly "how" they do that is not clear, though. (It *is* straightforward if you understand that this is Starbucks' purpose statement.)
- **Is it clear who they do it for?** It is not precisely clear whose "human spirit" will be inspired and nurtured. We might assume they aim to inspire and nurture customers, employees, and neighborhood members—but the company does not state this clearly.
- **Is it clear why employees put forth extraordinary effort—or why customers should care?** Yes—inspiration and nurturing are valuable outcomes to strive for, on both an individual and community level.

This statement is 90 percent there. We are confident this purpose statement is crystal clear in the hearts and minds of Starbucks' employees today. Still, the lack of clarity about what is in "one cup . . . at a time" makes the reader work too hard to understand what this company does.

We grade this 4 stars out of 5. So close!

Servant Purpose Statement #5:

To discover, develop and deliver innovative medicines that help patients prevail over serious diseases.[7]

- **Is it clear what the company does?** Yes—they discover, develop, and deliver innovative medicines.
- **Is it clear who they do it for?** Yes—they do it for patients who are battling serious diseases.
- **Is it clear why their employees put forth extraordinary effort—or why their customers should care?** Yes—they help those patients, their customers, win their medical battles; their work saves lives.

A full 5 stars! A highly effective servant purpose statement.

Now, let's analyze one more company's mission statement: yours—the one your company uses right now. (Of course, if your company does not yet have a mission statement, please feel free to skip this part of the book.)

Based on what you have learned so far, the temptation to edit your current mission statement might be strong. Resist!

Look at your mission statement. Do not just skim. *Read*. Take a moment to think about what it says to you, right now. Then ask the three questions we asked about the other mission statements we analyzed. (To help articulate your answers more constructively, please put your answers to paper.)

- Is it clear what your company does?
- Is it clear who you do it for?
- Is it clear why your employees put forth extraordinary effort—or why your customers should care?

By analyzing the examples above, rated from 1 to 5 stars—and your own company's purpose statement—it should be clear that it is not easy to craft a servant purpose statement that addresses all three questions crisply, invitingly, and succinctly.

As you have probably gathered by now, you should not include any form of "making money" in your statement. As we established, results matter. Profits are good. But making money is ultimately an uninspiring "reason for being."

If you do have some form of "making money" in your purpose statement, leave it there for now. In a few pages, we will guide you through creating (or refining) a more effective servant purpose statement for your team or company. But before we do, let's discuss how your statement will be communicated and lived—and how it should serve as your company's North Star.

COMMUNICATING YOUR COMPANY'S SERVANT PURPOSE

If your company has a mission or purpose statement now, how well do employees know it? Do they believe it? Do they believe *in* it?

They probably do not know it. After all, while the Institute for Corporate Productivity found that 84 percent of organizations studied have a mission statement, the majority of those companies also reported that only half of their employees could repeat the company mission statement.

And even if your employees do know your purpose statement, chances are they do not wholly believe in it.

This smells a lot like the logical consequences of "Managing by Announcements," a plague Chris referred to in *The Culture Engine* as "MbA."

When infected by MbA, leaders do an excellent job of *defining* purpose, policies, or procedures. They publish and announce the details. The problem comes in when those leaders expect all employees to align with the policies or procedures immediately. Leaders seem to believe, "We've told them. So now they'll do what they're told."

As history and precedent show, though, merely announcing new practices or policies or a purpose statement—and then expecting compliance—is not enough. Without reinforcement of the new model, without context for why these changes are necessary, employees do not have a compelling reason to embrace—let alone demonstrate—the new purpose, policies, or procedures.

To ensure desired changes take hold, leaders must first model the principles of the mission statement themselves. Then leaders must spend time and energy to ensure fellow leaders and employees embrace the desired changes. Leaders must coach to the changes, measure traction of the changes, celebrate progress as people welcome the changes, and redirect players who do not embrace them.

Hint: As you might have already figured out, the five-practice model known as the GCF Accountability Model introduced in Chapter 5 (and talked about in much more detail at the top of Chapter 10) is perfect for helping team members embrace your new servant purpose statement:

- *Model* the desired servant purpose
- *Coach* the desired servant purpose
- *Measure* the desired servant purpose
- *Celebrate* those who consistently demonstrate the servant purpose
- *Mentor* those not aligned to the servant purpose

Bottom line: Communicating your new or revised servant purpose statement is not enough. Managing by Announcements is not going to cut it. From the moment it is socialized (shared with your organization for feedback) and announced, a servant purpose statement—starting with you and your leadership team—must be *lived.*

YOUR SERVANT PURPOSE VERSUS YOUR "ACTUAL" PURPOSE

A typical purpose statement is often well written. In many cases, it is posted and promoted throughout the organization.

But it isn't lived.

In these situations, the *actual* purpose—the purpose demonstrated day-to-day—is much different than the *espoused* purpose of the company.

Here is a prime example:

To become the world's leading energy company—creating innovative and efficient energy solutions for growing economies and a better environment worldwide.

Let's again review the elements of a compelling purpose statement:

- **Is it clear what this company does?** Yes—they aspire to create innovative and efficient energy solutions.
- **Is it clear who they do it for?** Yes—they serve growing economies. (Granted, that is a pretty broad marketplace.)
- **Is it clear why their employees put forth extraordinary effort—or why their customers should care?** There seem to be two competing outcomes in this statement—being the world's leading energy company and creating a better environment worldwide.

Do you sense the underlying theme of this company's purpose statement? Their "reason for being" seems to be "making money." And that narrow focus wound up being their undoing.

Which company is this?

Enron—yes, *that* Enron.

Who would have thought Enron's servant purpose was, at least in part, "creating . . . a better environment worldwide"? Clearly, this is a company that did not live that part of their servant purpose.

As demonstrated by senior leaders, the company's actual purpose surfaced in an interview[8] with Enron vice president Sherron Watkins. Watkins, one of many senior leaders at Enron who raised questions, concerns, and fears with the CEO about its accounting practices, said the core problem at Enron was "greed and arrogance" among executives. She explained: "Enron's leaders set the wrong tone. So did Arthur Andersen's leaders [Andersen was Enron's external auditor]. In the end, both companies put revenues and earnings above all else. The means by which those earnings were generated did not matter."

Enron is not alone. Accounting scandals[9] have been the undoing of Waste Management, WorldCom, Tyco, Freddie Mac, American International Group, Lehman Brothers, and so many others. And should we track down the purpose statements of any of these organizations, we would learn their mission or purpose statements did not specifically say, "Company executives shall lie, cheat, and steal our way to billions of dollars in profits." Yet, in each case, that is precisely what happened. Based on their actions, that was these companies' actual purpose.

The credibility of any team or company—and its senior leaders—is based upon the team or company doing what it says it will do. They must live the carefully stated purpose and align with the values they defined in that purpose.

If the *actual* purpose is different from the *espoused* servant purpose, the organization is living a lie. In this situation, we cannot expect respect from workers. Even the best employees will struggle to live the company's values. Trust is impossible to establish. All of this makes a Good Comes First culture impossible to achieve.

GREAT PURPOSE INSPIRES HUMANS

In his best-selling book *Drive*, Daniel Pink examined what truly motivates people. He said, "[Humans], by their nature, seek purpose—a cause greater and more enduring than themselves."[10]

Howard Schultz, the former CEO of Starbucks, said,[11] "It's not what you do; it's why you do it that is important!" Schultz described the "spiritual crisis" Starbucks created for itself at the beginning of the global recession that started in 2008. At the time, despite record growth and profits, the company had unintentionally stepped away from its core purpose and values. Starbucks, Schultz said, measured and rewarded the wrong behaviors. Starbucks' purpose and values "were compromised by yields and profits," he said—and he took personal responsibility for that.

The turnaround began with an apology delivered in person by Schultz to over ten thousand store managers and employees (Starbucks calls them "partners"). To get back to the crux of their servant purpose, he asked these key players to help him and the company focus on "one." Schultz went on to say that "one" was "the only number that matters: *one* cup, *one* customer, *one* experience, *one* employee at a time."[12]

When considering what it would take to turn the culture around, Schultz realized that he and Starbucks' senior leaders first had to regain the trust of store managers and employees. His thinking: If they could regain the trust of these key partners over time, they might have a chance to regain customers' trust as well.

In the five years following Schultz's epiphany, Starbucks regained that trust. And ever since, it has maintained a company culture of which employees and customers are proud—all by living their passionate yet (as we saw earlier) imperfect (more on this later) servant purpose:

To inspire and nurture the human spirit—one person, one cup and one neighborhood at a time.

Before we move on to creating a purpose statement for your company, let's look at more tangible benefits to having and living an effective purpose statement. Your purpose statement serves as an active filter when assessing opportunities, plans, decisions, and actions. With the servant purpose statement at the forefront, leaders and team members can easily pose the tough questions:

- "Does this opportunity align with our defined purpose?"
- "Will this acquisition complement our 'reason for being'?"
- "Is this decision being made within our stated servant purpose?"

If the answers to those questions are yes, it makes sense to pursue that opportunity, take that action, and make that decision. If not, as is easy to see—and to communicate—it does *not* make sense to pursue that aspect of the business. In fact, as many organizations—including some of what were once considered the best of them—have learned (we're looking at you, Yahoo . . . what were you thinking with Tumblr?), pursuing a misaligned opportunity or action wastes time, money, and human energy.

When done well, a clear, effective servant purpose statement does more than just inspire your employees and customers. It describes more than what you and your team are passionate about or what you do well. The best servant purpose statements keep the entire organization singularly focused on what it is you, as a company, set out to accomplish.

As you begin to craft your organization's servant purpose statement, make sure you build one that will help you keep your eyes on the prize even during the worst economies and the most challenging circumstances.

WHAT COMPANY IS YOUR SERVANT PURPOSE ROLE MODEL?

Take a moment, please, to consider companies you regard highly—that you enjoy experiencing. It could be your local espresso bar. Or your dry cleaner. Your dog groomer. A favorite online retailer. The industry does not matter. Your admiration does.

One of Chris's favorite local providers is a tiny hair salon. Doreen, the owner-stylist, is happy, friendly, and extremely competent. She is very flexible, even offering to come to his house after the COVID-19 scare ends so that the entire family would feel safe.

One of Mark's favorites is a local gastropub. Not only does the food consistently impress, but the service is also outstanding—every time. There are no surprises, except maybe when the pub pulls the lobster roll off the menu. (Not their fault. New England crustaceans are sometimes hard to find in the Rocky Mountains.)

Whatever you choose as your favorite, they have consistently wowed you as a customer. Time and again, they have delivered more than you expected—and certainly more than their competitors.

Now, consider how your favorite providers make you *feel*. Then think about how they do that. For example, if they make you feel important or valued—perhaps "part of the family"—exactly how do they accomplish this? (Again, to inspire more profound thoughts, note where your organization can inspire this beneficial feeling in employees and customers.)

Finally, think about what you can learn from how they make you feel. How can you bring that feeling into your team's or company's purpose statement? Be specific: What do they *do* that makes *you* feel valued?

Got it? Understand the major differentiator of your favorite brand or service provider?

Good.

Keep that in mind as we look at one more excellent example of a servant purpose statement—this time from one of our clients, most definitely a Good Comes First company.

Servant Purpose Statement #6:

Our purpose is to deliver quality, on-time product marketing communications solutions that inspire consumers to purchase our customers' products and services.

This is a clear statement of *what* they do (quality marketing communication solutions), *for whom* (their customers), *why* their employees work so hard (they want to inspire), and *why their customers care* (their services inspire loyalty from consumers).

This company's crisp purpose statement is compelling for employees. The straightforward yet inspiring statement educates them about *why* their work is vital to their customers. More importantly, the clarity that comes from this purpose statement boosts employee pride and enthusiasm for their work each day.

Full disclosure: Building this "simple" servant purpose statement took weeks of honest assessment and intense discussions. Leaders, managers, team supervisors, and frontline team members all participated. When the senior leadership team took this statement (draft #40, give or take!) to organization members, employees smiled and nodded. They said, "Yes, that's what we do!"

Those smiles, nods, and responses told the senior leadership team they had removed all the jargon. They had avoided all the buzzwords and corporate speak. They had successfully crafted a concise statement that describes their organization's core compelling essence—its reason for being.

This is your goal. To create a servant purpose statement that captures your reason for being so well (and so absent of any jargon, buzzwords, trendy phrases, and corporate-speak) that, when socialized, all you get are smiles and nods. Only then will you know you have achieved your goal.

CRAFTING A COMPELLING, INSPIRING PURPOSE STATEMENT

Finally, let's get started on *your* organization's first (or new) servant purpose statement. The next few steps will help you create a meaningful *first draft* of your team's or company's purpose statement. But before you start, let's prepare your body, mind, and spirit for this task.

Take a deep breath—oxygen inspires your brain cells and heart muscles. Most of us take very short breaths—short in duration as well as in depth. Breathe deeply and slowly. Stand and stretch your muscles for a minute or two—maybe shake out your arms and legs like an Olympic swimmer getting ready for a race. Get your blood flowing.

Sit comfortably—and relax. Most of us do not relax much during our daily activities—we hold our muscles tight, inhibiting adequate blood flow and causing us to invest energy in the tightness. Consciously loosen your muscles.

Next, I encourage you to think beyond the first "right" answer that comes to mind. Jot those first answers down, of course, but know the essence of crafting this statement is getting to the "best" answer rather than the "right" answer. Also, know the "best" answer is rarely the first answer. So, at every opportunity, dig deeper and look for the messaging that will both educate and inspire team members.

To begin, answer these three questions:

1. **What does your company make or deliver?**
   List the core products or services your team or company delivers to customers day-to-day. If your organization has a wide variety of products or services, round up into standard business categories. For instance, rather than list "bookkeeping, tax returns, and financial audits" separately, say, succinctly: "Accounting services."

2. **Who are your primary customers? Who seeks out your products and services? Who do you primarily serve?**
   Create a list of the consumers, teams, and/or companies you serve. If an industry is more relevant than companies—"restaurant and food service" versus "Morton's Steakhouse," for example—list the specific industry or industries you serve.

3. **To what end do you and your team members work so hard? What benefits do customers gain when they receive or use your products and services? How do your products or services improve quality of life, boost efficiencies—or help move their organizations or communities or families toward desired goals?**

Yes, these questions are more challenging to answer than the first two sets of questions. But take your time. Precedent shows these carefully considered answers move you from the "right" answers—*what our team makes*—toward the "best" answers—*how our team inspires.*

Now, review your notes. Pull the most compelling, impactful answers from each of the three sets of questions above. Focus on what rings most true; what feels most right. With those answers in hand, craft a single servant purpose statement that clearly describes your team's or company's "reason for being." As you do, remember your goal is to create a sentence or two that:

- Explains what your company does
- For whom
- And "to what end"

Obviously, this is important. So maybe you will want to bring in senior leaders and key employees to talk this out. That is more than acceptable, but whether or not you go solo, do this work now—*right now.* Or at least before you keep reading this book. Because until you know your company's servant purpose, you cannot possibly create a Good Comes First culture.

Simple, right? Go ahead. Get started. We'll wait . . .

. . .

Insert the theme from Jeopardy! *here. Or maybe light up your favorite Spotify playlist . . .*

. . .

If it helps, take another look at the sole 5-star servant purpose statement from earlier in this chapter:

To discover, develop and deliver innovative medicines that help patients prevail over serious diseases.

Do we know what they do? Absolutely. Is it clear for whom they do it? Absolutely. Is it clear what inspires employees to come to work every day? Absolutely.

Now, using this as an emulation-worthy example, get back to work on your servant purpose statement . . .

More Jeopardy! *or Spotify music . . .*

. . .

Done? Feel good about this first draft? Great work!

But the real work is only just beginning.

Next, you must socialize these ideas—you must share this draft statement. Share it with peers, bosses, and mentors. And then, most important, communicate it with team members. If you feel confident, you might even share it with the key customers and influencers who know your team or company well enough to provide insight.

As you share, remember: Your goal during this sharing phase is not to justify or defend terms or concepts contained in the purpose statement. Instead, your goal is to learn what others see in it—to engage others and understand their perceptions. So, as tempting as it may be, do not "sell" the work you already did. Instead, simply ask the questions you have already done your best to answer:

- Is it clear what our company does?
- Is it clear who we do it for?
- Is it clear why our employees put forth extraordinary effort—or why our customers care?

Then listen to people's reactions. Do not just hear while you prepare what to say next—actively listen. As you do, take thorough notes. And if at the end of the listening session, the words in your draft statement do not ring true for 90 percent of your team's or company's members? Well, your work must continue.

When this happens, engage further. Ask team members for better words to describe your company's impact on customers. After all, words are powerful—and using the best possible words in your purpose statement will engage team members as well as customers. Keep searching for and testing better terms to describe your organization's beneficial impact on others. Become a wordsmith. For now, become a perfectionist. This time, good enough is not good enough.

Refine the statement. Find the next version of best. Then seek feedback again. If necessary, restart the theme from *Jeopardy!* again. Or start a new playlist.

Still not quite there?

Rinse and repeat. Further refine that sentence (or two) until the words *do* ring true for most team members. In the end, you may have to go through a few iterations—and a few different sets of test subjects—to reach a purpose statement you are satisfied with, and one that inspires team members to do good work.

We have seen this accomplished in a couple of hours. And as we said, we have also seen it take weeks. But there is no time limit. This is not a race. Take all the time you need to get the best answer, not the "right" (or, even worse, the "right enough") answer.

Done? Feel good?

Nice job. Step 1 of creating your Organizational Constitution is complete.

Now, take a moment and celebrate the crafting (or recrafting) of your company's servant purpose statement. When done and ready to move on, we will continue creating your Organizational Constitution. The next big step: adding the desired values and defined behaviors that will create high standards for great team or company citizenship.

CHAPTER 8

The Organizational Constitution: Values, Definitions, and Behaviors

Congratulations! You finished your servant purpose statement, which outlines your team's or company's reason for being. If you have not already, you will soon socialize this draft purpose statement by sharing it across your entire organization and seeking feedback. There is no doubt: You will learn a great deal. Every conversation will bring greater clarity to you and your team members about your team's servant purpose.

As we start this chapter, we shift our focus to defined values and desired behaviors. Or, more precisely, values defined as behaviors.

We understand that defining your values—and then choosing and defining the behaviors that will help demonstrate those values—may at first seem like a daunting task. Stay with us, though: Experience shows that the work flows well once you engage fully in the process. The leaders who went through this process before you tended to get on a roll, then stay there—and you will, too. This task is vital for creating your Organizational Constitution. In the rest of this chapter, we will show you exactly why—and how—you can do it.

WHY MUST VALUES BE DEFINED
IN BEHAVIORAL TERMS?

Every team seeks talented players enthused about their work and team-mates. Companies want players who are willing to learn, grow, and support their peers through cooperative teamwork. Employees who display a positive attitude, especially in times of change, are worth every penny we pay them, and perhaps more.

So how does a leader ensure consistently great attitudes from their team's or company's players?

Before you answer that question, allow us to ask another: Can a leader "manage" a person's attitude?

Our research and experience lead us to believe the answer to the second question is no. In fact, we would go so far as to say managing any team member's attitude is impossible. By definition, a person's attitude is intrinsic, internal. Because it organically comes from within, we cannot easily influence attitudes through outside efforts. So even though a leader may try hard to improve a less-than-positive attitude, the attitude rarely changes.

After all, in the history of human civilization, not one person's attitude has ever changed for the better because anyone else said, "You need to change your attitude!"

Therefore, let's agree leaders cannot manage a person's attitude. Let's also agree we should not try. This being the case, what are your other options for ensuring workers consistently have a good attitude?

Can you hire for attitude? Many leaders would say they do their best to hire people with good attitudes. The fact is, though, everyone is on their best behavior during the job interview process. That superficial dynamic makes it incredibly hard to tell what kind of attitude someone will have once they are on the job, let alone under pressure. We have seen some outstanding leaders experience frustration when an employee's initially terrific attitude goes downhill shortly after joining their team. In many cases, nothing the leader says or does halts this attitude erosion.

So, no, we cannot consistently hire for attitude.

Is attitude measurable? If it is, it is extraordinarily difficult to do in a scalable, repeatable way. Typically, all we can do is observe a person's behaviors—their plans, decisions, and actions—and attempt to interpret their attitude over time. In the end, measuring attitude is more of a guess than a reliable assessment. So let's agree that attitude is not consistently or reliably measurable.

In summation:

- We cannot manage—or perhaps even positively influence—a person's attitude.
- Despite our best intentions and herculean efforts, we cannot hire for attitude.
- And attitude, being subjective in nature, is not measurable.

As important as it is to have a positive attitude in the workplace, it is challenging to gauge an employee's ability to be a solid workplace citizen, as demonstrated by what we often refer to generically as a "good attitude."

Now, let's look at attitude from another angle: You have served with talented, engaged team members in the past. They showed enthusiasm. It was clear they shared a willingness to learn and grow. They supported fellow team members' work, and their emotional intelligence was on display as they actively participated in problem resolution. You might have said to yourself, "These people have great attitudes!"

But in a Good Comes First culture, acknowledging a great attitude is not enough. We must look deeper. We must look at *how* those players behaved. We must ask the question, "What *exactly* did those team members do to make them such strong, aligned players?"

Did they:

- Consistently treat others with dignity and respect?
- Expect the best of others?
- Give others the benefit of the doubt?
- Accept responsibility, even blame?
- Give credit where credit was due?
- Praise and encourage others?
- Express pride in the team's work?

Based on your experience, you can easily add a dozen other positive characteristics to this list, which means you are aware that your best team members demonstrate their enthusiasm, willingness, and support through dozens of *observable behaviors* every day. And, unlike their attitudes, these behaviors are not just observable—they are tangible and measurable. That makes them quality indicators of any team member's workplace citizenship. By observing and scoring (as we will learn in Chapter 11) how a team member acts, speaks, and the behaviors they demonstrate, we can quantify their alignment to company values.

Subjectively judging others by their attitudes is a fool's game. Instead, a Good Comes First leader focuses first on modeling, coaching, and measuring desired behaviors. That is why we must define values in behavioral terms—which is where our sights are set in the pages to come.

DECIDING WHICH VALUES YOU WILL DEFINE IN BEHAVIORAL TERMS

We now know *why* we must define values in terms of observable, tangible, measurable behaviors. Before we discuss *how* to define those values, though, let's talk about two questions on the minds of most leaders as they begin transitioning to a Good Comes First culture:

1. How do I know which values are right for my organization?
2. Is there a set of values that applies to nearly every organization?

Allow us to answer the first question with a question:

Which values (and desired behaviors) will best enable your organization to live its servant purpose?

We know that is not the most satisfying way to answer the first question. But we cannot answer. Or rather, we cannot answer for you. Only you, and perhaps other members of your leadership team on this journey with you, know the answer. Don't worry, though. We do not expect you to have the perfect answer to this question quite yet. Only by going through this chapter will you begin to learn the most appropriate values for your company.

Fortunately, you will find the answer to the second question more helpful: Yes, many of our clients choose many of the same values as many other clients. For that reason, we included a list of the most frequently chosen values later in this chapter. But even when choosing the same value, we often see widely varying definitions of that value. For example, let's look at a value desired by many organizations—regardless of size, industry, or place of origin:

Integrity.

Let's start our analysis of this popular value by asking you to answer a series of questions strictly from *your* perspective. (Yes, we want you to *answer* each question . . . *in writing*. So open your favorite note-taking app or gather up some scratch paper.)

- Specific to your company's or team's work environment, how would *you* define integrity?
- What phrase or sentence describes what *you* mean by integrity?

With those answers recorded, consider how you would like fellow leaders and team members to demonstrate integrity, as *you* defined it.

- How would leaders and team members act so that, when you observe them, you would see a demonstration of integrity? (Keep this simple; note three or four behaviors that would clearly demonstrate *your* definition of integrity.)

Next, answer these questions exclusively from your team members' perspective:

- How would your *team members* define integrity?
- How would *their* definition differ from yours? Why?
- What behaviors would employees feel they must model to demonstrate their integrity value properly? (Again, three or four behaviors will do.)
- How would their modeled behaviors differ from yours? Why?

We know what you might be thinking: *Why would the definitions of integrity, and associated behaviors modeled by employees, be that much different from mine?*

Based on our experience, though, it is quite likely that if you ask twenty frontline employees what integrity looks like, you will get twenty different answers. And if you ask twenty members of your leadership team what integrity means to them, you might get *thirty* different answers!

That is the problem: Everyone has a slightly different version of both the "integrity" value and the associated behaviors, which means everyone judges others on how well leaders and peers demonstrate *their* version. That is where an Organizational Constitution comes in.

An Organizational Constitution deliberately creates *common* agreements based on *shared* purpose and values.

These "rules of engagement" are formalized so that every team leader and team member lives by the same clearly defined value. They understand the expectations of that value. Just as important, they are enabled to model that value, coach to it, and celebrate when people and teams demonstrate the desired behaviors for that value. In the best working environments, team members, regardless of rank, understand they are free to respectfully redirect any behaviors not aligned to that value.

Defining values and behaviors, and then holding everyone in the company or team accountable for living them, creates continuity. That accountability provides psychological safety—and perhaps even preserves sanity—because, in the end, every player knows precisely what managers and leaders expect of him or her. And they know exactly what to expect from each other. When all cylinders are firing, having defined values and desired behaviors is liberating for every leader and every employee.

Why "liberating"?

Because clearly stating those definitions means nothing is open to interpretation. There are no unwritten rules, so players do not have to guess how they should treat others. Even better: They need not question how others should treat them. They know leaders and peers will not tolerate issues like rudeness, harassment, inequity, and workplace bullying.

By defining even one value as important—combined with choosing one set of behaviors that demonstrate that value—you have already moved that much closer to a Good Comes First Culture.

VALUES: DEFINITION, BEHAVIORS, AND THE POWER OF "DO" MESSAGES

So how do you—as efficiently and thoroughly as possible—decide on (and eventually communicate and live) each of your desired values?

Let's take a look at how one client, using the template we will discuss next in this chapter, simply—and in an inspiring tone—outlined their "integrity" value. As you read, compare your written notes on integrity to these:

Value:
Integrity

Definition:
We are accountable for our actions. We do what we say we will do. We do not compromise our organization's values, no matter what.

Desired Behaviors:
- I hold myself accountable for my commitments and actions; I keep my promises.
- I attack problems and processes, not people.
- I accept responsibility and apologize if I jeopardize respect or trust.
- I align my plans, decisions, and actions with the organization's purpose and values.

Now, take a moment to understand *how* this client sensibly outlined this value. As you do, please note:

- These behaviors are in the form of "I" statements. They describe how every employee, no matter their title, role, or responsibilities, behaves day-to-day. We define these statements to hold every team member accountable.

- The behaviors do not say "I will . . ." because "will" means "I might do it . . . later. I do not have to do it now." As a leader and change champion, you want every player to understand the sense of urgency: These are NOW behaviors.

- We *positively* define these behaviors; they outline what you want members of the organization to DO daily (not what you DO NOT want them to do).

Before we go further, let's talk a bit more about the power of "do" messages.

As many of us have learned, the human brain processes "do" messages more quickly and efficiently than "don't" messages. While declaring values and defining behaviors, this is important because those "do" messages tell every leader and team member how we expect them to behave. We do not tell them how they should *not* behave. This positive tone—which provides more clarity—allows for a much more consistent demonstration of the organization's defined values.

Here are a couple of examples that highlight the importance of stating desired behaviors framed in more positive "do" terms.

- You are riding your bike on a narrow trail. You tell yourself, "Don't fall!" Human nature being natural, your brain hears, "Fall!" You lose focus. You lose desired straight-line tracking and momentum. Then you fall, and donate blood to the narrow trail.

Or . . .

- You are playing golf. Driver in hand, you are on the first tee box. An expansive fairway lies before you. A ball-eating lake, though, runs along the entire left side. As you line up the tee shot, you say to yourself, "Don't hit it into the lake!" Your brain, of course, hears "Lake!" You lose focus, and—despite your best efforts—with a splash, your ball becomes another wet casualty.

We often use these "don't" messages in the work environment (and at home, for that matter). Workplace "don't" messages include such statements as:

- "Don't be late" (for meetings or project deadlines)
- "Don't be a jerk" (don't yell or be rude)
- "Don't promise what you can't deliver" (don't mis-set expectations)

Not exactly motivating, right?

On the other hand, positively stated messages like "I am on time," "I am kind," or "How can I be of service" are much more inspiring, and much more actionable. These actionable behaviors become the inspiration for excellent corporate citizenship. So, when defining your values and selecting the model behaviors, choose your words carefully. Strive for accountability. Create a NOW sense of urgency. Be positive.

STEP-BY-STEP: HOW TO DEFINE VALUES IN BEHAVIORAL TERMS

When creating this portion of the Organizational Constitution, you will need to formalize three to five values with definitions and desired model behaviors. Why three to five? Frankly, more than five is hard for us humans to remember, let alone embrace! Our advice: Do not complicate things by offering too much content; keep it simple and easy to remember.

The template for declaring those three to five values and defining their associated behaviors, as you just saw, looks like this:

Value:
A one- or two-word title for each value.

Definition:
A two- or three-sentence description that clearly states what this value means in your workplace.

Desired Behaviors:

- First "I" statement
- Second "I" statement
- Third "I" statement
- Fourth "I" statement

List no more than four behaviors per value for the same reason you do not want more than five values in total. You must simplify, simplify, simplify. Each additional behavior beyond that fourth one starts to feel prescriptive. And with each addition, you run the risk of muddying the waters of the previous behaviors. In the end, there is a reason people frequently use the "when everything is a high priority, nothing is a high priority" cliché.

To help the process for declaring values and defining behaviors sink in a bit, let's now examine some well-defined values, definitions, and desired behaviors from some of our culture clients.

Value:

Service

Definition:

Our customers are the reason we are in business. By giving them superior service at every opportunity, we exceed their expectations. When we exceed their expectations, we are at our best.

Desired Behaviors:

- I initiate friendly hospitality by promptly and enthusiastically smiling and acknowledging everyone that comes within ten feet.

- I passionately exceed customers' expectations by offering actionable solutions.
- I promptly assist each customer to find requested items.
- I deliver a fast, friendly experience to every customer.

In this customer-focused value, is it clear what this retailer wants demonstrated? Yes. As good as the definition is, however, the behaviors are where the values come to life. In "now" terms, the behaviors definitively state how the company expects every organizational member to behave when modeling this value.

Another example:

Value:

Mutual Respect

Definition:

I work with my customers (internal and external) openly, honestly, sincerely, and ethically. I follow through on my commitments and expect the same from others.

Desired Behaviors:

- I trust that everyone has the customers' and the company's best interests in mind. So I attack problems and processes—not people.
- I do not take it personally when someone challenges a process I own. I listen to the input and implement changes to improve the process.
- I do not lie, betray a confidence, stretch the truth, or withhold information from a peer, customer, or stakeholder.
- If I am unable to keep a commitment or meet a deadline, I immediately inform all people potentially impacted.

Is it clear what this manufacturer wants demonstrated regarding their mutual respect value? Again, yes.

When teaching clients how to generate this portion of an Organizational Constitution, these "mutual respect" behaviors struck a chord with a number of them. Many used these behaviors in their own "respect" or "trust" values, so this good work has lived on and on. Since there is nothing worse than being asked to read between the lines, we will create a new line:

Rather than reinvent the wheel each time we take a drive, whenever and wherever possible—emulate!

Use the best of what the Good Comes First community offers . . . every time.

We will give you one more example, this one from a small, family-owned business:

Value:
Dedication and Contribution

Definition:
Our company deserves our best. Each of us demonstrates dedication by applying our service skills to company goals and customers, refining our skills to improve efficiency, boosting our own contributions, and valuing others' contributions, daily.

Desired Behaviors:
- I contribute my time, talent, and skills to the long-term viability of the company.
- I complete my tasks on time and under budget, fully responsible for my commitments.
- I embrace opportunities to build needed skills and increase my contributions as the business evolves.

Are these behaviors measurable? Can peers and customers provide feedback about the degree to which any leader or employee of this company demonstrates these desired behaviors? We are sure you will agree: They are—and they can.

High-performing, values-aligned teams and companies embrace the promises they make to each other and to their customers. We base those promises on performance expectations, which must be delivered daily. They are also rooted in the values expectations demonstrated daily by everyone—senior leaders, managers, team leaders, frontline experts, and everybody in between.

This is how you foster great corporate citizens. This is how you build a Good Comes First work culture.

Now, let's do it for your company and team.

YOUR COMPANY'S VALUES AND BEHAVIORS

Way back in Chapter 2, we said defining "good" is personal—that everyone has their own definition. We also said the ultimate goal in a Good Comes First company is:

Good people. Doing good work. In a good place to work.

To clearly demonstrate what "good" means to your company, you will choose values that bring your company the closest to your version of "good." Soon after you make your value selections, you will thoroughly define each value (otherwise, people will perform based on their own definitions). Finally, to complete your view of "good" and to ensure the values chosen are observable and measurable, you will supply desirable behaviors that, when on display, undeniably demonstrate those values.

The first step in this process, then, is to consider which values best help you define your company's "good."

A hint: Start with those values you already demonstrate well. And, if it helps, think about the good people (High Performance / High Values Match or, if you do not yet know in which quadrant they spend the most time, a "talent match" from Chapter 5) doing good work in your team or company today. What values do they demonstrate? What behaviors indicate they live those values? And, since cloning still is not legal as of press time, who are the people worthy of emulation? As we complete this section, who can you best learn from?

Ask yourself (and, using your preferred note-taking method again, write down your answers):

- What values are we already proud of? What are we already known for?
- How do our company's or team's great corporate citizens behave today?
- What do they do today that makes me, as a leader, proud?

To this list, add any additional values you would like to see leaders and employees demonstrate with peers, leaders, vendors, and customers. To spark some ideas, we listed many of the values our clients chose over the years:

- Abundant
- Agile
- Audacious
- Autonomous
- Aware
- Bold
- Brilliance
- Caring
- Classy
- Community
- Creative
- Dedicated
- Diverse
- Dreamer
- Educational
- Equality
- Excellence
- Freedom
- Fun
- Generous
- Grateful
- Great Place to Work
- Harmonious
- Human
- Humble
- Imaginative
- Integrity
- Irreverent
- Learning
- Loyal
- Mentorship
- Mutual Respect
- Noble
- Outrageous
- Passionate
- Philanthropic
- Poise
- Respect
- Responsive
- Safety
- Service
- Significant
- Social Justice
- Stable
- Unconventional

One last step: Think about your competition. From their demonstrated values, what do you envy most? Or, if they make it hard to think positively about them, what is the opposite of the traits you despise most? For example, if they are arrogant, include "humble" in your list.

Finally, from all your notes, whittle down your list to seven to ten values. Don't over-think this; your only job is to narrow your thoughts to the top 10 (or so). What values make the cut?

Once you compile that top 10 list, you have our permission to over-think. Because your job now is to select the three to five values you expect everyone in your organization to model in daily interactions. Remember, these values and their assigned behaviors must be observable and measurable—or they cannot be on the final list.

DEFINE YOUR CHOSEN VALUES

In this next step, your goal is simple: Clearly define your organization's values. When you complete this task, there will be no question in anyone's mind about what those values mean to the company. Otherwise, in the absence of clear definitions, team leaders and members are left to define the values on their own.

For example, let's say one of your values is "excellence." This word seems universal, so you may assume everyone knows what excellence means. And you will be unpleasantly surprised when, as you start to expect people to model that value, you learn just how differently people view "excellence." Consider the real-world views of five different people, all committed to doing quality work:

- Player 1 defines excellence as keeping the customer happy.
- Player 2 defines excellence as giving her personal best every day.
- Player 3 defines excellence as hitting his minimum daily quota all week.
- Player 4's definition of excellence is exceeding all goals by year-end.
- And to Player 5, excellence means delivering the promised product or service before the deadline, at better than required quality, and at below the budgeted cost.

Given these widely different interpretations of the same term, what happens when each of these players performs to their definition of excellence? Despite their hard work, they will most likely:

1. be disappointed in their peers because their peers' values definition does not align to their personal definition, or

2. be a disappointment to their peers because their definition does not align with their peers' personal definition.

When the dust settles, five people did their job to the best of their abilities and well within *their* definition of "excellence"—and yet *no one* is happy. Obviously, this is a recipe for confusion, frustration, and conflict.

A clear, succinct values definition helps everyone know the standard associated with each value. This definition enhances clarity and, in doing so, increases your employees' confidence. To add positivity to this healthy mix: As you define each value, be sure to use *desirable* terms—say what it *is*, not what it *isn't*. The bottom line is that, rather than leave your values definitions to chance, provide a definition that is not only understood, but is shared and modeled throughout your organization.

A FEW MORE EXAMPLES OF DESIRED VALUES

Before we turn you loose to define your three to five desired values, let's look at two more solid examples from our Good Comes First clients. Remember, emulate whenever and wherever possible. After all, emulation—not imitation—is the sincerest form of flattery. Feel free to use these examples as you start to craft definitions for your team's or company's desired values. Then, make them your own.

Value:

Excellence

Definition:

I exceed the expectations of internal and external customers in every interaction.

Value:

Respect

Definition:

We treat everyone—team leaders and members, customers and prospects—with the utmost dignity and honor. Every interaction leaves people feeling valued and trusted.

Now you are ready. It is time to define your uncompromising values.

Take all the time you need. Again, no more than three to five primary values, and no definition longer than two or three sentences—after all, we are not writing a novel. We are writing a one-page how-to guide. Our suggestion: Use the template you are already familiar with.

Value:

A one- or two-word title.

Definition:

A two- or three-sentence description that clearly states what this value means in your workplace.

INCLUDING OBSERVABLE AND MEASURABLE BEHAVIORS

By now, you carefully chose the values that define your company's "good." You crafted definitions for those values that are not open to interpretation. The final and most crucial step in crafting your team's or company's values remains: adding desired behaviors to each value.

Ultimately, the behaviors you choose reinforce the values' definitions by describing exactly how you want members of your team or company to interact. In other words, these behaviors define the ground rules for great citizenship. Here are two examples of defined behaviors from clients. (Keep these examples in mind as we brainstorm potential behaviors for each value.)

Value:

Respect

Definition:

We treat everyone—team leaders and members, customers and prospects—with the utmost dignity and honor. Every interaction leaves people feeling valued and trusted.

Desired Behaviors:

- I actively cheer others on by giving sincere praise and encouraging positive behaviors.
- I take personal responsibility to understand, respect, and appreciate others who are different from myself.
- I give honest and direct feedback by communicating in a respectful and timely manner.
- I respect customers and peers by using appropriate language at all times.

Value:

Excellence

Definition:

I exceed the expectations of internal and external customers in every interaction.

Desired Behaviors:
- I embrace constructive feedback by taking personal ownership and changing my behavior to improve my contributions.
- I teach, train, and support the development of others by sharing my knowledge.
- I adapt to changing priorities by keeping myself informed about the business.
- I represent the company with pride by always following the dress code.

The first step to creating your list of behaviors is simple: For each of your defined values, note behaviors you would be proud to see team leaders and members *demonstrate* while modeling this value. As you do, please note:

- We write each in the form of an "I" statement.
- We use the term "demonstrate" intentionally.

After all, we cannot measure or hold people accountable for what they "think," what they "believe," what they "meant"—and especially what they "promise" to do. As agreed upon earlier, we cannot manage their attitudes—no matter how bad (or good). We can, however, measure and hold players accountable for demonstrating clearly defined behaviors. We can measure actions, not words.

Once you have several possible behaviors for each value, cull through the behaviors you noted. Your goal is to reduce the list of behaviors for each value to the three or four most impactful. As we already said, no more than four, please—simplify, simplify, simplify.

To help with your selection process, for the behaviors you consider, ask yourself:

- **Is this an observable behavior?** Can I assess someone's demonstration of this behavior by watching and/or listening to their interactions with peers, leaders, customers, and vendors?
- If not, refine it, or toss it in favor of a more robust entry.

- **Is this behavior measurable?** Based on my observations of a player, can I reliably "score" this behavior (perhaps on a 1 to 5 scale)? Can I rank how a player models or demonstrates this behavior at any point in time?
- If not, refine it or toss it.
- **Is this behavior globally applicable across our company? Or is it unique to a particular function or unit?** The behaviors for "team- or company-wide" values must be relevant to all team members no matter their role or function within the organization.

- If the behavior is only applicable and appropriate for one team or a select group of team members, toss it or refine it.

YOUR VALUES, DEFINITIONS, AND BEHAVIORS

Now, pull these essential elements—values, definitions, and behaviors— together. Do so knowing that this pivotal moment:

- Sets the tone for your Good Comes First culture; it defines "good."
- Provides an uncompromising view of each of your desired values.
- Outlines how leaders and team members model or demonstrate each behavior.
- Adds depth and substance to the "values match" axis of the Performance-Values Matrix.

If your values and behaviors need a little more polish, that is entirely normal. We would be surprised if you did *not* need to spend more time getting each value and behavior just right.

If you think another pass is necessary, be sure to wordsmith your values and definitions first. After all, we cannot get the desired behaviors right until the value, including the definition, is perfect. And by perfect, we mean perfect for your team or company.

Done? Great work!

You crafted a solid draft of your team's or company's values, definitions, and behaviors. Like the first draft of your servant purpose, though, the real work has just begun. Next, you must socialize these ideas. You must share them with peers, other leaders, and team members. Again, like your servant purpose statement, you might even share them with key customers or vendors who know your operations and purpose well enough to provide helpful insights.

Just as before, your stance during this sharing phase is not to defend the terms or concepts used in the values, definitions, or behaviors. Instead, actively listen, learn, and understand people's perceptions. Again, if the words in your draft statement do not ring true for 90 percent of your team's or company's members, you are not quite done—which, again, is 100 percent normal. Be patient. The right words—and the right tone—will come at the right time.

Before we move on from this important element of defining and building your Good Comes First culture, let us remind you again about the danger of "MbA"—Managing by Announcements. Simply publishing your values, definitions, and behaviors is not enough. Good Comes First leaders must also model these values and behaviors. They must hold everyone accountable for embracing them. Otherwise, creating high-values, high-performance teams will be difficult at best—which makes your team's or company's transition to a Good Comes First culture much harder than you can imagine.

This section of the Organizational Constitution is *that important*. Your role as a leader—making sure people live these values and behaviors—is *that important*.

Dig in. This is where stuff starts to get real.

Our next chapter will incorporate the last two areas of our Organizational Constitution: strategies and goals. For now, take another well-deserved break. We will be here when you get back.

CHAPTER 9

The Organizational Constitution:
Strategies and Goals

By now, you have created your company's servant purpose. You've also crafted a short list of defined values, their definitions, and the observable and measurable behaviors associated with them. Now it is time to add strategies and goals to your Organizational Constitution.

"Why?" you might ask.

Think of it this way:

- Your servant purpose is your "Why."
- Your values and defined behaviors are your "How."
- And your strategies and goals are your "Who," "What," When," and "Where."

As any good communicator would tell us, you need "Who, What, When, Where, Why, and How" to fully communicate. To leave out even one of the five "Ws" or the one "H" means you have not told the whole story. Without all the information, people fill in the blanks—and when that happens, if anyone comes to the same conclusion, or if the same call to action inspires anyone, it is purely by accident.

For example, say you receive the following message:

"Zoom meeting after lunch to discuss the new culture initiative."

Sounds important, right? But all you know is the "Why" (to talk about the culture initiative) and "How" (a Zoom meeting). Assuming everyone works the same shift and the same number of hours, taking lunch around the same time, you can narrow down "When" to within four hours or so. But the only "Who" you know is the sender of the message. That leaves out the majority of the "What," other than "Zoom." And without the actual Zoom link—you cannot even begin to guess the "Where."

As a business leader, you have most likely given a great deal of thought to your corporate strategies and goals. After all, effective leaders must clarify and consistently communicate strategies and goals to their employees. They must then manage performance toward executing those strategies and achieving those goals. But as we have already established, since the Industrial Age began, that is where the communication from too many leaders ends. The "Why" (other than "making money") and "How" ("just get the job done") were obvious. So was the "When" ("now" or maybe "this quarter") and "Where" (up until the COVID-19 crisis, in the "office/campus/ plant/factory").

So, we as business leaders have been very good at strategies and goals. That is not a bad thing. In fact, it is critical to remain diligent about setting challenging goals and executing the right strategy to achieve those goals. Just for a second, though, let us go back to the Good Comes First foundational principle:

Equally value respect and results.

Now, as we begin to complete this last section of your Organizational Constitution, consider this:

- Your servant purpose, combined with your values and behaviors, clarify your expectations of *respect*.
- Your strategies and goals clarify your expectations of *results*.

Here is another way to look at it:

- To determine if any player meets the standards for "High Performance," we must understand how well they executed a clearly communicated strategy and whether they achieved their agreed-upon performance goals.

- And to know if that player is a "High Values Match," we must observe and measure their alignment to clearly stated values and defined behaviors.

You get it. We cannot have a Good Comes First culture unless we pay equal attention to both respect and results. One can live without the other. But without both, the life span of your ideal company culture is much shorter.

In other words (and we can't emphasize this enough):

In a Good Comes First company, respect and results are not two separate entities; they are forever intertwined.

They are like sales and service. Product development and production. Peanut butter and jelly.

And that, for the remainder of this chapter, is the mindset we will use. That is how we will combine your current strategies and goals with your servant purpose and values and behaviors, to create one formidable Organizational Constitution.

MORE PARALLELS BETWEEN RESPECT AND RESULTS

In our research and experience, we find many teams and companies struggle to meet their performance commitments for many of the same reasons:

- Targets are set too high.
- People do not have the skills required to meet performance standards.
- Goals are not explicitly defined; they are not specific, measurable, or trackable.
- They do not share goals with key players and mentors who serve as role models, teach skill sets, objectively monitor progress, and so on.

These performance commitments represent a formal promise made to customers, both internal and external. If we do not meet our commitments, we don't keep our promises. When we do not keep our promises, the perception of the team's or company's integrity erodes. Trust becomes hard to find. Customers stop expecting you to keep your promises. And when customers lose faith, it becomes difficult to meet business goals. This is an unhealthy cycle that costs you and your team not just time and money—but *results*. This cycle also costs you *respect*. And the loss of respect further erodes *results*.

The antidote to this spin cycle, and performance issues in general—whether newly diagnosed or chronic in nature—is a formal strategic plan. A plan that aligns deliberately to your team's or company's servant purpose as well as its values and behaviors. This strategic plan sets specific performance goals tied not just to your "Who," "What," "When," and "Where"—but also to your "Why" and "How."

This means people are not just doing the work assigned to them—they understand the "Why" behind the work, and they know "How" they work together. Inspired by the servant purpose and fully aware of the ground rules (the values and behaviors they agreed to model), not only is a business strategy easier set, but the goals are more easily met.

All this because you focused equally on *respect* and *results*.

CREATING YOUR STRATEGIC PLAN AND SETTING GOALS

Continuing to think back to your servant purpose and values and behaviors, let's now focus on your business's strategic plan and performance goals. We will start, as has become our standard, with a question:

In summary form, perhaps three to five sentences, what is your team's or company's current strategy?

Do not look it up!

Answer from memory. You do not have to recite the strategy perfectly. Just list, in writing, what you believe are your team's or company's top three strategic objectives right now.

If yours is like most organizations, reciting your team's or company's primary strategy (or strategies)—without looking it up—is not easy. Because for most companies, business strategy is not very clear—not only is it rarely socialized (as we have asked you to do with the first two components of your Organizational Constitution), but a company's strategy is typically not communicated outside the C-suite.

Good Comes First companies, however, are intentional about their business strategy. Because with a formalized strategic plan—effectively communicated and reinforced—the right path is crystal clear. The right decisions are crystal clear—to every leader, every employee, and every stakeholder. Once everyone at your organization embraces the strategy, your company's goals—from the highest reaches of the organization to the newly hired interns—perfectly align to its strategy. Everyone knows the expectations placed upon them and on each other; just as important, everyone knows which goals are the highest priorities. Each team member works toward accomplishing those goals, so they know their work matters—*really* matters.

Remember how your servant purpose served as a filter for other business opportunities, possible new products, markets, and even acquisitions, allowing you to identify right away if a pursuit aligned with your values? Your strategic plan—from a performance perspective—does the same. It becomes the filter that stops disruptions from finding their way into your business model. Those programs or potential distractions—the proverbial shiny objects we are all tempted to chase—can be assessed (and dismissed) quickly using a carefully crafted strategic plan. If that program, product, service, or acquisition advances the strategy and helps meet long-term goals, it deserves further consideration. If it does not—if it does not align well with your "Who, What, When, and Where," and especially your "Why and How"—let a competitor chase the shiny object.

You focus on working the plan and meeting your goals. Because without a formalized business strategy, any "path"—any number of plans, decisions, and actions—can *seem* aligned to leaders and team members. But they are not *aligned* so much as *assumed*.

As a result, people inevitably make competing decisions. For example, a CFO's decision to reduce overtime might conflict with Production's need to meet a customer deadline.

Decisions within a company based on assumptions, as you can see from this example, are often misaligned with those of teams with their own priorities. Perhaps worse yet, they are also often out of step with the C-suite's perception of the overall strategy. Work will start, stop, and start again—this time in closer alignment to the person offering the correction based on their own assumption. As you as a business leader already know, this leadership miss results in frustration (at minimum) and chaos (at worst). It also leads to inconsistent performance, missed deadlines, and, eventually, less-than-satisfactory customer experiences.

Other than that, everything is great!

A SECOND CHANCE AT GETTING IT RIGHT THE FIRST TIME

Now, with all this in mind, answer this question again (again, in writing and in about three to five sentences):

What is your team's or company's strategy now?

This time, if it helps, bring up all the resource material you need. Of course, first you have to figure out where to find your company's formalized strategic plan—*if* it is in writing. Either way, based on what you have learned in the last few pages, construct a new summary version of your company's strategic plan.

A highly effective strategic plan should:

- Help everyone on the team (or in the division or company) understand the business's primary objectives for a specific planning period (quarter, year, period, etc.).
- Outline how to allocate the resources of the team or company, aligned to deliver promised goals.
- Help every leader and team member communicate your strategy, in lay terms, to anyone they work with—which helps every leader and team member get on, and stay on, the same page.
- At any point in the performance period, answer the question, "Why are we focused on this goal, project, or task *now*?"
- Remove any mystery; instead, it creates clarity and generates confidence.

Take your time. We will wait right here.

When you have your three to five sentences, come back this way.

HOW LONG? AND HOW LONG?

With your summary strategic plan in hand, and before we move forward with expanding that plan, let's talk about two questions leaders often ask us about strategies and goals:

- How long should my performance period be?
- How long should my strategies and goals document be?

For most companies, under normal circumstances, we recommend you set strategies and goals for two years. Even in the best of circumstances, a time frame longer than two years does not offer many benefits in this shrinking global marketplace. In fact, a more prolonged time frame can cause your strategic plan to become antiquated way too soon. Little good can come of that.

However, the COVID-19 pandemic has had a significant impact on our ability to look ahead. Not too long ago, business leaders—in shock from the effects of the pandemic—were trying to keep their heads above water. And every time it looked like they could make that post-shipwreck swim to shore, another wave would knock them backward.

For them—and perhaps for you—even now, looking ahead more than a year seems counterproductive. But the worst decision we can make is to remain reactive. We must plan ahead. We must set at least modest goals— even if they are "just survive" in nature. Otherwise, we will just tread water. So, even if it is only six months at a time, build a plan. Then—in what you will soon see is a recurring theme—execute the plan.

So how long should your strategies and goals document be?

Ideally, one page. Yes, *one page.*

Of course, your source docs and notes will be much more than one page. But the document you first socialize and then live by is . . . one page.

Maybe your strategic plan is in infographic form. Perhaps in the style of an executive summary. As long as your intended audience can digest the most critical points in small bites, the format does not matter. If you are still not sure how your strategies and goals document should look, go to GoodComesFirst.com. We have some great examples there. Again: emulate.

THE FLUID NATURE OF STRATEGY AND GOALS

You now have an idea of your basic company strategy. You know how far ahead to look. And you now know how the strategies and goals component of your Organizational Constitution should look and feel. So, at this point, some of you are thinking:

Strategic plans are different than servant purpose and values. Servant purpose and values are firm. Uncompromising. But strategies and goals evolve constantly.

You are exactly right—especially if dealing with any unpredictable, post-pandemic realities.

A company's servant purpose statement rarely changes, nor does its values (though we refine these critical Good Comes First items as your company evolves, as you will see in Chapter 11).

However, strategies and goals change regularly—and sometimes quickly (and in the best cases, nimbly). As we have learned, your overall strategy acts as the filter that stops the company from going off on tangents. So, as your market changes, your industry evolves, and customer requirements shift, specific elements of your strategy must be flexible enough to remain relevant amid these changes. You and your leadership team should monitor your company strategies closely. You should plan to make a formal reassessment of your team or company strategies at least every year—more frequently if your strategies are not serving your customers, stakeholders, and employees effectively. And even *more* often if faced with major disruptions from a natural disaster like a hurricane or a human-made disaster like a merger. (Kidding! Not all mergers are disasters. Right?)

Of course, if strategies change often, so must goals. After all, goals are the tactical, day-to-day targets that ensure traction toward accomplishing your stated strategies. You will also cycle in new goals and performance targets as your team or company learns, evolves, and grows. Six months from now, even after you did your best to set impactful, challenging goals, you might find some goals to be irrelevant or unneeded. When that happens, set your sights on new goals and new challenges—all within your defined performance period.

In the end, strategies and goals become complicated because they are, by definition, fluid. But at the same time, they are also resolute. To set strategies and goals, and then ignore them, is a leadership failure waiting to happen. And to fail to update them as real-world conditions demand is a missed opportunity to lead. However, guided by your servant purpose and by modeling your values and defined behaviors, you will find the right balance—even if that balance requires redirection along the way.

WHO, WHAT, WHEN, AND WHERE

In the Organizational Constitution work already completed, you have defined your servant purpose (your "Why") and your values and defined behaviors (your "How"). You already know your reason for being, the principles that guide every effort, and the behaviors you expect of great team citizens. Now you are charged with defining your "Who, What, When, and Where."

Let's start by looking at each of these four Ws to better understand the role they play in the strategies and goals segment of your Organizational Constitution.

Who | Who are we now? From a team perspective, where do our strengths lie? What weaknesses must we overcome? From a people perspective, what is our current percentage of High Performance–High Values Match team members? Conversely, what is our rate of Low Performance–Low Values Match leaders and employees? Finally, how are our people viewed within our community? Do we, as human beings, contribute positively to wellness on a local, regional, and global scale?

What | What is working well now? What is not? Going back to our servant purpose, what do we do now? Does what we do help us live that servant purpose? What opportunities shall we consider? What are our customers looking for that might be in our team's or company's "wheelhouse" (we do it well or can realign our skills to do it well)? What would allow us to scale quickly to take advantage of those wheelhouse opportunities? Once we decide to pursue those opportunities, what would serve as a barrier to success?

When | When will we accomplish our major goals? When will we achieve our goal of having all High Performance–High Value Match leaders and team members? At what point in time will we be perceived as a Good Comes First company? When will we be ready to expand into other markets and product lines? From both a culture and financial perspective, when will we be prepared to pursue merger and acquisition opportunities? Finally, when should we expect to begin mentoring replacements for those currently in leadership positions?

Where | From a performance and productivity perspective, where are we now? Where do we excel? Where do we not? From a product perspective, where do we do well within our marketplace? Where can we do better? From a value perspective, where are we improving the lives of our customers? And where are our products seen as a commodity? Finally, from a more traditional definition of where: Where should we consider expansion? And where, if anywhere, should we pull back current operations?

These are all critical questions. So, before you can begin laying out a detailed strategic plan, we must answer them. You will, within the strategies and goals segment of your Organizational Constitution leverage your team's or company's "sweet spot," the combination of skills, as well as your collective vision and ingenuity. Without a doubt, this step typically requires the most focus and resolve.

For that reason, our experience shows that one person—one leader—should provide the first draft of answers for the "Who, What, When, and Where." And many of our clients do just that. They go somewhere quiet, a place that allows both a time for reflection and the opportunity for forward thinking. They carefully craft the answers, without interruption or opposing thoughts. Once they have that first set of answers, our experience also shows that leaders—like with so many other aspects of the Organizational Constitution—must socialize their thoughts. They must ask for input. They must actively listen. Eventually, they must create answers the leadership team believes in wholeheartedly and without reservation.

Everything related to strategies and goals depends on these answers and this work. There are no shortcuts. No "I will just keep reading and do this later." As a Good Comes First leadership team, and with "Why" and

"How" already articulated in your company's servant purpose, you must get the "Who, What, When, and Where" right. Right now.

STRATEGIC IMPERATIVES: WHAT MATTERS MOST

You constructed definitive answers to the remaining four Ws. To make them even better, you socialized them. Now, the entire leadership team believes in them. You are ready to move on.

Nice work!

Next, you will begin mapping out your strategic imperatives—the business goals or objectives that will have the highest priority during the next performance period—for your team or company.

How does an actionable strategic imperative look? Consider these examples:

Business and Financial:

- Become known as the top provider of accounting services in the Pacific Northwest.
- Grow revenue by 25 percent annually; maintain a 20 percent Net Profit Margin.
- Become a strategic partner in our customers' long-term success.
- Take the company public by 2025.

Culture and People:

- Develop and maintain an infrastructure that enables an engaged remote workforce.
- Create and sustain a culture that equally values respect and results.
- Build a team that is a 95 percent High Performance–High Values Match.
- Become known for making our employees' and customers' lives better.

As we have discussed, Industrial Age leaders were focused almost exclusively on business and financial objectives. So we used to believe that limiting strategic objectives to a maximum of three to five of these bottom-line-oriented goals was best. Now, however, we know that focusing exclusively on business and financial objectives—*results*—is not in the best interests of the company or its employees.

To that end, as you craft your company's strategic imperatives, carefully select an equal number of imperatives from both the "business and financial" and "culture and people" designations. We suggest two—and a maximum of three—from each. Keep this as simple as possible. Again, when everything is a high priority . . . *nothing* is a high priority.

PLAN THE WORK, WORK THE PLAN

We are both whitewater rafting enthusiasts. Chris has used rafting as a team-building strategy since his days at the YMCA. Mark's first-ever business was a guiding company based in the High Sierra. Equating whitewater rafting to the business strategy may seem like a stretch. But stay with us. We will explain.

Before each trip, a rafting guide must take as much time as necessary to explain how the team will work as it makes its way downriver. This is especially important with beginners. But even with experienced paddlers, each team member must know how best to pull their weight while working together. So the guide emphasizes both paddling and team skills.

As you can imagine, rafting companies and guides design most rafting trips to give the team time to master these new skills. Rather than go straight into the more challenging Class III and IV rapids, each trip starts with Class I and II water, or "float" trips. While not as exciting as the bigger water, the moments invested in adjusting to the guide's commands and learning how to execute the guide's strategy is time well spent.

If you have ever been on a whitewater rafting trip, you know guides do not say much on Class I water. While they become more vocal and act with a higher sense of urgency in Class II rapids, they do not scout the routes. Those rapids typically have clear channels the guides navigate rather effortlessly.

Class III rapids—where the fun really starts, but the danger of dumping what guides call a "swimmer" into the water also increases—are much more challenging. Depending on the water level, a guide might take a moment to scout out the Class III rapid before proceeding downriver. Class IV water—without exception—is always scouted, every time. Or six rafters will very suddenly become six swimmers in very cold, very treacherous water that courses rapidly among very big rocks.

This is especially true on dam-controlled rivers, where the water flow and the degree of difficulty can change in an hour's time. As engineers release new water from the dam, a Class III rapid can quickly become a Class IV. In these conditions, scouting three hours in advance or, worse yet, using the same strategy used yesterday, might lead a guide to take a particular route that seems safe—but is not.

So the guides scout the bigger rapids in real time. They watch the river flow. They look for the safest passage. Then, among themselves, they discuss and agree on that passage. They map out which rafts will go first, second, third, and so on. Once guides set the strategy, they trek back to where the rafters are enjoying the beach while building up adrenaline for the stretch of water ahead. The guides explain what they saw. They carefully outline to the paddlers the passage the team will take.

The rafting team makes sure their personal flotation devices (PFDs) and helmets are well secured. They jump in the raft. They turn on their ears; they are ready to listen to and execute every command. And when the guide—the leader—and the team come out the other side of the rapids without coming out of the raft, everyone knows they did their job.

They planned the work. They worked the plan.

Just as a whitewater rafting guide scouts each stretch of the river, you will do the same for your strategic plan. This means, once you decide on the best passage forward, you will design a plan that ensures each team, and each team member, can execute the plan.

Your goal is to help every leader and team member navigate the challenging waters ahead.

First, you have some scouting to do.

SETTING QUANTIFIABLE GOALS

Before you ask your team to execute a plan or work toward achieving goals, you must set expectations. How will you get where you are going? How will you know when you have arrived?

So, similar to the work you did to define the behaviors that best model each value in the last chapter, you will state two to four quantifiable goals for each strategic imperative.

For example:

Strategic Imperative:

Build a team that is 95 percent High Performance–High Values Match.

Quantifiable Goals:

- Through quarterly performance reviews and annual performance evaluations, measure each leader's and team member's ability to reach agreed-upon performance standards.
- Through quarterly pulse surveys, measure alignment of all team members to defined behaviors.
- Consistently serve as a mentor when redirecting areas of misalignment; celebrate areas of improved alignment.
- Frequently assess the capability of all team members to become High Performance–High Values Match contributors. Lovingly set free those people incapable of reaching that status.

As we are sure you will agree, this is a plan that will work—if you work the plan. And, of course, if all the fires we need to put out each day do not stop us from working the plan. This, dear reader, is why these are called strategic *imperatives*. You specifically chose them because they are your company's highest priorities for a given performance period.

Those fires? They are like those big rocks in the river that the rafters bang into; no matter how hard they try, they cannot seem to miss them. Those rocks—and those fires—keep us from getting where we want to go.

They prevent us from focusing on what matters most. And at the end of the journey, they become our excuses for not meeting established goals.

Should a leader or team member not work the plan as designed, then by default, they have not performed well. The chances are that leader is not aligned with defined values such as integrity and trust. By definition, they—at least for this task in this performance period—find themselves in the Low Performance–Low Values Match quadrant (we will discuss this much more in our next chapter).

And if you, as a leader, tolerate this misaligned conduct, if you do not serve as a mentor and redirect those leaders and team members, then you—at least in this moment—are also in the Low Performance–Low Values Match quadrant. Stay here long enough and you will erode employee confidence in the company's direction and in you as a leader.

However, this is also an opportunity to demonstrate that your ideal culture—and the values and defined behaviors that serve as the backbone of that culture—will not be compromised. At every occurrence of misalignment, you can clearly demonstrate that you, the well-prepared guide, know how to get your teams where they need to go. You planned the work. Now you are working the plan. And in the process, you are making it clear you expect others to do precisely the same.

With all this in mind, let us move on to the next step. Take as much time as you need to create two to four quantifiable goals for each of your strategic imperatives. Once done, socialize each of them with insightful—and perhaps influential—leaders and team members. Refine them. Socialize again.

You know the deal: When 90 percent of the stakeholders smile and nod . . . you are done.

PRESENTING YOUR STRATEGIES AND GOALS

When we talked about how long your strategies and goals document might be, we also talked about using an infographic-style format or perhaps an executive-summary-style layout to present your one-page document. Now, for just a moment, let's review what else—besides your strategic imperatives and quantifiable goals—might also appear within that document.

Why is this relevant now? Because this last segment of your Organizational Constitution is not just a place to list strategic imperatives. Yes, those imperatives are front and center. But to paint the complete picture, and with your "Why" and "How" already established in your servant purpose, you, as a leader, should include as many elements of your "Who, What, When, and Where" as possible. For this reason, your strategies and goals one-pager might also include:

- **Projected Growth (Who)** | Who will help get our work done? Who is responsible for helping us achieve our goals, and who will help identify new opportunities?
- **Competitive Advantages (What)** | For employees' and leaders' awareness, a list of what we do best now broken down by business sector or team.
- **Anticipated Timelines (When)** | By quarter or year, when we expect to accomplish our established goals—and when we should move on to our next set of goals.
- **Key Performance Indicators (Where)** | State where we will focus our primary efforts, where our plans will take us—and how we will know when we arrive.

Each of these areas adds to a sense of completeness in your strategic plan. Together with the strategic imperatives, they communicate your overall vision in a concrete, uncompromising way. Just like your values and defined behaviors, each person will know exactly what to expect—and exactly what you expect of them.

NEXT STEPS

In our rafting analogy, it was clear that every leader and rafting team member was responsible for strategic clarity. Each team—leader/guide and member/paddler—had to understand the best passage forward, and their role in helping the team get there. When the time came, they had to execute their part of the plan.

Executing your strategic plan is no different. Each team member must know the plan. They must know how their work contributes to the plan and how they help achieve the primary goals. So they can execute their part of the plan, every player must understand what performance is expected, at what quality standard, by when.

The only way to make this happen is to ensure everyone understands and can verbalize the company's strategic plan and goals. Everyone must also know how you expect them to contribute to achieving the plan and goals. Reinforce your plan and goals regularly, and carefully communicate everyone's role. Validate individual effort and celebrate every team win—every day.

With your strategies and goals in hand, you have now completed the last segment of your company's Organizational Constitution. Now it is time to pull it all together.

If you are not sure how, or you are not sure what form the finished Organizational Constitution will take, don't worry. That is our intent. There is no right or wrong way to pull all this together. Your constitution is unique to you and to the people who follow you. As long as the chosen format works for your desired culture—and includes your servant purpose statement, defined values and desired behaviors, and strategies and goals— that works!

(We have clients, though, who appreciate a more prescriptive approach. And for that reason, on GoodComesFirst.com we have three examples of how an Organizational Constitution, in finished form, may look. If you would like, take a look and even emulate.)

No matter how your Organizational Constitution looks when done, take time to celebrate. You have accomplished much in a relatively short amount of time. You have defined exactly why your company exists, how it will operate, and the "Who, What, When, and Where" behind its primary strategic objectives. You deserve some downtime—and you will need it. After all, we are only one-third of the way through our "Define, Align, and Refine" process for culture transformation. There is still plenty of big water to navigate.

When you are ready, let's move on to our next chapter. We will discuss how best to align to the unique Good Comes First culture you have so deliberately defined.

Living Your Constitution: Aligning to Desired Values and Behaviors

Through Chapter 9, you completed the "Design" phase of "Design, Align, and Refine." But the acts of defining and publishing your servant purpose, values and behaviors, and strategies and goals do *not* make your culture better on their own. That change does not happen until you begin actively *living* your Organizational Constitution. The moment you align all plans, decisions, and actions to your desired culture—as specified in your Organizational Constitution—is the moment your culture begins to make significant gains in respectful interactions, proactive problem solving, and consistent performance.

In this tenth chapter, we discuss the "Align" stage of "Design, Align, and Refine." Here, we equip you with five proven practices for holding yourself and others accountable for performance and values.

As you will soon learn, this alignment phase is hard work and takes time. In fact, most clients spend eighteen to twenty-four months on this stage alone. It takes that long for a Good Comes First culture to gain credibility and traction, in large part because it takes time for senior leaders to champion the change effectively. And it takes that long to model, coach, measure, celebrate, and mentor the consistent demonstration of your company's values—all while continuing to meet or exceed performance standards.

That does not mean you will not see *any* results until the twelve- to eighteen-month mark.

It will not take that long for next-level leaders to learn this change is essential—and not optional. After all, if senior leaders embrace and model the valued behaviors, the fact that change is already here should be evident to those next-level leaders in a matter of weeks, maybe even days. This timeline does not mean pockets of excellence and small armies of change champions cannot rise up soon after the change initiative is socialized. Person to person and team by team, change will be evident nearly immediately.

But the ultimate transformation into a Good Comes First work culture happens when everyone—from the C-suite to the front lines—embraces respect and drives results. It happens when everyone operates from the High Performance–High Values match quadrant—in every interaction, every day. Only when every formal leader in your company models, coaches, measures, celebrates, and mentors the demonstration of your values and valued behaviors will team members—employees—embrace those values and valued behaviors of their own free will.

There is a reason why we are adamant about senior leaders leading, modeling, and driving culture change in organizations: Senior leaders are the only players in your company that have the authority to change policies, procedures, incentives, and recognition practices. They alone have the burden—or maybe a better term is *opportunity*—to serve as champions for your Good Comes First work culture.

That authority—that opportunity—cannot be delegated to others in your organization; it is not the HR team's responsibility; it is not the organizational development group's responsibility; it is not the cross-functional culture committee's responsibility. None of those players have the authority, opportunity, and—dare we say it—the *firepower* necessary to define your desired culture, align your desired culture, and refine your desired culture over time.

Senior leaders must be the champions of your Good Comes First work culture, or that desired culture will never come to fruition.

Defining and publishing your servant purpose, formalizing your Organizational Constitution, and sharing it throughout your company make up a critically important first step. After all, the align phase cannot happen without a defined, clear statement of your company's servant purpose, values and behaviors, and strategies and goals. It is not until you begin to align your actions toward your desired culture, holding everyone accountable for both respect and results, that you start to see tangible proof that your efforts are paying off. That is when you realize you are that much closer to a Good Comes First culture.

PERFORMANCE ACCOUNTABILITY

Over the years, we have learned that most organizations have established systems and structures in place to manage performance. They all have some form of goal-setting processes: HR ensures every player has an updated annual performance plan that outlines that person's goals for the year. HR also makes sure every boss has a copy of every player's plan. Companies have mid-year reporting forms. They have year-end performance review forms. They have interim performance plans. HR publishes a schedule of due dates and nudges leaders at all levels to get their forms in on time. And so on.

We have also learned all these systems and forms do not truly improve accountability. They do not help deliver promised results, nor do they substantially change behaviors and levels of engagement. True, performance accountability varies wildly within most companies and from company to company. But for the most part, nearly every performance evaluation process—especially considering all the money and time invested in them—sucks.

The good news is that every organization wants to be efficient and effective at managing performance.

The bad news is that they do not have the right tools. Not yet.

The five accountability practices that follow—which, as we first learned in Chapter 5, make up the Good Comes First Accountability Model (GCF Accountability Model, for short)—help boost expected performance. Simultaneously, this model enables demonstration of your company's desired values and behaviors.

In other words, the model works for both results *and* respect.

Our experience shows this model can help you embed *any* desired change into your organization. For example: If you want greater diversity and inclusion, this model can help align recruiting practices, interviewing processes, hiring practices, and orientation approaches to ensure new hires have the best possible opportunity to thrive in your Good Comes First work culture.

Let's learn more about this model and the five change practices that make it up. Then we will apply it as we align all plans, decisions, and actions—company-wide—to your Organizational Constitution.

THE GOOD COMES FIRST ACCOUNTABILITY MODEL

First introduced in Chapter 5, we designed the GCF Accountability Model to help you align behaviors and performance to a formalized desired change or outcome. That formalization must happen first. Without that clarity, this model will not help you. If you have not yet specified the change you want (or need), set this model aside until you complete that vital clarification.

As a reminder, the five separate but constantly entwined practices that formulate the GCF Accountability Model include:

- **Model** the desired process and outcomes
- **Coach** the desired process and outcomes
- **Measure** the desired process and outcomes
- **Celebrate** the desired process and outcomes
- **Mentor** misaligned processes and outcomes

Here is the visual representation of the Good Comes First Accountability Model we use to help guide our clients through the entire align stage:

The outer ring of this graphic provides examples of areas where we apply the five practices to build and sustain accountability. Examples include building accountability for your servant purpose, increasing demonstration of your company's defined values and desired behaviors by all players, meeting performance metrics, and developing desirable leadership traits. Notice that these are just examples; while these areas are common areas of concern for many organizations, you should supplement and customize your own list of concerns that are unique to your company.

The graphic's interior ring notes the five practices needed to implement change—Model, Coach, Measure, Celebrate, and Mentor. At the center, the bi-directional arrows help leaders visualize this accountability model's fluid and organic nature; they demonstrate that a leader might flow from one practice to another at any time, and that the practices are not sequential.

Humans are complex. It is unlikely that you will apply only one of these practices with a given team member. Steady progress toward account-ability is sometimes more art than science; it requires leaders to be nimble, moving fluidly from one needed practice to another, depending on each player's specific needs. Effective leaders observe their players closely, then shift to a practice as discussions continue.

To apply the accountability model well requires a leader to be skilled in all five practices—and to be committed to applying this approach to build and sustain desired accountability.

The most beneficial impact of these five practices on accountability within your organization occurs when two things happen concurrently:

1. Formal leaders do the modeling, coaching, measuring, celebrating, and mentoring.
2. All five components of the model are applied; a leader does not skip or ignore any one practice.

Why must formal leaders demonstrate the five practices?

When senior leaders lead change by actively employing these five practices, that builds credibility for the organization's change process. Since they proactively serve the needs of their most important customers—employees—it also increases credibility for the leaders themselves. When next-level leaders see senior leaders deliberately and consistently leverage these five practices daily, they will begin using the GCF Accountability Model themselves.

The acceptance of a common model throughout your company helps everyone understand that this change initiative is real. And, from the top down, so are the leaders' behaviors and actions.

Even informal leaders—for example, project team leads—can effectively influence accountability by demonstrating these five practices. However, those informal leaders will not be able to effectively embrace this model until formal leaders build credibility for the model by applying the five practices nimbly and effectively.

We have all seen this: We build credibility and optimism when team members see formal leaders demonstrating these practices over time. We build momentum when those team members observe *all* leaders across the organization embracing this system. And it is the combination of momentum and confidence that encourages team members to embrace the new behaviors themselves.

In other words, change becomes not just consistent—it becomes contagious. And when team members embrace the new behaviors themselves, they begin to celebrate each other when they observe aligned behaviors from leaders and peers. Just as important, those team members actively mentor others when they observe misaligned behaviors in colleagues.

Why are all five practices required for the most beneficial impact?

Each practice addresses specific needs. For example, if you choose not to apply the "Celebrate" best practice, you will miss out on addressing the human need for validation and recognition. Suppose you decide to ignore the "Measure" practice. In that case, you will not address everyone's need for undeniable proof—of progress on values and behaviors, traction on innovation, leadership team effectiveness, and more.

THE FIVE PRACTICES OF THE GCF ACCOUNTABILITY MODEL

Now let's take a look at each of the five practices—because once you understand the needs each practice addresses and what each accomplishes, you will be far more likely to invest the time necessary to build the skills and passion for each practice.

Model

Once a company creates and publishes its Organizational Constitution, scrutiny from employees—naturally—goes way up. By definition, employee scrutiny means they are hyper-observant of every plan and decision leaders make, and every action leaders take. In the face of declared change, this makes perfect sense; after all, employees have learned over the years that "MbA" (Managing by Announcements) is very real. What gets announced does not always get embedded in the operation. The antidote to this skepticism is effectively applying the first practice within our GCF Accountability Model: modeling.

Employees will not initially believe the Organizational Constitution is there to stay. Many have been conditioned not to believe because of multiple change initiatives they have seen come and go during their careers. Whether it is an announcement of a new or changed policy, practice, or procedure, they will not believe it until they see leaders embracing the new initiative. The announced change is purely hypothetical for employees until they see leaders doing it—*modeling* it—over and over again, over time. Employees will judge you and your fellow leaders by how well you model the proposed changes. In a Good Comes First company, that starts with adhering to your company's valued behaviors and supporting traction on your company's servant purpose.

For example, pretend one of your company's values is respect, and one of that value's behaviors is "I resolve differences by directly communicating with the people involved." If a senior leader has a difference of opinion with someone—even a customer—and complains about how frustrated they are with that person, then, clearly, that leader is not adhering to the "resolve differences directly with the people involved" valued behavior. That is a miss—and employees will notice. They will first internalize what they saw, and then they will talk to each other about the miss. Credibility—and momentum—will be lost.

As a leader, you must understand this reality. You must know, due to this intense level of scrutiny, you are *always* "onstage." There will never be a time when you, as a leader, are not being carefully observed. We can tell you this scrutiny is unfair, but it has been happening for eons. As we say to our clients, you will never be able to run a yellow light in town again—or take twelve items through the "Ten Items or Less" checkout line at the grocery store. If a defined value at your company is "respect" and you treat a fellow leader or team member harshly, judgment will soon follow.

Embracing this reality—knowing you will be watched closely at all times and owning it—helps you be fully present as a leader, each day. It also encourages you to be a positive role model 24/7 (or as close to "all the time" as possible).

Let's go back for a moment to the demonstration of the "respect" value mentioned a moment ago—and specifically, to another dynamic you as a leader must be aware of as you serve as a change champion: the importance of consistency.

Suppose thirty wholly aligned leaders demonstrate valued behaviors that are consistent with "respect" for a week straight—with dozens of issues being addressed respectfully and constructively—but *one leader* blows it on the afternoon of the seventh day. Employees will judge the entire leadership group harshly—they will quickly forget all the good that happened over the previous six-and-a-half days.

Modeling requires the intention and attention of *every formal leader, every day.*

Coach

In the context of Good Comes First, coaching is a means to improve others' citizenship within the defined work environment. The design of the coaching practice enables the modeling of defined values (respect) and boosts demonstrated performance (results) during day-to-day operations.

Coaching now has a wide variety of applications in our world beyond athletics—from health coaching (fitness training or diet guidance, for example) to skill building (taking an archery course from a champion archer) to life coaching (career planning or relationship skills) to workplace performance coaching.

The problem is that most of us are not naturally talented coaches. In Western society, Industrial Age thinking continues to influence our leadership actions—and not in healthy ways: Many of us did not have bosses who were effective coaches. Instead, we had bosses who told us what to do and were then quick to chastise us if we did not meet their high standards.

Here is an example: A colleague was facilitating a coaching course at an automobile manufacturing plant. During the program, she asked how managers trained new employees for production line tasks. One gruff team leader explained, "First, we tell them what to do. Then they ask stupid questions. We sigh heavily and say, 'Here's all you gotta do,' and show them how to do it, once. They never get it right."

She asked for a show of hands, saying, "How many of you learned how to do your jobs that same way when you started here?" Ninety percent of the people in the program raised their hands.

That's *not* effective coaching.

An effective coach is genuinely optimistic about the person they are coaching. They are committed to that person's growth. And they are willing to try (and try again) to help their "coachee" (the person they are coaching) improve their results and increase the level of respect they offer others. Citizenship coaching is usually conducted in a one-to-one partnership and is the most common in workplaces. Yes, as systemic team or company situations arise, coaching could include group coaching. However, most coaching conversations are typically between two individuals. As you might guess, to serve the needs of team leaders and team members across the organization, formal leaders must learn to be skilled, engaged coaches. Because the requirements section of a leader's job description does not typically include "effective coaching," you will likely need to train on coaching techniques as part of your transition to a Good Comes First culture.

In the end, if a leader is not skilled in effective coaching and/or is not optimistic about the likelihood of coaching having a beneficial impact on a player, that coaching will fail. That means alignment is impossible, which means that team members will never reach the High Performance–High Values Match quadrant in our Performance-Values Matrix.

This unfortunate reality also means the leader—*the person who failed to be an effective coach*—has failed to model the defined behaviors. In effect, that leader expected results without showing enough respect to the team member to want to become a good coach.

The team member then talks to other team members. Quickly, the team members learn to lose faith in the leader. In the end, nothing changes; the employees never hit the High Performance–High Values quadrant—and the team is back to square one.

Good Comes First coaching requires effective coaching skills. Effective coaching takes time, energy, conversation, observation, facilitation, reflection, and action planning daily. It also requires optimism that coaching will move people forward and a willingness to partner, grow, and learn together.

Measure

Of the GCF Accountability Model's five practices, Measure requires the most explanation—both in this book and in our work in the field. The reason is simple: Many business leaders still believe values and behaviors are difficult—maybe even impossible—to measure. And if your values are lofty ideals that are not grounded in observable behavior, then it is true—they are challenging to quantify. However, values are not difficult to measure when defined as observable, tangible behaviors—precisely as you did in Chapter 8.

As you will learn much more about in our next chapter—and a bit here—values *are* measurable—just as results are measurable. Just as performance metrics provide hard data for results, the "Measure" practice, executed properly and consistently, presents hard data in the form of how well aligned an individual, leader, team, division, or company is to your defined values and behaviors.

How? By collecting insights from team members and leaders using two low-impact surveys and one more comprehensive assessment:

- **Values and Behaviors Survey** | In a quick survey conducted every six months, employees rate leaders on the degree to which they demonstrate defined values and behaviors in daily interactions. This survey provides every formal leader in your organization with a profile, noting employee perceptions of how that leader aligns to values and behaviors.

- **Executive Team Effectiveness Survey** | A formal survey conducted every six months, where all staff members provide feedback on how well your senior leadership team operates according to ten best practices. Like the values survey, the company provides each executive with a report that shows how employees view that executive's alignment to values and behaviors.

- **Workplace Intelligence (WQ) Assessment** | Conducted annually, this assessment asks all staff members to provide feedback on how well your organization models the Good Comes First foundational principle and all four culture cornerstones. This assessment provides insight into five WQ components and a total overall WQ score for each team, department, division, or for the entire company. We will explore the concept of WQ much more in the next chapter.

As we have often said, it is leadership that has the power to drive change. So we design the two surveys to collect data on the impact of leaders only.

Because the emphasis is on the leaders' abilities to both demonstrate the values and behaviors and operate within them, the structure of your surveys is vitally important. Each must be customized and based on your formalized and socialized Organizational Constitution.

The WQ Assessment also takes an in-depth look into values and behaviors; however, this more extensive assessment, through the lenses of both respect and results, looks deeper into the impact of your Organizational Constitution on overall operations. Rather than focusing on "them" or "they" (the leaders and executive team), this assessment focuses on the "me," "we," and "us." Once the WQ report is published, you as a leader will have an in-depth view of which teams—and perhaps entire departments and divisions—already put good first. And which do not.

That makes the Measure practice an integral part of the GCF Accountability Model. This is the one practice that informs all others because, without this data, you will not know if leaders serve as effective Models of all three areas of your Organizational Constitution (servant purpose, values and behaviors, strategies and goals). Your leaders will not know what aspects of your desired culture to Coach. They will not know when to Celebrate. And they will not have the data that enables them to identify areas of misalignment objectively—so they will not know whom to Mentor.

Yeah. Measuring is kind of a big deal.

Celebrate

As we do keynote presentations, we challenge audiences: "Raise your hands if you get enough praise on the job." Typically, 10 to 20 percent of the audience members raise their hands. These informal responses parallel current research. A 2019 study[1] by TINYpulse found that one-third of employees had not received recognition in the past two weeks. The same percentage said they were not well recognized the last time they went "over and above" at work.

On top of that, only 26 percent of respondents said they felt highly valued, with 33 percent reporting that they felt *under*valued. This highlights the reality that people do good work all the time, but most leaders either do not notice or fail to express praise or encouragement. By default, that means they do not leverage that good work to create a better working environment.

The Celebrate practice changes that. It requires leaders to pay attention—and to pay attention to what they pay attention to! Celebration simply means expressing praise and encouragement for ideas, efforts, and accomplishments. Of these three things, accomplishments are the most likely to be celebrated because leaders are looking out for them. Ideas and efforts, however, are rarely celebrated. Leaders are not looking for those. Ideas and efforts are not as flashy—but good ideas and good efforts, over time, earn respect and lead to better results.

That is why Good Comes First bosses are on the lookout for good ideas and good efforts! They seek out accomplishments and achievements. Just as important, they promptly and appropriately celebrate and validate good work.

What types of celebration are the most effective? For individuals, a handshake (or a fist or elbow bump in the days of COVID-19) and verbal appreciation are easy and impactful. A heartfelt, handwritten note (or text or email if working virtually) is compelling. While your introverted players will likely not find the public limelight to be comfortable, extroverted team leaders or team members might welcome a more public celebration. Teams that generate good ideas and produce solid effort—that play well together and accomplish expected results—deserve thanks, praise, and maybe even pizza! (Paid for by the company, of course.)

As you consider how you and your leaders may celebrate good work, please note the difference between praise and encouragement:

- Praise comes *after* the desired behavior.
- Encouragement comes *before* the desired behavior.

Humans need both. And in a Good Comes First work culture, employees will come to expect both. Praise and encouragement are each forms of celebration. The combination of praise and encouragement inspires satisfaction, validation, teamwork, and proactive problem solving. As you have come to learn, those characteristics are hallmarks of a Good Comes First work culture. So, as soon as you hear about them or observe them, praise ideas, efforts, and accomplishments. As soon as you see the need, encourage future aligned ideas, efforts, and achievements.

As a leader, you can observe many actions worthy of praise by strolling around your work environment intentionally. As we say, "Walk the floor." Observe meetings and production where you can. Pay attention. Focus on how the work is getting done and notice who best demonstrates defined values and desired behaviors. In a remote work environment, it is much tougher to "wander and observe." So consider recruiting internal "scouts"—peers who can look out for reasons to celebrate and who will gladly report back others' aligned ideas, efforts, and accomplishments. Once you hear about deserving behavior, celebrate! Say thanks, send a note of appreciation, perhaps call or text them. Promptly.

If a day passes and you have not celebrated individual or team ideas, efforts, or accomplishments—you are not paying close enough attention.

Praise and encourage daily, and be ready to go into full-blown celebration mode often. Allocate a budget for this purpose if necessary. Because in a Good Comes First culture, having a reason to celebrate is a common occurrence.

Mentor

The Cambridge Dictionary defines a mentor[2] as "an experienced and trusted person who gives another person advice and help, especially related to work or school, over a period of time." An alternate definition is "to support and advise someone with less experience to help them develop in their work."

The Mentor practice in our Accountability Model focuses on the latter. In a Good Comes First work culture, mentoring is focused on redirection, helping someone who does not currently model your organization's desired valued behaviors to embrace those valued behaviors—or face the consequences. While we Westerners tend to react to a term like "consequences" with an "oh no" look on our faces, not all consequences are bad—they are simply logical extensions of a plan to align every player to your desired valued behaviors.

There are positive consequences—like the Celebration practice just discussed. Effective leaders are adept—comfortable, willing, and skilled—at providing positive consequences. But though we no longer live or work in the Industrial Age, when we taught leaders to exclusively wield negative consequences, even in a Good Comes First culture, there are negative consequences—there must be. After all, Good Comes First leaders do not tolerate bad behavior.

Let's say the leader sees a player missing performance deadlines, producing poor quality work, interacting in rude or demeaning ways, or not operating ethically. The leader must apply earned and deserved negative consequences—with no excuses and no lengthy delays.

When leaders effectively apply the other practices in the GCF Accountability Model—Modeling, Coaching, Measuring, and Celebrating—they provide the best opportunity for everyone to embrace the Organizational Constitution and align to specific values and behaviors. The Mentoring practice can be no different. We must allow each leader and team member to better align to the new culture, which means tough conversations must be started—and finished.

At the end of a percentage of those mentoring conversations, it will become evident that some players do not fit into your Good Comes First work culture. When that happens, it is important to remember that the mentor practice does not mean every person will embrace change. It simply ensures leaders do everything possible to help everyone be—or become—great citizens, delivering promised results while treating others respectfully.

Consequences that originate in the mentoring process (positive and negative) can vary in degree. You will likely start mentoring by identifying the problem and getting the mentee's agreement that change is required. You may commit to regular one-on-one meetings each week to create expectations, strategize action plans, and monitor your mentee's progress toward the upper right quadrant. If they align, you have another reason to celebrate, though you must continue measuring and mentoring. If they do not align, you must apply more restrictive consequences until they do.

You know your team best, but our experience shows that a "Let's work together to improve _____ (specific goal) _____ by _____ (specific date) _____" approach works best. Your primary goal is to set clear expectations on exactly when you, as a mentor, need to see improved behaviors or results.

Granted, some mentees will not last through the mentoring practice. They will not agree with your valued behaviors, so they will not embrace them—or they may disagree with your assessment of their ability to demonstrate the values and behaviors. Either way, they will become members of the "opt-out-and-leave" group.

Let them go.

The Mentor practice is the ultimate accountability lever. It is a fair, calm, consistent way to reinforce your desired culture, and it has proven to be a requirement in every organization we have helped become a Good Comes First company. Just remember: Mentors who approach this practice from a positive perspective and who remain focused on the mentee's growth are often fondly remembered. However, team members see those leaders who view this practice as a disciplinary tool as just another autocratic boss.

In the end, the Mentor practice is the only way you will reach Good Comes First nirvana—where every senior leader, team leader, and team member consistently delivers both respect and results.

Remember in earlier chapters, when we discussed companies like Southwest Airlines, Trader Joe's, and Radio Flyer? Leaders throughout those companies defined the human-centered, trusting work environment they wanted in their companies. Their desired culture included directions like remove bureaucracy. Let people be themselves. Act with integrity. Hold everyone accountable for results and respect. Validate employees through fair pay, fair benefits, and great coworkers. And so much more.

Leaders at each of those companies drove and sustained their desired culture by modeling, coaching, measuring, and celebrating accountability for their standards. And—using a positive approach—they mentored misaligned behaviors and practices.

In a video post from April 2019, Chris reported on a viral social media thread that asked why Trader Joe's employees are so happy. One employee replied, "Because we're treated very well."[3] You defined your unique Good Comes First culture—one similar to Southwest Airlines, Trader Joe's, or Radio Flyer—in your Organizational Constitution. Now you must *live* that culture by aligning all plans, decisions, and actions to that Organizational Constitution.

You must treat your employees very well.

The GCF Accountability Model ensures that we make every effort to inspire respectful interactions while delivering expected results. At every opportunity, it allows you to increase demonstrated alignment to performance expectations and values standards. As a leader and change champion, all you have to do is apply these five practices daily.

In our next chapter, we will discuss the third phase of "Define, Align, and Refine." Once there, we will look more closely at exactly how to measure the very human characteristics a Good Comes First culture depends on so much. Along the way, we will familiarize you with Workplace Intelligence (WQ)—and show you how best to leverage WQ as you enter the Refine phase of your Good Comes First culture.

Get ready for the light bulb over your head to turn on!

CHAPTER 11

Measuring and Refining Your Good Comes First Work Culture

In Section II of *Good Comes First*, we have learned how to *define* your Good Comes First culture through creating an Organizational Constitution. In the last chapter, we learned how to *align* our organizational culture and climate to the constitution. In this chapter, we take on the third leg of our "Define, Align, and Refine" journey: *Refine*.

Here, we learn how to objectively measure how well all your employees—including formal leaders and especially members of your leadership team—align with the ideals defined in your Organizational Constitution. Based on the objective data you collect, you then have the opportunity to refine your leadership efforts and your company's culture.

Your ultimate goal is to thoroughly understand how far your Good Comes First culture has come . . . and how far it still must go.

You do not know it yet. But you cannot wait to learn more—and for a good reason. After all, this is our favorite part—this is when the light bulb goes on for nearly every executive in the room.

This is when everything starts to make sense.

This is the moment every ounce of the work you have done so far becomes actionable!

But we are not going to start yet. First, please do us a favor: Take just a minute to jot down how your company measures and monitors performance. In other words, how do you track results?

Because we do not want this to take too long or use up too many brain cells, here are some of the common reports and tools that clients typically rely upon to gauge results:

- Accounts receivable
- Accrued overtime, company-wide and by division
- Accrued PTO
- Actual sales to sales projections comparison
- Annual report
- Balance sheet
- Cash-flow statement
- Income statement, company-wide and by division
- Market share by product and by region
- Profit and loss statement, company-wide and by division
- Quarterly reports
- Rolling twelve-month revenue projections
- Sales projections
- Stock price
- Total labor hours by division
- Valuation
- Work-in-progress, showing mid-project progress

How many ways to track results are on your list?

Chances are this task will not take you long to complete because, for many business leaders, these methodologies are top of mind. You use them every day. Plus, organizations and leaders have been building systems and dashboards to monitor and measure these key performance indicators forever. Since the beginning of the Industrial Age, leaders have learned to pay very close attention to these metrics. Their jobs depend on it.

Now, please take a minute to note how your organization measures and monitors your company values. If your company has not formalized values or behaviors yet, share how your company measures the degree to which employees are treated respectfully in daily interactions.

This task may not take a whole minute because if you are like most organizations, you do not have a system or structure to measure or monitor respect. Granted, some companies have one report that usually qualifies as a "values" data point: an employee engagement (or employee satisfaction) survey. But even with that one data point in hand, it is highly likely your organization has far fewer systems, reports, or dashboards monitoring the health of your organization's work culture than you do monitoring performance and results.

But now you know better. You are committed to our foundational principle: to equally value respect and results. And you now understand your company must be as thorough about measuring and monitoring values as you are about performance. Unlike performance-related monitoring, you do not need to create a dozen systems or a set of complex dashboards to measure values alignment effectively.

You just need to create and utilize the three methods of data collection introduced in the last chapter.

GOOD COMES FIRST DATA COLLECTION METHODOLOGY

- Values and Behaviors Survey
- Executive Team Effectiveness Survey
- Workplace Intelligence (WQ) Assessment

So let's take a closer look at each method for collecting objective data.

VALUES AND BEHAVIORS SURVEY

Formalized within your Organizational Constitution, you have values defined in observable, measurable, behavioral terms. We measure alignment to the values and behaviors using the appropriately named **Values and Behaviors Survey**.

The structure of your survey is vitally important. So we strongly suggest you derive your questions from those defined behaviors. For example, say one of your values is "integrity." Let's also say the defined behavior for that value is "I do what I say I will do." To ensure this behavior-defined value becomes highly relevant in your survey, we convert that behavior into a personalized statement that becomes a rating of that leader, like so:

- "Roberta Garcia does what she says she will do."

This item on your survey measures this specific leader (Roberta Garcia) on a single, distinct, observable behavior (she does what she says she will do). Naturally, the quantified responses from employees who have firsthand knowledge of Roberta's behavior provide actionable insight into Roberta's ability to demonstrate the defined value (integrity).

The concept of a "single, distinct" behavior is an important one. If your survey item presents more than one behavior to be rated, respondents will be confused. For example, if your item states "Roberta Garcia openly shares information that helps individuals and teams," this statement is hard to score because you are asking for a rating on two different contexts—individuals *and* teams. What if Roberta excels at informing teams but rarely shares information with individuals? That is why it is best to separate these contexts into two separate items:

- "Roberta Garcia openly shares information that helps me."
- "Roberta Garcia openly shares information that helps our team."

Each of these two survey items now presents a single, distinct behavior or context that is simple for employees to rate.

The rating scale used in your survey is also important. Depending on the scale used, the ratings collected can help or hinder how actionable the data is. For this reason, we highly recommend using this 6-point scale:

- Strongly Agree (6 points)
- Agree (5 points)
- Slightly Agree (4 points)
- Slightly Disagree (3 points)
- Disagree (2 points)
- Strongly Disagree (1 point)

Over the last thirty years, we have experimented with several rating scales and determined that this approach offers the most significant benefit.

An odd-numbered response scale ensures that a neutral, mid-scale response is available to employees (e.g., a 3 out of 5). The trouble with that mid-scale response is that it is, by design, neutral; therefore, a mid-point response is not actionable. Since every question in your survey will be stated in favorable terms—meaning the item will present a desirable behavior (not an undesirable one)—you strive for scores on the higher end of the scale. Offering a neutral response defeats that purpose.

Why not a 10-point scale? For behavioral observations like your values survey, a 6-point continuum provides plenty of choices. While a 10-point scale would offer more options, the additional range does not provide greater impact. Instead, it creates a more extensive but less specific scale that makes the feedback less actionable. Ultimately, a 6-point scale includes fewer nuanced points to consider, which means a less-intrusive survey that is faster to complete.

When the data is collected, you as a leader (and your organization as a whole) want responses in the 5 to 6 range—Strongly Agree and Agree. Responses in this range mean that leader demonstrates the desired behavior stated in that question. Ratings in the 3 to 4 range mean your leader does not consistently model the desired valued behavior, and constructive redirection from a mentor is required. Ratings in the 1 to 2 range mean a rapid intervention is needed. Those scores indicate a leader, even if they are considered a high performer, is absolutely not in alignment with the change effort underway—and may never be.

From our experience, fewer than one out of five leaders who receives a score of 2 responds well to redirection. Fewer than one out of ten leaders with a score of 1 will recover well enough, over time, to be considered a member of the High Performance–High Values Match Club.

To help visualize the reporting that might come from a Values and Behaviors Survey (and for possible emulation), there are some client examples on the following pages. The first client has defined six values and fifteen model behaviors. This bar chart summarizes the first-ever Values and Behaviors scores collected for the company president:

In the survey, each value has two to four questions derived from the company's fifteen valued behaviors. The bars represent the president's average scores for each value.

Valued Behaviors Report Card

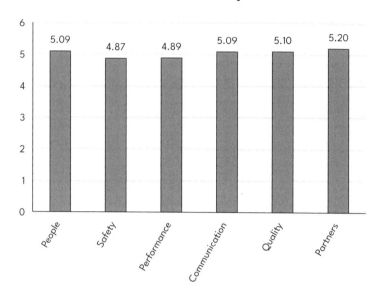

Here you can see the president's scores are quite good. Four out of the six values ratings are in the 5 to 6 range. As you can also see, this leader falls short, below the 5 to 6 range, in two values. Because of this executive's standing as the most senior leader of the organization, the response pool included everyone impacted by his leadership. That means direct reports, as well as everyone else in the organization (indirect reports), were surveyed. The survey includes ratings by question for each value in the alignment profile. This approach allows this leader to understand how many respondents rated him a 6, how many rated him a 5, and so on, for each valued behavior/survey question.

The survey, to maintain confidentiality, does not report ratings by individual respondents. Employees' identities are never shared. So there is no way a leader can see that "George" gave the president a 3 on valued behavior question 11, for example. One notable caveat: In smaller teams, determining who said what becomes less of a challenge.

For instance, in a three-person team, the leader has a 33 percent chance of guessing the source of any one score. For this reason, we suggest broadening the scope of small-team leaders to include peers and perhaps indirect reports with knowledge of that leader's day-to-day behaviors. No matter what, because of the strict need for confidentiality, it is imperative that no leader receive their full profile unless they receive ratings from at least three respondents.

Let's look at the bar chart from another formal leader in this client's organization. This person is a frontline supervisor rated by his direct reports:

The bar chart's visual nature lets us quickly see this group of direct reports does not feel their leader effectively models the organization's desired values in daily interactions. Average scores in the 2 to 4 range for all values means this supervisor needs near-immediate coaching and mentoring to embrace respect and results fully. (And if a CEO received these same

Valued Behaviors Report Card

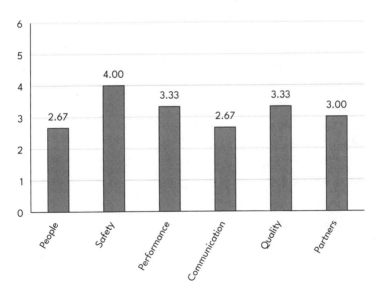

scores, that executive is well served by securing an external mentor able to be direct with his advice.)

With performance data that shows strengths and opportunities for improvement, you coach toward strengths while improving perceived weaknesses. The same is true when leveraging data from the Values and Behaviors survey. We coach and mentor leaders toward their strengths (the values and behaviors demonstrated consistently). We redirect leaders in the areas where they fall short of values expectations.

This coaching and mentoring is typically not a one-off experience. In fact, most of our clients include values profile strengths and opportunities in the leaders' annual review. Some clients go so far as to make raises and bonuses contingent upon exceeding performance goals *and* exceeding values standards. If that leader fails to excel, or at least improve, in the areas of respect and results, the company does not grant those financial rewards.

While often counter to a company's "old" culture, this type of policy reinforces that values are as important as performance. It also almost instantaneously moves those much-maligned annual performance reviews from the "reviews suck" category to "these actually mean something" status.

EXECUTIVE TEAM EFFECTIVENESS SURVEY

We designed the Values and Behaviors Survey to provide a snapshot of how well an individual leader is aligned to the company's defined values and desired behaviors. Chances are good that each member of the executive team has been the subject of the Values and Behaviors Survey and has rated their peers on that survey. The feedback provided helps them better model and coach the defined values and behaviors. That survey, however, does not tell us how the executives respond to that feedback as a leadership team. For that reason, we designed the *Executive Team Effectiveness Survey.*

In the ten-question Executive Team Effectiveness Survey—again customized based on the concepts contained in the company's unique Organizational Constitution—we gather perceptions from everyone in the company. From fellow executive team members to the newest employees, the survey asks every person how effectively the company's executive team leads the organization.

While executives are used to quantifying performance-based contributions of managers and employees, few leadership teams receive regular feedback about their key responsibilities. They often are not aware of how their actions and decisions impact the company's overall operations. Even fewer companies measure an executive team's ability to serve as a role model for demonstrating values and behaviors.

In Good Comes First companies, though, leaders stay in tune and in touch with employee perceptions. They know that is the *only* way to gauge the leadership team's effectiveness.

In this survey, the responses—based on ten personalized questions, and measured using the 6-point scale—help gather the perceptions of the executive team in several areas. They cover topics ranging from how well the executive team communicates examples of meaningful work to the members' ability to serve as positive role models. They also include culture-defining topics like accountability, validation of good work, and steering the organization in the right direction.

An example of the data collected during another client's first-ever Executive Team Effectiveness Survey is shown on the next page.

Here, you can quickly see this leadership team meets or exceeds standards in two of ten areas. Just as clear: Employees rate this leadership team as less-than-effective in the other eight leadership areas.

While these scores may not seem overly positive, this wide range of scores is quite typical for the first run of this survey at any company. Indeed, these executives hoped for better scores. At the same time, they readily admitted they previously saw their job as "managing results." As they continue to work toward creating a Good Comes First work culture, they know they must do more to validate, communicate, connect, reflect, and more.

Of course, human nature dictates that we focus most on the lower scores. A golfer will agonize over the quadruple-bogey shot on the fourteenth hole and ignore three earlier birdies. A parent will skim over the five A grades and then drill down into the one C+ grade by asking, "What happened in Science?" However, with this data, we ask executive teams to

Executive Team Effectiveness Survey

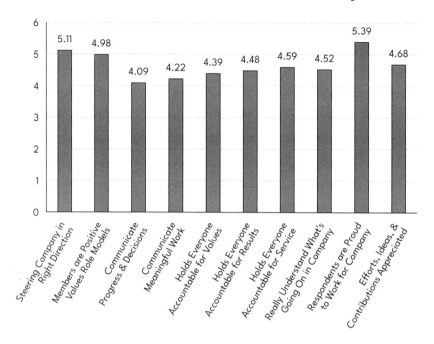

resist that temptation to focus on the negative. We encourage them first to celebrate areas of excellence.

When taking on a culture change, every little win matters; sure, leaders must address the lower scores—and they will. The executive team will create and execute action plans to improve the areas where they fail to meet their responsibilities. But when they do, over time, there will be more to celebrate.

WORKPLACE INTELLIGENCE (WQ) ASSESSMENT

We will begin talking about our most extensive data collection device, the Workplace Intelligence (or WQ) Assessment, in just a few paragraphs. But first, for context and clarity, let's look at the little brother of Workplace Intelligence, Emotional Intelligence (or EQ).

Certainly, everyone in Human Resources, and many of us in leadership circles, understands the importance of Emotional Intelligence (EQ) when hiring, team building, and promoting our next set of leaders. But just to get us all on the same thought plane, we'll start with a quick primer on EQ.

Experts define EQ[1] as:

The capacity to be aware of, control, and express one's emotions, and to handle interpersonal relationships judiciously and empathetically.

EQ—which exploded into prominence in the 1990s after the publication of *Emotional Intelligence: Why It Can Matter More Than IQ*[2] by Daniel Goleman—consists of five primary components:

- **Self-awareness** | The ability to recognize and understand the personal emotions that affect behaviors
- **Self-regulation** | The capacity to control or redirect disruptive emotional impulses and moods
- **Internal Motivation** | A capability to work within an inner vision of what is important—both individually and from a mission perspective
- **Empathy** | The ability to understand the emotional makeup of others, combined with the skill to treat people according to their emotional reactions
- **Social Skills** | An ability to effectively manage one-on-one relationships and to deftly build personal and professional networks

As you can surmise, and most likely already knew, a person with a higher EQ level tends to be more mature, is more likely to work independently, and is less prone to confrontation. In addition, someone with higher EQ is more capable of creating mutually beneficial relationships. Perhaps because they are more able to focus on the mission rather than "What's in it for me," they are also considered better leaders.

Starting in the last couple of decades, if two candidates had the same level of technical proficiency and experience, or two people up for promotion had the same qualifications and experience, most employers would choose the person with higher EQ. The same is true when building a Good

Comes First culture: Always, without fail or excuses, like your grandma's life depended on it, hire and promote the person with higher EQ.

While EQ is important because your upcoming culture change depends on a company full of high-EQ leaders and employees, it is also vital because . . .

What EQ is to an individual, WQ is to a team and organization:

- EQ is an indicator of how well any one person might work given a particular task, especially under pressure.
- WQ is an indicator of how a team or company might function when facing either an opportunity to excel or a mounting challenge (for example, when asked to help change company culture).

A low collective WQ means a lower chance of success with current personnel. Higher team and organizational WQ, especially after the "Align" portion of "Define, Align, and Refine," creates a much better chance of success, both operationally and from a culture change perspective.

Simply put, a company with a high collective level of WQ is far more likely to be able to place respect on the same pedestal as results. There will be much less, "Who cares how it gets done? Let's just get it done!" and, "But that's the way we've always done it" and far more, "Let's do this right. Let's put good first."

High WQ = function. Low WQ = dysfunction.

THE FIVE COMPONENTS OF
WORKPLACE INTELLIGENCE (WQ)

Just as EQ has five major components, so does WQ. Each of these five areas is an integral part of the Good Comes First model and is deliberately labeled to correlate to more traditional business metrics, such as "employee experience" and "sense of community." These labels are important because many senior leaders want a baseline snapshot of their WQ before they begin the transition to a Good Comes First culture. And they do not yet want to hint that a culture change might be coming. Other leaders are not yet sure a culture change is necessary. After all, if they already show a high

WQ level within their company, why invest—at least for now—in a culture change initiative?

This WQ snapshot enables you to see the state of your company culture, without the need to announce a culture change initiative is forthcoming. Even better, data from the WQ Assessment can let you know definitively whether a culture change effort is necessary.

We assume you, dear reader, already believe a culture change is necessary, or you would not have picked up this little green book—and chances are you would not have made it this far into the pages. So, for you, it is essential to note that each WQ business category aligns directly to the foundational principle and four cornerstones you have learned thus far. Each is directly related to the stated values and desired behaviors you listed in your Organizational Constitution. With that in mind, let's take a quick look at the five components of WQ.

Intentional Culture and Climate Change | *Aligns to "Equally Value Respect and Results"*

In this component, we measure how well we put respect and results on the same pedestal. This is also where we determine if we are building an uncompromising company culture—or whether we are still somewhere between what was and what could be. Other elements of culture change measured in this segment include the degree to which culture change happens organically (or, even better, contagiously).

This first component also critically allows us to measure how well we hire and retain team members according to their ability to consistently model the defined behaviors.

Transformational Leadership | *Aligns to "Live Our Servant Purpose"*

In this WQ component, we quantify exactly how well we live our servant purpose daily. Specifically, do we "walk the talk"? Or are we still in our infancy, like a fifteen-month-old baby who feels ready to walk, but maybe has not quite found their footing? We also take a close look at our transition from "manager" to "mentor."

Specifically, do we demonstrate a genuine concern for the growth and well-being of each of our employees? Finally, we ask the tough questions around equality and inclusivity—are we truly building a culture where we treat every contributor and stakeholder fairly, and with dignity?

Employee Experience | *Aligns to "Lean on Trust, Validation, and Growth"*
As we take a close look at the experience of work from the employee perspective, we quantify our ability to develop trust. We measure how often and how well we show appreciation for our team members' work, and we learn how focused on personal and professional growth we are as an organization.

These behaviors may seem tough to measure. However, employees and leaders instinctively know just how vital this WQ component is to a Good Comes First culture, so they tend to be more than forthcoming with their observations and suggestions, which will provide you with plenty of data. When done, you will know exactly how your employees feel about their employee experience.

Values-Driven Performance | *Aligns to "Understand Behavior's Impact on Performance"*
In a Good Comes First culture, we deliberately tie desired behaviors to tangible outcomes, to performance, and, of course, to results. We cannot do any of that, though, if we do not understand precisely how modeling those behaviors affects not just our culture, but our productivity. So we ask: Is living our defined values and desired behaviors having the anticipated impact? Have we leveraged our values and behaviors to maximum effect? Just as crucial: Have we done a thorough job demonstrating that we have a zero-tolerance policy for unproductive behaviors? If there is a leak in the Good Comes First boat, this is where we will find it.

A Sense of Community | *Aligns to "Use Our Voice for Good"*
When an organization has built a strong sense of community, people feel like they belong there. For the most part, they know this is the right place for them and feel good about coming to work every day. They have likely built lasting friendships, so they are even more incentivized to stay. They believe leaders and peers hear their voices, that their work matters—and that they matter. They believe so strongly in their company's servant purpose

and are so aligned with its values and behaviors and strategy and goals, they refer friends and colleagues to HR for employment opportunities. They also believe the leaders of their company will do what is right, at the right time, every time.

Before beginning a culture change transformation, you must obtain insight into just how strong the sense of community at your company is now. Yes, it takes courage to ask the questions necessary to obtain this data. But when you have the answers—and know how close your employees are to speaking with a united voice—you can confidently use that voice for good.

By measuring all five of these components, you will understand your organization's current level of WQ. You will know exactly where you are now. And, as you continue to work toward a Good Comes First culture, where you need to go next. This assessment becomes a road map for your leadership team. Without it, you are playing a guessing game you cannot win. With it, you will have an excellent idea of which teams, and which leaders—and perhaps which influential individuals and informal leaders—operate in the High Performance–High Values Match quadrant. And which do not.

WHY WQ IS CRITICAL TO A GOOD COMES FIRST CULTURE

The "which do not" types—those who do not operate in the High Performance–High Values Match quadrant—are another reason WQ is a critical concept to grasp. During the "refine" process, you, as a leader, will find out exactly which teams are all in on culture change. You also will learn which of your teams has the most members who fall into the third category of employees described in Chapter 5 as "opt-out-and-stayers."

Ranging from hopeful-but-it-just-didn't-work-out to full-blown pretenders, these employees and leaders will require most of your attention over the coming months. Of course, this is not necessarily fair to those employees who have already become change champions, and those who are about to be. But remember the last sentence of Chapter 2:

"We build company culture by rewarding desired behaviors. We tear down culture by tolerating disrespectful, unproductive behaviors."

So, although not necessarily easy, our mission in this phase is simple: to measure the WQ of each team, department, division, and company. More specifically, we must determine how well each team member—from the mail room to the boardroom—is personally aligned to the values and behaviors defined in the Organizational Constitution.

Once we have the WQ report in hand (and especially when combined with the results of the Values and Behaviors Survey), we now have objective data to show which teams need the most work. We know what areas of the company are being torn down by disrespectful, unproductive behaviors. You might think discussing these results with your employees sounds like a confrontation waiting to happen—but it does not have to be. The intent is to build each conversation that happens as a result of what we learn from the WQ Assessment upon the foundational principle of respect, so those discussions should not be innately confrontational.

Furthermore, because we are not focused exclusively on personal productivity and results, but instead on how a leader's team does as a whole, the WQ Assessment provides us with an interactive opportunity. It enables us to apply the Mentor practice from the GCF Accountability Model as we respectfully guide team members back into alignment. As a result, the human-to-human conversations that occur are typically positive, productive, and purposeful—just like your Good Comes First culture.

From the leader's perspective, it is best to view each of these candid, constructive conversations as an opportunity for improvement, a moment of growth, and a chance to build a relationship with their mentor. And yes, their boss.

Sound too good to be true? To some, it may be. As we will learn in Chapter 12, not everyone takes responsibility for living the company's values and behaviors, and not every leader makes the leap from manager to mentor. Obviously, confrontation is still possible.

However, once the conversations start, both people in the room understand that each data point in the WQ Assessment shows the behaviors the team consistently models—and the areas where a mentor might need to provide some redirection. They celebrate the "Here is what you have done well." Then they coach the "Here is where you can do better." And before the conversation is over, the mentor has motivated the team with "Here is how we will grow, together."

With the WQ Assessment in hand, this is where our GCF Accountability Model becomes actionable. This is where a mentor demonstrates full commitment to a leader's or team member's personal and professional growth. And once that happens, this is where each leader or team member shows a commitment to change. Workplace Intelligence is critical to a GCF culture because it enables you to guide every member of your company into the upper right quadrant of the Performance-Values Matrix.

Respect. Trust. Validation. Growth. Engagement. Commitment. Good. All in one thirty-minute conversation.

EXAMPLES OF THE WORKPLACE INTELLIGENCE (WQ) ASSESSMENT

The WQ Assessment has many similarities to the Values and Behaviors and Executive Team Effectiveness Surveys in that:

- The questions asked are based on your company's Organizational Constitution.
- We score each question on a 6-point scale (there are no neutral answers).
- We design each question to address a single, distinct aspect of current culture.

Unlike the two surveys, however, the WQ Assessment provides a score for each of WQ's five components as well as a total score. The best possible score is 20 for each component, making the best possible score on a WQ Assessment a 100.

Here is an example of one client's WQ summary data report for their outbound sales team:

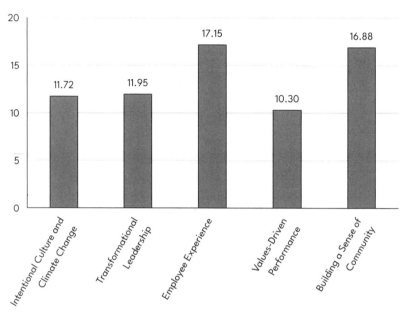

WQ Assessment | Sales Team

Based on these WQ team scores, we can deduce (from left to right):

- With a score down near 11 for **Intentional Culture and Climate Change,** this team has not yet embraced the culture change initiative. Furthermore, the low score here indicates they might not believe a culture change was/is necessary.
  — *Here, you should* ***Coach.***

- A score of <12 for **Transformational Leadership** indicates the leaders of this team are not yet living the company's servant purpose; in fact, they may be hanging on to the previous company culture.
  — *Here, you should **Mentor.***

- With a score of around 17 for **Employee Experience**, it appears this is a close team that finds fulfillment in the work and understands the value of its contributions.
  — *Here, you should **Celebrate**—the sooner, the better.*

- The score of 10+ for **Values-Driven Performance** indicates this team is not yet inspired enough to demonstrate the company's values and behaviors; a score this low might also imply they do not see a connection between those values and behaviors and results.
  — *Here, you should **Coach.***

- With a score close to 17 for **Building a Sense of Community**, members of this team share a sense of belonging; they also most likely work well together (even if it might currently be at the expense of the defined culture).
  — *This is an opportunity to **Celebrate.***

Of course, our analysis cannot stop there. To see how the sales team wound up with a score of <12 in the summary report, let's take a close look at this client's responses to the ten questions in the Transformational Leadership category of the WQ Assessment on the following page.

Based on this team's WQ Transformational Leadership scores, we can deduce (again, from left to right):

- The low scores in the first two bars—for "Understanding the Company's Servant Purpose" and "I Am Aligned with the Company's Servant Purpose"—perhaps demonstrate an unwillingness to embrace the purpose.
  — *Here, **Coach.***

WQ Assessment I Sales Team I Transformational Leadership

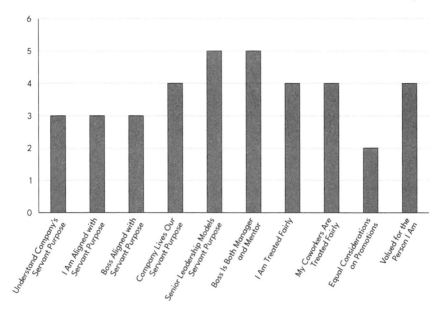

- Another low score for "Boss Aligned with Servant Purpose" shows the team's leader has not personally embraced the culture change and/or does not believe in (or does not feel they need to believe in) the company's servant purpose.
  — *Here, **Coach/Mentor.***
- If this "Company Lives Our Servant Purpose," this team has not seen it.
  — *Here, **Coach.***
- The higher score for "Senior Leadership Models Servant Purpose" means this team sees executives as good role models.
  — *A metric to **Celebrate.***
- With the high score for "Boss Is Both Manager and Mentor," it is clear this team considers their direct supervisor a mentor.
  — *Again, **Celebrate.***

- Based on the scores for the next two bars—"I Am Treated Fairly" and "My Coworkers Are Treated Fairly"—some members of this team report they and others are treated fairly while others do not; this might indicate the existence of a pervasive bias.
  — *Here,* **Coach.**
- The meager score for "Equal Consideration When Applying for Promotion" indicates the existence of a pervasive and perhaps systemic bias.
  — *Here,* **Mentor,** *perhaps to the point of intervention.*
- Some members of this team report they are "Valued for the Person I Am" while others do not; again, this might indicate a bias exists.
  — *Here,* **Coach.**

To see if we have a company-wide issue, or, rather, a team (and perhaps a leadership) issue with the sales group, compare the sales team's overall report to that of the customer service team within the same company (see the chart on the next page).

As you can see, the customer service team's WQ report shows much higher scores across the five categories. There is much to celebrate with this team's data.

If this report (and, perhaps, the reports of other teams) had shown low scores in the same areas as the sales team, the conclusion might be that we have a systemic culture issue. When comparing the scores of the two teams, however, we can objectively state we most likely do not have a company-wide problem; that the customer service team, at least, has responded well to the concept of a Good Comes First culture. They are living the servant purpose, demonstrating the values and behaviors defined in your Organizational Constitution, and are performing well. We also can see the customer service team responds well to the Transformational Leadership provided by their team leaders and mentors.

Our conclusion (based on these three reports): The members of the sales team seem to have admiration, and perhaps affection, for their leaders. Clearly, those leaders influence how their team works—and thinks.

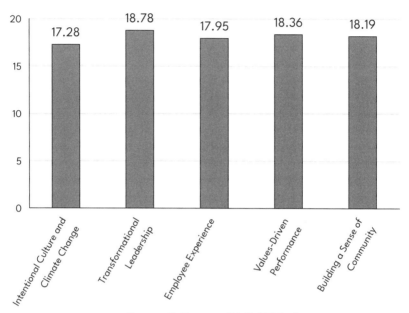

WQ Assessment | Customer Service Team

Overall Score: 91.0/100.0

Perhaps because they admire their leadership team, this seems to be a unified sales team. However, those leaders have not embraced the Organizational Constitution. Nor do they expect their team members to demonstrate the stated values and behaviors. This team's leaders seem to require extensive coaching; a good mentor would work with those leaders to help them understand how to use their influence for good.

These leaders must be made aware that they are measured not just by results, but by the respect shown to and by all team members, and to internal and external customers. In addition, the issue of treating people differently when applying for a promotion seems to be worthy of immediate intervention.

As you can see, the WQ Assessment is an integral part of our Measure practice—and one that informs how you apply the other practices from the

GCF Accountability Model. Administered once a year, and typically a couple of months before the performance review cycle begins, this survey provides valuable feedback for you as a business leader. Of course, by design, it also provides feedback for every leader on your team.

And for those organizations that choose to be wholly transparent, this presents an opportunity to show every team member exactly where your organization stands now, where you still need to go, and what you—as a leader—are doing to close that gap.

Before we close out this chapter, let us share a question we often field from clients and those leaders interested in knowing where they stand right now:

I don't want to wait six months to obtain my baseline. Are there other ways of measuring the effectiveness of our leaders and the executive team now? Is there any way to gain some insight into our company's WQ without waiting a year?

We wholeheartedly believe in this process and want more leaders—and companies—to start putting good first. So we have sample surveys and a sample WQ Assessment online at GoodComesFirst.com. Should you want to go the DIY route, there are also sample reports there to get you started down the right path.

OTHER METHODS OF DATA COLLECTION

Of course, there are other ways to collect data. In addition to the three data collection methods outlined in this chapter, we recommend conducting pulse surveys. Instead of having all questions answered every three to six months, pulse surveys ask one question per week. Some people feel this administration is more straightforward. Others believe it is more complex; they do not enjoy starting a company-wide survey cycle every seven days. Plus, they believe the input from the pulse surveys can cause overly assertive reactions from leadership. (We have certainly seen that happen.)

But often, pulse surveys are worth the effort, and the main benefit of weekly pulse surveys over quarterly or bi-annual surveys is compelling: Your organization can see, and act upon, trends much more quickly.

No matter what collection method you choose, the primary purpose of consistently gathering data in the Measure practice remains constant: to present "undeniable truth"—based on perceptions of the employees you serve as a leader—of your company's progress toward building an uncompromising culture. This critical data helps senior leaders leverage the other four practices—Model, Coach, Celebrate, and Mentor. Ultimately, the action taken based on the data collected helps move capable team leaders and team members into the upper-right quadrant in the Performance-Values Matrix: High Performance *and* High Values. Simultaneously, it helps those not in the upper-right quadrant of the Performance-Values Matrix understand their approach to work might be a better fit elsewhere.

And that, dear reader, is the pathway to becoming a Good Comes First company. Do everything possible to keep the good people ready to do good work in a good company. And lovingly and respectfully let everyone else go.

Congratulations! You have now made it through Section II of *Good Comes First*. You now have the tactical and practical knowledge—and hopefully, the inspiration—to Define, Align, and Refine a Good Comes First culture in your organization.

In Section III, we will share some tips on how best to lead your culture change effort, how to intentionally build teams capable of thriving within a Good Comes First culture, and so much more.

Take a big, deep breath. Then let's keep moving.

SECTION III

Actionable Inspiration: Building Your Culture from the Inside Out

CHAPTER 12

Leadership Qualities Within a Good Comes First Culture

So far, you have come to realize why culture change is important. You understand how a Good Comes First culture will positively impact your business. And you have learned that you, as a leader, are responsible for leading the coming change. You are the banner carrier. You are the primary change champion.

As you probably guessed, this responsibility comes with significant demands. Over the next several months and years, you will need to invest time and energy in communicating, coaching, and celebrating your desired culture. You will spend even more time modeling and measuring your company's values and behaviors. Starting very soon, you will think your title should be Chief Redirection Officer.

You cannot delegate any of these primary responsibilities. This job is entirely yours.

The good news is you are the right person for the job.

THE CHALLENGES AHEAD

So, as you lead this change effort, what should you expect? What challenges should you anticipate? What demands will be placed on you personally?

Here—based on the collective experiences of those leaders who have built a Good Comes First culture before you—are the major challenges you will face very soon:

- **Resetting Priorities** | The daily grind you have experienced so far will not end. You were already working maybe eighty to one hundred hours per week. Working another forty is not possible, which means you cannot simply add culture change activities to your existing workload. Instead, you must focus your time and energy on the highest priority tasks associated with a culture champion and stay away from less critical activities. The time required to implement this change has to come from somewhere—and you must decide where.

- **Becoming a Poster Child** | Your change effort's credibility will rely on the degree to which you, as the culture champion, consistently model the desired values and behaviors. Scrutiny of your every plan, decision, action, and reaction will increase tenfold. You will be under a microscope, both in and out of the workplace. Employees will construe any misstep on your part as, "See? Told you. This change isn't real." Get ready. You are now the poster child for change.

- **Channeling Optimism** | Even if your demonstration of optimism is not currently a core strength, it soon will be. It must be. Any sense of hope, at least initially, will come from you. When something goes wrong (and it *will* go wrong), people will look to you for signs of commitment to the cause. When something goes right, you will need to promptly and genuinely praise and encourage team members and the teams' aligned efforts. The first authentic smile must be yours.

- **Showing Resiliency** | Unlike most projects, a culture initiative is never finished. Yes, you and your fellow change champions will see contagious pockets of excellence in just a few weeks. And you will begin to notice company-wide alignment in the first eighteen to twenty-four months. But working budgets change, new opportunities arise, challenging issues plop in front of you, and people come and go—which means new forms of resistance come and go. Your work environment is always evolving; you are always modeling, always aligning, always refining. Resiliency is the key—and cannot ever be in short supply.

- **Providing Clarity** | Most leaders and team members have never lived in an intentional, high-performance, values-aligned work environment. They do not know how this will work. They do not yet know what you expect of them. As with any change, humans would rather not follow an unknown path; they would rather stay in the known (even if the known sucks). To get them to venture into the unknown, you must leverage clarity; specifically, you must let every member of your team know exactly what the company expects of them within your Good Comes First work culture. Clarity breeds confidence and inspires commitment and competence. And you are the most vital source of that clarity.

As we said before, as a change champion, there will be no more running of yellow lights. No going through the express lane with too many items. No more telling little white lies to avoid a tough conversation. No more—*not a single instance*—of allowing disrespect. No tolerating unproductive behaviors. No more praising the performance of people who fail to demonstrate expected values and behaviors. No making excuses for those who choose not to live the servant purpose.

Team members will perceive any one of these workplace events as proof that your Organizational Constitution is not important to you—and that you are not serious about this change effort. By definition, every allowed exception shows you are not committed to building an uncompromising company culture. That is a lot of pressure—a lot to deal with on a daily, even hourly, basis.

This change process will not be easy. More specifically, it will not be easy on *you*.

So, right now, you better decide what kind of leader you want to be.

Before you can do that, though, you need to know what kind of leader you are *now*. Most leaders have not thought about this. Even more troubling, they do not know what kind of leader they must become to lead a Good Comes First company.

Perhaps you can relate. Whether or not you think you know what kind of leader you are now, keep reading—this will come in handy.

THREE TYPES OF LEADERS (WHICH ARE YOU?)

Let's look at the three most common types of leaders we see in the workplace now. As we do, please note that despite the labels (e.g., "old" and "new") placed on the groups, age is not the dominant factor in any of these three types. Age does not matter: Actions matter. Behaviors matter. The willingness to be vulnerable and transparent matters. So does the desire to serve the people you lead—to be a mentor. And, except for moments of reflection and self-awareness, the sincere desire to see work more as "we" than "me" matters—a lot.

We have worked with all three leader types. We have seen amazing work, and spectacular fails, from all three. Most important, we have seen enough to know all three types are capable of tremendous personal growth. Leaders from all three groups can value respect and results equally, which means all three types of leaders are more than qualified to lead a Good Comes First company.

As we seek to understand these leadership styles, we will offer a quick look at the observed strengths and perceived weaknesses of each. Just as important, we will look at what happens when their apparent strengths go into overdrive.

Of course, the strengths and weaknesses are not brands burned into the hides of any one type of leader. An old-school leader, for example, may have learned to situationally display traits more commonly associated with a new-school leader. However, the described characteristics tend to be the default position of each. When their back is against the wall, these are the traits they will most often display—even when they know another strength may be more appropriate at that moment.

Old School

An old-school leader is often highly influenced by their Industrial Age mentors and predecessors. They, until recently, have been much more focused on results. We see old-school leaders as "Get Shit Done" people.

Strengths:

- Self-confidence
- Decisiveness
- Strategic Mindedness
- Results-focused
- Persuasiveness

Weaknesses:

- Empathy
- Flexibility
- Self-improvement

When Strengths Are in Overdrive:

- **Self-confidence** | Too often does not feel the need to query knowledgeable people around them; combined with decisiveness, self-confidence in overdrive means being quick to form conclusions, even the wrong conclusions.
- **Decisiveness** | Strategic decisions tend to be impulsive; combined with self-confidence, decisiveness can mean stepping into decisions without using all data and expertise available. "Ready, fire, aim," even when it is the wrong way to go.
- **Strategic Mindedness** | Becomes frustrated when allies and partners do not see the big picture quickly enough; fails to delegate, and can be guilty of micro-management.
- **Results-Focus** | Sacrifices respect while over-emphasizing results; too often fails to role-model (or expect others to model) values and behaviors.
- **Persuasiveness** | Tends to over-sell their strategic vision and passion; becomes frustrated when others do not share that vision and passion.

New School

A new-school leader, perhaps instinctively and maybe through an experience with an old-school leader in overdrive, always knows there is a better way to manage their employees. Until proven wrong—about a decision or a direction or a solution—they want to be the "good guy." So we think of them as cheerleaders who can get off track when plans do not work as expected.

Strengths:

- Optimism
- Empathy
- Self-improvement
- Flexibility
- Development of Others

Weaknesses:

- Decisiveness
- Results-Focus
- Strategic Mindedness

When Strengths Are in Overdrive:

- **Optimism** | Can become blind to strategic challenges and potentially miss milestones and deadlines; in general, a failure to look at objectives and people realistically.
- **Empathy** | Enables unproductive and disrespectful behaviors from leaders and team members; hangs on to people outside the High Performance–High Values Match quadrant.
- **Self-improvement** | Tends to work on themself more than leaders and team members; continuous attempts to be better negatively impacts team and company goals.
- **Flexibility** | Deadlines and milestones become fluid; satisfied as long as the company makes progress; commitments to results and performance too often take a back seat to growth.

- **Development of Others** | Often takes the role of mentor too seriously at the expense of applying consequences. When combined with empathy in overdrive, the development of others in overdrive fails to hold others accountable, or to lovingly set non-upper-right performers free.

Middle School

As the name implies, the middle-school leader has a combination of old and new leadership styles. When times are good, they strive to be the good guy. When facing a tough challenge, however, they immediately revert to old-school tendencies. Perhaps unfairly, we think of these leaders as "Oh Shit . . . It's Not Done!" types.

Strengths:

- Efficiency
- Critical Thinking
- Relationship Building
- Common Sense
- Self-awareness

Weaknesses:

- Flexibility
- Situational Optimism
- Consistency

When Strengths Are in Overdrive:

- **Efficiency** | Prone to expecting others to work as efficiently as themselves; tend to expect others to work long hours in an effort to meet milestones and achieve goals.
- **Critical Thinking** | Inclined to seek more data in order to form a judgment; apt to take an "I need to see this for myself" approach, rather than showing trust in others' recommendations.

- **Relationship Building** | Places a high priority on existing relationships while seeking out the next one-on-one relationship; a "people pleaser."
- **Common Sense** | Apt to make "hunch" decisions and promote pivots; fails to use available data or expertise to support those decisions.
- **Self-awareness** | Leans toward themself more than team or company; often holds themself to impossible standards while aligning to values and behavior.

A Fourth Leadership Style—Boomer Male Syndrome (BMS)

It is important to note that none of these three leadership types has led to what your authors see, throughout Western civilization, as a crisis in leadership today. In fact, each of the three types we have discussed so far consistently contributes to performance that gives so many of us hope for the future.

Instead, we firmly believe the root cause of our ongoing leadership crisis is a fourth category of leaders: those afflicted with what we call Boomer Male Syndrome, or BMS. By taking this stand, we realize we risk alienating a segment of people we want to enlighten with this book. However, the risk is overshadowed by the rewards that will undoubtedly come from starting this tough conversation.

Our goal is to inspire current BMS leaders to become ideological converts—to make them think twice about how they lead and why. To help that person—regardless of age, gender, race, religion, sexual orientation, or any other demographic—put good first. If we enable even one former toxic leader to create a purposeful, positive, productive work culture, we will have reached this book's full potential.

To be clear, not all people suffering from BMS are Boomers. Not all are male—and we understand placing a label on anyone included in a certain age bracket or gender can be unhealthy and unproductive—but here, it is necessary. The reality is that most of the continuous confrontation, failures to actively listen and effectively compromise, and the current dissatisfaction too many people experience in the workplace is directly due to the failures of BMS leaders. At the risk of being even more specific with labels, Boomer *white* males often lead this charge into crisis. From Wall Street to Pennsylvania Avenue to El Camino Real in Silicon Valley, we have all felt their negative influence for decades. The very worst of the afflicted, frankly put, seem to want us to revert to the business practices of the 1950s: a time when white males were firmly in charge—and we did not expect them or their companies to address diversity, equality, and fairness in the workplace.

Boomer Male Syndrome, we suggest, is characterized by authoritative, ego-driven leadership. Yes, this leadership style worked well for most of the Industrial Age, when workers traded hours for dollars. Over time, though, it slowly killed workers' enthusiasm, company cultures, and entire organizations. Now that awakened knowledge workers have replaced manual laborers as the most dominant contributors in the workforce, this leadership style adds toxicity to the workplace that is difficult for workers to tolerate. These stubborn leaders become the problem rather than the solution.

The problem is that, for decades, BMS leaders have been so entrenched in the way they have always led that they are seemingly incapable of recognizing the symptoms of BMS—or its weaknesses. To this day, they are unaware they have unconsciously built unhealthy company cultures. They do not understand the tremendous toll BMS has taken on our customers, people, organizations, and our global economy.

If exposure to the traits of a BMS leader seems like a real possibility, or you are beginning to feel like you are personally exhibiting BMS symptoms, then take a step back. Take a big, deep breath. And realize that before you can lead a successful culture change effort, you must first be willing to change yourself.

DESIRED LEADERSHIP TRAITS OF CHANGE CHAMPIONS

The first step of building your Organizational Constitution was crafting your company's servant purpose. It may not surprise you, then, that many of the desired leadership traits we are about to discuss fall entirely into the "servant leadership" bucket—which, as you'll recall from Chapter 2, is a term first coined by Robert K. Greenleaf in 1970.

(It also will not surprise you that we subscribe to this leadership philosophy more than any other. Chris, in fact, spent the better part of almost three decades with The Ken Blanchard Companies teaching this foundational leadership principle. In his work, Mark has helped usher in the concept of social leadership, which is essentially servant leadership that leverages a significant online presence.)

What is servant leadership?

Serving others is the foundation of citizenship in our families, workplaces, and communities. Found in nearly every one of the world's religions, the call to service has been around for centuries.

Essentially, servant leaders believe:

- Every person has value and deserves civility, trust, and respect.
- People can accomplish much when inspired by a servant purpose beyond themselves. And as we learned in Chapter 7, beyond making money.

Within a Good Comes First culture, a servant leader's primary role and responsibility is to enable others to bring their best to every moment and every interaction. At work, certainly, but also in their communities, with friends, or with strangers. Servant leaders, then, typically:

- **Reinforce the Need for Service to Others** | Servant leaders educate others through their words and actions. They help create a clearer understanding of the greater purpose of serving others. As their influence grows, they pose questions to help those around them consider setting aside self-serving behaviors and embrace servant leadership behaviors.
- **Listen Intently; Observe Closely** | Servant leaders understand that to inspire the best in others, they must understand the world in which others live. They do not make assumptions about others, nor do they judge. Over time, they learn about their players' unique worldviews and opportunities to serve by listening more than talking, observing more than preaching.

- **Demonstrate Persistence** | Servant leaders understand a conversation or two may not change a player's mindset or assumptions. Therefore, servant leaders are not afraid to be tenacious. They are willing to invest hours in conversations to help educate and, hopefully, inspire change in others—both personally and professionally.
- **Foster Accountability** | Servant leaders hold themselves and others accountable for their commitments. Servant leaders are human; they make mistakes. They know those they work with and for will also make mistakes. Still, they push for high standards of performance, values alignment, and service quality. When people meet those standards, servant leaders offer abundant praise.
- **Develop a Mentor Mindset** | In terms of developing a Good Comes First culture, no element of servant leadership is more important than the development of a mentor-first mindset. Rather than looking for credit, they look to help others grow personally and professionally. They do not care just about the work—they care about the person doing the work.

These servant leadership practices are vitally important for you as a leader of a culture change effort. Chances are, regardless of which of the three leadership types discussed a moment ago you identify with most, you already demonstrate many of these traits.

How do you know if you are a full-fledged servant leader now?

You do not have a vote! The only people who get a vote are those who interact with you daily: fellow leaders, team members, customers, strategic partners, mentors, friends, and family members. You must ask them regularly, "How can I be of greater service to you?" In doing so, you will get a clearer understanding of how a servant leader behaves within your sphere of influence. Then you must actively listen to—and then align to—their answers. Finally, you must refine your behaviors to serve more people more effectively. Again: Define, Align, Refine.

If you determine you have not been serving as a servant leader, nothing is stopping you from becoming one. The reality is that servant leadership is type-agnostic. Anyone—and any type of leader, from old school to new school and everything in between—can adopt servant leadership practices as their own.

Servant leadership principles are universal. And for those serving as change champions, they are essential.

STRONG LEADER VERSUS STRONG LEADERSHIP TEAM

As you reviewed the three leader types capable of transforming their company culture toward Good Comes First (and the one that is not), where did you see yourself? What strengths most applied to you? Which weaknesses? As you read what happens when strengths go into overdrive, which resonated most with you? Which desirable traits do you demonstrate now? Which servant leadership practices do you exhibit? And which must you learn?

Keep your answers to those questions in mind as you answer the most important ones:

- How can you leverage current strengths, traits, and practices to lead your company culture transformation?
- Who do you have by your side to help balance your weaknesses and overdrive tendencies?

We ask all these questions not to put you in a corner, or to place a leadership type label on your forehead, or to make you feel bad for any piece missing in your leadership-style puzzle.

We ask to help you think about exactly how you will pull this off and what kind of help you will need along the way. After all, there is no one right way to lead, and no wrong way. As we have learned, every leadership type has advantages. But each type also needs help in the form of balance. For example, the world is full of case studies of what happens when an old-school leader surrounds themself exclusively with more old-school leaders. That covey of results-driven personalities only serves to embolden the decisiveness and raise the self-confidence of the person in charge. By hearing nothing but how righteous they are—how just their decisions and strategies are—their way becomes the only way. Their model, no matter how faulty, becomes the only option. Eventually, that leader comes to believe their only job is to persuade others they are right—and everyone else is wrong.

In the end, that is no way to run a company.

To become a change champion, you must pull from the strengths of everyone around you. Not known for being a critical thinker? Trust someone who exhibits that trait. Your default position is to judge others quickly? Invite someone capable of empathy to join your change team. Prone to pleasing everyone instead of making hard decisions? Bring along someone who excels at critical thinking and decisiveness.

As a leader and change champion, the challenge before you will soon become real. The pressure will mount. The resistance will intensify. Eventually, the responsibility might become too much for one person—one leader, no matter how strong—to bear. Soon, your weaknesses will become apparent; your strengths will go into overdrive.

The only way to prevent this scenario from becoming inevitable is to surround yourself with complementary leaders. As you begin the change process, and throughout the change journey, determine which holes in your leadership style you must plug first. Then make it a priority to build a change team strong enough to battle the resistance that will come.

Ultimately, the answer to the "what type of leader am *I*" question we asked earlier is not anywhere near as important as the one you must answer now: "What kind of leadership *team* must I build?"

YOUR LEADERSHIP LEGACY

Before we leave this chapter, let's discuss one more beneficial impact to creating a Good Comes First culture—something personal. Something, for once, that is all about you: your leadership legacy. To this point, others in your organization have defined your legacy by your actions, decisions, and results—and your track record may be exemplary. However, we ask you to consider that your professional accomplishments to date are not so much your legacy. Instead, they are the line items on your resume.

Your legacy is so much more. For many leaders, legacy is not a conscious consideration. Too many leaders do not even think about their legacy until after they have finished the last glass of champagne at their retirement party. Instead, they are steadfastly intentional about getting stuff done, getting products out the door, getting services delivered, and so on.

"Legacy?" one leader asked us. "I'm not thinking about my leadership legacy. I'm just trying to keep the doors open. I'm trying to make more money today than I spend!"

We understand the need for leaders to manage results. After all, leaders must keep the results-based promises they make. We are not asking you to make those promises less of a priority. Instead, we ask you to make more promises. Start by looking back to what we said about the challenges facing today's leaders way back in Chapter 1:

> *After all, at no time in the past did we task any leader with coalescing four generations of workers—each with different working models, motivators, and priorities. We did not ask leaders to integrate massive amounts of technology into the workforce. We did not require leaders to manage quickly assembled micro-teams, entrepreneurial subgroups, and remote contributors in the Industrial Age. And we certainly did not expect leaders to be active, let alone approachable, on social media (we did not even have social media!).*
>
> *We also did not hold our past executives accountable for gender parity, inclusion, and unbalanced work-life integration. Focusing almost exclusively on shareholders and often motivated by self-interest, we never asked corporate leaders to join the fight against poverty. We did not ask them to fight social injustices, take a stand against politically motivated decisions, or actively work to prevent climate change.*

Every one of those issues is real. Each is a real challenge for you and your fellow business leaders. We realize those two paragraphs could become a ninety-thousand-word book all on their own, but that is not this book. Here, we are working toward one goal: putting good first. It is our hope that more business leaders like you will all work toward ending the divisiveness so prevalent in all our lives, that collaboration will eventually win out over deliberate confrontation, and that you will help drive hate, racism, sexism, and inequity toward extinction.

As you ponder your legacy as a leader, consider taking a stand on some of these issues—or, at least, the ones you have some control over. From just being kind to making sure every person in your company is paid equally for equal work—regardless of gender, race, or any other factor—you can make a difference.

When you finally walk away from the work you love, the people who admire you will not remember how much money the company made. They will not care about the exit strategy or the stock splits. Instead, they will talk about how you cared about many of the issues above, and so much more. They will remember you for how you treated people along the way. They will remember that you served as a mentor—and that you cared just as much about respect as results. They will remember you as a difference-maker. Above all, they will remember that you put good first.

No matter your past, your legacy as not just a difference-maker to individuals but also as a change-maker to your organization as a whole begins now. From this point forward, you form that legacy with every interaction, behavior, and decision. What you value now and in the future becomes transparent through your actions. Everything you do as a leader tells peers, team members, and customers what you stand for—and what you will not stand for.

Now, make some more promises . . .

Promise to be known as a coach. A mentor. A good partner. And a good human being.

Promise to serve others, not self. Promise to validate the good work of others. To build trust. To show respect.

Promise to build a culture of curiosity and commitment. And a sense of community.

Promise to bring people together rather than drive them apart.

Finally, promise to use your voice for good.

Then, keep your promises.

CHAPTER 13

Team Building and Hiring
While Putting Good First

Perhaps you have taken a business trip with someone you thought might be a decent travel companion. But after a tolerable hour waiting to board the aircraft, that person becomes intolerable. The careless placing of the elbow on the armrest was the first clue, followed by the loud popping of "I-still-have-a-thing-with-my-ears" gum. The flight is not the only non-stop part of your trip . . . the talking! And the squirming. Your middle seat-mate is apparently a nervous flyer. So he talks. And squirms. A lot. Clearly, you will not enjoy this trip as much as you planned.

This is what happens when you have begun your Good Comes First adventure, then realize you did not surround yourself with people ready to find joy in the journey.

Your Good Comes First journey is a long one—and while it is more than worth it in the end, like any good trip, it is made better by being with people who share your vision for the journey. This is why team building and hiring are critical steps in the culture change process.

After all, it only takes one gum-chewing, small-bladdered companion to make you regret getting on the airplane.

As you are nearing the end of this book, you probably already started thinking about:

- Who among your current leaders and team members can contribute to this adventure, and who cannot
- Those who will share your vision of the company's culture, and those who will not
- Which of those leaders and team members will join you in the effort to change your organization's culture, and which will not
- What percentage of your staff are members of the High Performance–High Values Match Club, hanging out in the upper-right quadrant, and what to do with those who are not
- How to replace those who cannot, do not, will not, and are not— with those people who can, do, will, and are

This challenge is common among change champions, and, like the culture change itself, this challenge never ends. For a company going in the right direction, building new teams and bringing on new people is the best possible problem to have.

This chapter will discuss building great teams and hiring the right candidates for your Good Comes First culture. Specifically, we will discuss the importance of hiring High Performance–High Values Match (or, at least, Talent Match) candidates. We will also jump into how to build high-WQ teams capable of helping you gain some quick wins. Let's get started!

TEAM BUILDING IN A GOOD COMES FIRST COMPANY

We have dedicated many of the pages you have read so far to the "Align, Define, and Refine" process. We also introduced the concept of Workplace Intelligence and how WQ helps us measure human behaviors. And we have shown how the WQ Assessment can tell you which teams thrive within your desired culture, and which teams need you as a mentor. You also know team building requires you to Model, Coach, Measure, Celebrate, and Mentor.

In short, you know you need to rely on the GCF Accountability Model to implement a lasting culture change. But you also need to remember that the travel between the five Accountability Model practices is often not linear. At different times, your teams will take you through every one of the model's 120 possible nuanced variations. Sure, as you help, some teams will need you to go "Model-Coach-Measure-Celebrate" in that order. As they excel, you might not ever get to the Mentor stage; they may only need validation, not redirection. In those instances, your work as a mentor, for now, is not necessary.

However, other teams, especially those with low WQ, will go more like this:

Model-Coach-Measure-Coach-Mentor-Model-Coach-Mentor-
***again?**-Measure-Mentor-Celebrate-**crap!**-Model-Coach-Measure-*
*Celebrate-and-Mentor-Measure-**dammit!**-Coach-Mentor-**lovingly-***
***set-someone-free**-Model-Coach-Measure-Mentor-Celebrate-*
Mentor . . . and so on . . . and so forth.

As we said before, the leaders of these teams will require most of your attention, time, and energy. When it is clear further investment in the team leader is no longer worth the effort, do yourself a favor: Lovingly set that team leader free. As soon as you land, for the next leg of your flight, upgrade to First Class by hiring a better fit in that leadership role. There is no saving your original companion; there is nothing you can do to help them enjoy the journey. Sure, you do not know your new row-mate as well. But at least there is a chance you will enjoy the rest of the trip.

As you start down the metaphorical runway, the "cannot, do not, will not, and are nots" will become apparent. So, early on, spend all the time necessary in the Mentor practice. Give them every opportunity to become a "can, do, will, and/or are." But if and when it becomes clear any one person will not share the armrest? Lovingly, respectfully, and *quickly* set that leader free.

On the other hand, if the leader is not at fault—but a key employee is blocking progress toward a positive, productive, purposeful team culture—do not tolerate that key person's poor performance or disrespectful treatment of others. That toxic player is holding your team back—eroding purpose, positivity, and productivity.

In our experience, the identity of that one toxic person may be a surprise to you, but the entire team already knows it. They have tolerated that person's subversive, unproductive behavior for quite some time. So when it is finally time for that person to go, the team will applaud you. They will exhale all that has been bad. The team will inhale all that can be good.

And once again, they will become a team of good people doing good work.

CONTAGIOUS POCKETS OF EXCELLENCE

Most of your teams will not have a hugely toxic player like the person above. A few of your teams may be toxic—it happens. The reality is, however, that most of your work teams will fall short of the absolute best possible teams, which we call contagious pockets of excellence. These contagious pockets of excellence are the teams that generate quick wins for your culture change initiative. They show other teams what is possible. Even better, they are not some lone wolf crew working to make a rebellious name for themselves. They wholly align their work with the company's Organizational Constitution. They live it. They breathe it.

These teams are not just good: They are so good other teams look up and say, "Dang! What are those guys doing over there?" Other groups—other leaders—want to learn more. Especially when leadership publicly celebrates those excellent teams, their peers strive to understand what those teams do and how they do it. They want to know why that workgroup—out of all the other teams—was so immediately successful.

The answers those curious leaders seek are not much of a secret. Once we analyze our client's work, they become apparent. Rapid growth and success within small teams happens when the team leaders focus on what their respective teams need—within the desired culture. Rather than apply a one-size-fits-all solution to every team, each team leader is enabled to set their own autonomous pace.

Even better, those team leaders state the challenge in front of the team, ensure they have the proper resources to get the job done, then get the hell out of the way. Innovative thinking happens from the very start. Autonomy and a sense of commitment fuel the journey. Respect and validation for a job well done make it a round trip.

These nimble teams—these contagious pockets of excellence—soon make noticeable progress toward team goals. They contribute clearly to the company's strategic objectives, which creates undeniable forward momentum—one small pocket at a time. Their enthusiasm for the work and their work style itself becomes (of course) contagious.

Over the years, we have learned this is how—once the company's Organizational Constitution is not just socialized but adopted—even the largest, most entrenched organizations can initiate and sustain real change. It is not the size of the company that matters. It is the courage of each micro-team and its leader. Big change happens one small team at a time.

This approach is simple, repeatable, and scalable—yet some teams just cannot seem to do it. The responsibility for that failure usually falls on the team leader. For some team leaders, achieving excellence in any form is a challenge, so the contagious variety of excellence may seem impossible. For this approach to work, that leader must be willing to learn, both by looking at available data and by talking with their people, what their *team* needs to thrive—not themselves. In other words, that leader must have wholly embraced the spirit of not just servant leadership, but the company's servant purpose. Their people and the mission must come first—not ego, personal agenda, or taking credit when it all starts to go right.

As you will soon learn (perhaps the hard way), that is not an easy transition for some leaders. They will need your help. They will need your mentorship. The BMS leaders who refuse to change will need you to show them the door.

For the leaders who remain, how do you, as a mentor and change champion, help them assume a servant leader's role? Then help them lead an emulation-worthy team? Here are some proven tips to help small teams become contagious pockets of excellence:

- **Take Small Bites** | Rather than take on the entire company culture at once, enable that leader to focus on improving that specific team's work habits—they must know precisely what it feels like to work within that group.
- **Leverage Strengths** | Within that team, ask the leader first to identify each employee's strengths, then assign work and assignments that energize and motivate while building on existing skills.

- **Enable Team Purpose** | The team leader knows the company's servant purpose, but do they know *this team's* servant purpose? Encourage the small team leader to learn what meaningful work looks and feels like for them.
- **Foster Belonging** | Empower the leader to create a sense of belonging among the team members and stakeholders; their job is to enable each team member to feel bone-deep pride in their work, and the team itself.
- **Build Respectful Relationships** | Encourage the team leader to build high-quality, mutually beneficial relationships and connections with—and also among—employees; the more they know about each other, the more they will care.
- **Create Wisdom Loops** | Ask the team leader to help their employees share knowledge and develop ongoing learning opportunities; this creates team-focused experiences that promote trust, confidence, and growth.
- **Become an Advocate** | Rather than focus on just the work, encourage the leader to care about who gets the job done; ask them to serve as an advocate for employee well-being and work recovery.
- **Set Boundaries** | This is always important, but especially in a post-pandemic work environment where many people still work from home: Support the leader as they set boundaries that indicate when the work is done—and other aspects of life begin.

This seems like a lot. We get it. Not every small team leader will be ready to take all this on. But remember what we said just a moment ago:

"Rapid growth and success within small teams happens when the team leaders focus on what their respective teams need . . ."

With this in mind, every small team leader's goal—and the goal of every potential contagious pocket of excellence—must be clear. The small team leader must determine which of these elements have the highest value for their team. They must know what is most important to those team members. And when those team members come to you with what they know? You must listen and mentor—and then get the hell out of their way.

TEAM-TO-TEAM COLLABORATION: BRINGING BACK BARN RAISING

How do you know if your company's servant purpose is taking hold? How do you know if team leaders and members demonstrate the values and behaviors? These answers are simple. But sometimes, as your new culture gains traction, they are difficult to witness. You must continuously be on the lookout, paying attention to both subtle desired changes in individuals and larger beneficial shifts in the team.

Watch what happens when a team leader shares their team's successes with the next levels of leadership, and with fellow small team leaders. Watch how people react when they see clear, definitive examples of how to achieve results are communicated upward and with peers. Do leaders share in the joy? Do they bask in the knowledge placed before them? Does every celebration inspire them to do better? Over time, do they get better? Or do they get bitter? Maybe they go all-out Amazon and turn ultra-competitive. Perhaps they become professionally jealous or some workplace anger surfaces. All of these are signs that your desired workplace culture has not taken root yet—at least not across all workgroups.

Of course, every culture change initiative seeks out quick wins. Every company and business leader hopes for social proof that the desired change is happening. They clamor for evidence that people and teams are putting good first. However, in many companies, especially those that do not fully embrace their Organizational Constitution—these early pockets of excellence can be seen as competitive threats.

Instead of living by a "When they get better, we get better" philosophy, teams and departments can take the success of others personally. In those cases, those pockets of excellence become contagious—but not in the right way. The fact is that many business leaders, as culture change propagates, do not see huge problems *within* small teams. Instead, they see conflict between one unit and another.

In Chapter 11, we showed you the WQ results for one company's sales and customer service teams. It was not important to mention then, but those two teams were a classic example of an unproductive "team versus team" dynamic. The BMS leader of the sales team, as you can imagine, was sure the new-school leader of the customer service team was out to get him. The rivalry went from a tolerable level of over-competitiveness to unhealthy to toxic in a hurry—and it stayed that way until the sales team leader was lovingly set free (and half his team went with him). Only then did the two teams start caring about each other's success. Only then did they start working well together in service of their customers.

This type of confrontation between teams can significantly stall any change momentum. Depending on how high up the BMS leader is, how much influence they have, and the resolve of senior leaders, we have seen change efforts completely halted by similar situations. (Remember The Other Company from Chapter 2? The one with what we now know was a BMS leader? That is a prime example of culture change aborted.)

So how do we avoid this culture change, hard stop? We bring back barn raising.

Yes, barn raising.

Once upon a time (and in some parts of the world to this day[1]), entire communities would gather to take part in a barn raising. At this simple gathering, people would cooperatively construct the framework of a neighbor's barn, or perhaps even their home. Typically, the collective hard work would be followed by a celebration that did not just celebrate the erection of a new structure but reveled in the feeling of good work being done by good people for good reasons. At the time, this was the very definition of "discretionary effort."

That sense of collective effort and accomplishment—that sense of togetherness and belonging—created an emotional attachment similar to how one might feel in a close family (or in a Good Comes First company) because, at its core, barn raising was a form of social interaction. Working side by side with your neighbor was a highly valued form of engagement. It was the best of cooperation and collaboration—every person serving one purpose, even if the work did not benefit them personally. As the day ended, there was no stronger feeling of collaboration than when everyone would look up at the barn frame and say, "We did that." The feeling was all about "When they get better, we get better"—and it was contagious.

How would it feel to be part of a culture where:

- Every person in every team worked selflessly to benefit others?
- When faced with challenging projects, you worked with values-aligned, skilled peers who were actively engaged while helping solve problems?
- Once a team finished the work, with all team members living the servant purpose, everyone—face-to-face or virtually—celebrated joint accomplishments?
- When a "neighbor" needed help next time, the entire community was there for them?

This is the concept of barn raising.

Yes, many people in your organization—at first—might believe barn raising is an outdated mindset. However, we have seen this uniquely human approach to community-based work become the basis of exemplary team-to-team cooperation. So introduce the barn raising mindset to your team leaders. Set it as the standard by which your company's teams will work together.

Then watch this centuries-old concept become a critical factor in building tomorrow's Good Comes First company culture.

HIRING FOR A GOOD COMES FIRST COMPANY CULTURE

For many leaders, efficient team building quickly becomes a natural element of your culture change process. After all, teams—and team leaders—are expected to welcome the change. And most do. However, one team typically embraces the changes unique to your Good Comes First company culture more enthusiastically than any other: Human Resources.

For years, many of us have considered the traditional hiring model to be broken: HR professionals (or hiring managers or small business owners) identify a need for more talent. They post a poorly written job description to a crappy job board. Then—*surprise!*—a bunch of poorly written resumes are submitted by what any objective observer would call crappy candidates.

An even crappier Applicant Tracking System, using the qualifications provided by the poorly written job description, spits out the best of the crappy candidates. HR then filters the crappy candidates based on technical ability, experience, and so-called "culture fit" (even though most companies have not defined their culture, let alone their servant purpose—and do not know how the crappy candidates will "fit"). HR schedules interviews; a couple of months later, someone gets hired. And almost half the time, according to a study by Leadership IQ, those crappy hires fail within eighteen months.[2] So the crappy process starts over. And over. And over.

That is the way hiring has gone for the past twenty years. Somehow, over more than two decades, we have taken the "human" out of "human resources." We are all automated, all the time.

No wonder the HR team embraces the coming change! Within a failed system that offers little or no fulfillment, they are working impossible hours on an impossible task that never ends.

A Good Comes First culture changes the systemically broken hiring process in many ways, including:

- **Establishment of an Intentional Culture** | The culture, including the company's servant purpose, has been clearly defined. Rather than being just another "fast-paced, dynamic" company, the HR team—and even the candidates themselves—can qualify applicants based on their alignment to the desired culture.

- **Proper Setting of Expectations** | The values and behaviors expected of every employee—and every new hire—are clearly defined. The company explicitly designs behavioral questions and observations during the screening process and interview to determine the candidate's ability to demonstrate those values and behaviors.

- **Alignment to Mission** | The company's strategies and goals are available to everyone, including new hires. So when HR or the hiring manager asks the candidate the inevitable "Where do you see yourself in five years" question, they and a member of the HR team can assess the probability of a long-term match.

- **Invitation to Join the High-High Club** | During the job interview, HR shows each candidate the company-branded

Performance-Values Matrix. The interviewer explains that the company expects all hires to be a potential member of the High Performance–High Values Match Club. Not only does this set proper expectations, but this step in the hiring process also scares off the candidates who had no intention of achieving any form of excellence—and just wanted a paycheck.

- **Introduction to Good Comes First Models** | Also during the interview, the candidate is shown branded versions of the Good Comes First Culture Cornerstones diagram that outlines the foundational principle and four cornerstones. HR also introduces each candidate to the GCF Accountability Model. As another potential fall-off point in the hiring funnel, candidates are asked their thoughts on both models. Again, HR has the opportunity to filter out those who cannot, do not, will not, and are not.

Within a Good Comes First company, HR professionals—perhaps for the first time in their careers—hire not just for technical skills and some generic view of culture fit. They hire based on alignment to a specific ideal. They hire for purpose. No more playing a crappy game they only have a 50 percent chance of winning. Knowing that their hiring process makes a real difference in a Good Comes First culture, the HR professional and hiring managers feel valued—and they know their work matters.

And the entire hiring team? Well, do not be surprised if they become one of your first contagious pockets of excellence.

A HIRING BONUS: EMPLOYEE REFERRALS

Another distinct advantage of a Good Comes First culture: a dramatic increase in the number of employee referrals that come into the hiring team. Consider:[3&4]

- Candidates who come into HR from employee referrals are four times more likely to be hired.
- Eighty-two percent of all *employees/candidates* rated employee referrals more desirable than any other sourcing options.

- Eighty-eight percent of *employers* said referrals are the best source for above-average applicants.
- While only 25 percent of employees sourced through job boards stay over *two* years, 45 percent of employees sourced from employee referrals stay longer than *four* years.
- Every time the company hires an employee referral, an employer saves $7,500 in overhead costs.
- Requisitions not filled with an employee referral take sixty days to fill; jobs filled by employee referrals take thirty-five to forty days to fill.

These employee referrals come from employees wholly aligned with the company's servant purpose and values. The referrals come from engaged employees who feel trusted and feel a sense of community—and who believe the work they do matters. They see their boss as more mentor than manager—and they know the senior leadership team will use their voice for good.

It is the team members who thrive within a Good Comes First culture who invite their friends and colleagues to join them at your company. That is the best possible compliment—and one heck of a hiring bonus.

You now know how to build the best possible teams. You know how to guide your HR professionals to hire aligned talent that makes those teams even better. Very soon, you will have good people, doing good work, in a good company.

In our next—and final—chapter, we will discuss how to reboot your current culture. We will provide actionable, proven tips to help you lead the transition to a Good Comes First company.

Hang in there. You will soon have read almost everything there is to know about putting good first.

CHAPTER 14

Rebooting Your Current Company Culture Toward Good Comes First

We presented the business case for proactive culture refinement. We outlined a proven, three-phase approach to create an Organizational Constitution. Specifically, we detailed how to:

- Define your servant purpose and desired work culture.
- Align all plans, decisions, and actions to that desired culture.
- Refine your desired work culture to ensure everyone models your valued behaviors.

Despite the dedication you have shown to learning the concepts in this book, as well as the proven steps and tools, you still have an important decision to make: You must decide whether to implement these practices in your organization.

The decision to reboot your company's current work culture is not one to make casually—or quickly. After all, starting a process like this without the full commitment of all senior leaders means there is little chance of success. And partial commitment typically leads to disappointment—primarily in team leaders' and team members' heads, hearts, and hands. Without a full commitment from senior leaders to help drive your culture refinement, the rest of the organization cannot confidently apply their knowledge (heads), passion (hearts), and skills (hands) in service to that culture shift.

This chapter presents the challenges senior leaders typically face when rebooting their organization's work culture and offers "go / no go" decision points leaders must address along the way.

ORGANIZATIONAL READINESS

Right now, you are probably thinking you should start the Good Comes First process by evaluating your organization's readiness for a culture reboot—but that conclusion is entirely incorrect.

Your organization, its leaders, and team members only know what they know today. Your organization, in many of their eyes, is "perfectly normal." In this sense, "perfectly" does not mean it is operationally perfect. It just means the company operates perfectly within the beliefs, flaws, norms, and myths that have been reinforced and embedded over time. The company's culture is "normal" for your company—it is by no means perfect. You already know this, or you would not be reading the last chapter of this book.

As you're now aware, to boost organizational readiness for the change to a Good Comes First culture, you must follow a planned, proven, step-by-step process. You also know you must define your desired culture, align your desired culture, and—over the next eighteen to twenty-four months—refine your desired culture.

As you move through this process, the team leaders and team members in your organization will learn—from you and your senior leaders—how a Good Comes First work culture will look. They will learn what it acts like, talks like—and respects like. Over time, with senior leaders' consistent modeling, coaching, measuring, celebrating, and mentoring, the players right for your organization will align with your servant purpose, values and behaviors, and strategies and goals.

In short, the best of your team members will fully engage. They will sign up and go all in. For years to come, they will be your strongest, most respectful, and most productive citizens.

But this change does not start with them. Every element of this culture change begins with you.

THE TRUE STARTING POINT: YOU

If you are not wholly committed to leading this change, do not start it. Not yet, anyway.

First, to be certain you are ready and willing for the "Good Comes First Change Champion" role, see if you have these vital characteristics:

1. You have come to the undeniable conclusion that your organization's work culture is not entirely purposeful, perfectly positive, or fully productive. You examined the available evidence. You analyzed your organization's treatment of its primary customers—its employees—and you know your team leaders and team members do not experience respect in every interaction.

2. You understand your senior leadership team must lead this change—especially you. You accept the responsibility to drive this reboot. You know you cannot delegate this responsibility to anyone else. You have resolved to embrace the obligation to champion this shift.

3. You are willing to invest the time and energy required to be the voice, face, and heart of this culture transition. You have a plan to free up your calendar to manage the health of your organization's work culture proactively. You know what tasks you can delegate—and what tasks simply do not need doing anymore.

4. You are willing to learn to be—and are prepared to evolve as—an effective culture leader. You are ready to engage daily with employees in town hall meetings. You are committed to embracing data from the Values and Behaviors Survey, Executive Team Effectiveness Survey, and Workplace Intelligence Assessment. Most important, you are willing to actively listen to customers (both the happy and not-so-happy ones). In short, in an effort to learn and evolve, you are eager to review every credible data point, both quantitative and qualitative.

5. You understand that you are *not* letting go of the need to ensure your organization delivers on its performance promises. You accept that driving results is just half your job, and that driving respect requires equal billing, equal emphasis, and equal celebration.

BUILD THE CASE

Once you are fully committed to the change champion role, you must be ready to help every senior leader embrace their responsibility and obligation to do the same. Those executives will want to see numbers that reflect current reality and support the need to change. They trust numbers. So before you meet with them about their roles in the change plan, gather reports from across your organization—but not just financial statements and performance-related metrics. Secure every data point we've gone over in this book that shows a shift to a Good Comes First work culture is not change for the sake of change—it is a necessary evolution.

Specifically, gather evidence that your company may not be performing as effectively as the executive team planned. If production is below standard, or quality is suffering, or maybe sales are not meeting forecasts, all those numbers are important to share with senior leaders. They may have already seen some of these metrics, but they have not seen all of them. You can show the big picture and bring all those numbers to the table.

Gather customer satisfaction data. Your customers may be thrilled with you—or maybe they are thrilled with some of what you do and driven batty by other aspects of the business. Bring net promoter scores (even if you have not yet acted on the recommendations) if you have them. Examine customer purchasing trends. Find out who your top customers are—by volume and sales—and how long those customers have been with you. Compare top customers today to those of five and ten years ago to figure out what causes customer spending to move up or down. Track down this data, analyze it, and prepare to share the results.

Your company may not be retaining talented team leaders and team members. Perhaps you are not consistently attracting top talent—maybe employee referrals do not come in as expected, or those referred candidates may not convert well. If the data is available, compare retention and attraction data from five years ago, or even ten years ago, to today's targets. Bring those reports to the table.

Also, bring evidence of your employees' daily experiences. Track them down to see if they have been positive, validating, and rewarding.

Gather satisfaction, employee engagement / experience, and/or morale data. (If your last employee opinion survey was two years ago or longer, it is time for a fresh survey of employee perspectives.) Examine your company's scores on Glassdoor. Dig into your brand reputation on Yelp or niche sites like Tripadvisor.

It may be even more important to monitor social media platforms. On Facebook, Twitter, Instagram, and others, what do customers love about your company? Your products and services? What do they not love? What does your company say about social justice issues—if it says anything at all? Bring that data—and include examples.

The answers to these questions will supply other much-needed data:

- How do different generations of team leaders and team members impact your work environment?
- What are your diversity and inclusion targets?
- What is the employee base by race and gender across your company?
- Does your employee population mix reflect the racial and gender percentages of your communities?
- How many women or people of color are in senior positions in your organization?
- Are people of all races and genders paid equally for equal responsibility?

Get these numbers. Get these answers. Bring them to the table. You may have other powerful data about culture gaps that exist today, so bring those reports, too—every number matters.

ENGAGE YOUR LEADERSHIP TEAM

Once you have all that data in hand, you are ready to invite your leadership team into the conversation. Do not, though, schedule a meeting with those senior leaders to tell them what you already decided! They may not be of the same mind as you. Not yet, anyway. After all, you took the time necessary to come to your conclusion. You read this book—and maybe other books—about the benefits of a purposeful, positive, productive work culture. You researched how your work culture operates today—the good and the not so good.

Your senior leaders have not done that thinking, studying, reflecting, and analysis. They have not come to their conclusion. Out of the blue, at this point in time, how might your senior leaders respond if you asked them to help you drive culture change? To spend the next eighteen to twenty-four months changing everything they know? To lose 10 percent, 25 percent, or more of their leaders and staff, and then help train their replacements? What would they say if you told them they need to model the agreed-upon values and behaviors? And that they must stop being managers so much, and instead focus on being coaches and mentors?

If they are respectful, the majority will likely say, "No, thank you." If they are a bit rougher around the edges, precedent shows some will employ blue language as they ask themselves, and you, if you have lost your mind.

A better approach to this first conversation is to invite your senior leaders to examine existing pain points in your operations today. Some of those pain points might be well known; some might not. Your data and reports will clearly outline misses, gaps, and frustrations employees and customers experience daily. The data might also show where the company excels; where organic pockets of excellence already exist. Ask your senior leaders to celebrate those pockets, and then learn to emulate them.

Another way to gain objective support is to give leadership team members time to review the reports before your meeting. Invite them to ask and answer questions about the health and quality of your work culture. Some of those questions might include:

- Do our employees feel strongly validated at work for their ideas, efforts, and accomplishments?
- Do employees proactively identify and solve tough problems to improve quality and efficiency and wow customers?
- Do our employees have the opportunity to leverage their strengths, skills, and passions at work on a daily basis?
- What systemic problems do we never fully resolve that waste time and money?

- Do employees have a solid one-on-one relationship with their direct supervisors, or is it more transactional?
- Do people like working here? Or is this just a way for them to pay the bills?

So you will ask them to consider these questions. You will set proper expectations. You will ask that everyone on the leadership team does their "homework." You will expect each person to review the reports and answer the questions. *In your mind,* they will not just come to your meeting prepared—they will arrive ready to consider better ways of acting, operating, and performing.

Unfortunately, that rarely happens—because most company cultures tolerate certain unproductive behaviors. So some people will come prepared and ready to engage; others will have made no effort to do their homework. Some will understand the need to improve work culture; some will not. Most will not understand why you are asking these questions, but they will have questions about how you—and they—will create and sustain an uncompromising work culture.

A decent outcome of this prework and the meeting is that your senior leaders agree some gaps between current company culture and ideal culture must be closed. The best possible outcome is their willingness to learn more about how they can help lead this coming change. But no matter how your organization goes about gaining reasonable consensus on the need to change culture and next steps, do not leave the meeting without that consensus. Stay in the room until you have a plan. If you disagree on the presence of specific culture gaps or do not agree on the need to close those gaps during this meeting, do not start the culture change process. Not yet.

(For your thoughtful consideration: Our experience shows this learning is best accomplished by an off-site meeting—perhaps led by an objective, outside facilitator. This environment best enables the focus needed to map out a proven process, answer questions, and build knowledge and skills about culture refinement.)

Instead, keep coaching. Keep the efficiency, customer service, employee expectations, and all other gaps top of mind for everyone. Continuously reinforce "what is" versus "what could be." Watch the numbers and update your reports. In the meantime, learn even more about your current culture. Then keep comparing that to your vision of the ideal culture—those are the gaps that must be closed. Ultimately, it may take weeks or months for the team to come to the same conclusion you have: that the company must engage in proactive culture refinement. And no matter how long it takes, that has to be okay.

Of course, they may never come to that conclusion. Your executive team might show signs that an embedded old-school leadership style will prevent progress toward a Good Comes First culture. Worse yet, you may have a leader or two afflicted with Boomer Male Syndrome. As you have learned in this book, those senior leaders may not be able to evolve past their current thinking. If that is the case, you have other big decisions ahead of you—like who to lovingly set free first.

As you—and your leadership team—contemplate the challenges in front of you, do something to show what is possible. For example, you might have a proactive team, department, or division leader willing to engage in culture refinement. Great! Start small (or at least smaller). Let their division pilot this process. They will get positive traction, happier employees, and better results. Soon, they will be known as a pocket of excellence. Their hard number gains will help other senior leaders lower their guard—and step up. In the worst-case scenario, you have one outstanding team performing well; in the best-case scenario, their work becomes contagious—more people want to do whatever they are doing, and your fellow senior team leaders see the momentum for change building.

WHAT TO EXPECT FROM TEAM LEADERS AND TEAM MEMBERS

Even as that momentum builds—and even when you do everything right—people will react differently. To get to this point, you carefully followed the Define, Align, and Refine phases. You thoroughly engaged in every practice within the GCF Accountability Model. And yet, you will *still* get a wide range of responses from senior leaders, team leaders, and team members as you spearhead this culture change.

Players typically align in one or more of these categories:

- **Active Resistance** | The firm denial of proposed values and behaviors. These players actively engage in debate—sometimes loudly—to express their frustration with the new demands.
- **Passive Resistance** | The withholding of cooperation. Without actively resisting change, these players will not align to defined values and desired behaviors.
- **Passive Observation** | This shows up as opting out—not participating in meetings and not completing values surveys, for example. These players sit on the sidelines, watching.
- **Passive Acceptance** | A form of, "I like this, I understand this, but I am waiting to see if my bosses model these new rules." These players wait and watch to see if it is real.
- **Active Engagement** | The early adopters, these players get your culture drive, want to be a part of the change immediately, and are optimistic about the changes to come.

Getting every team member to align with the active engagement category is your goal. Many leaders and team members will self-select this group when a steady hand, rather than force, is used to guide the organization through the Good Comes First process. Even if they do not, you do not need to aggressively "fix" those in the other four categories. They will often take care of themselves in one of two ways.

First, the passive folks see this change is not optional. Over weeks and months, they learn the best way to get along is to embrace new methods. And second, the resisters see this change is not optional. So many self-select out of the organization. They say to themselves, "This values crap is not for me. I'm out!" They join the "opt-out-and-leave" group. Let them go, kindly and without judgment.

Other resisters join the "opt-out-and-stay" club. They decide to battle the new demands, waiting to see if there are any "teeth" in the new culture. These are the ones you need to stay on; coach and mentor them. You need to show them, through the values surveys, how their direct reports and peers perceive them. By providing this information and coaching and mentoring, you give these players the best opportunity to choose to align. If they do not align with your Good Comes First work culture's purposeful, positive, productive norms, you must lovingly set them free. After all, their resistance does nothing beneficial for them, their teams, or their customers in your Good Comes First work environment. Even more critical to creating your new culture: Neither you nor your senior leaders can afford to tolerate their misalignment.

This stage of the change journey will not be easy. At many points along the way, you will be tempted to compromise your vision. That is why, while all this is happening, you must remember that a driver does not win the 24 Hours of Le Mans by coasting. Drivers win by remaining focused on the most desirable outcome, working the plan, and adapting to challenges that arise. You will do the same. With resisters or passive players, you must consistently and assertively Model, Coach, Measure, Celebrate, and Mentor. That is the only way to keep the message, direction, and expectations clear.

You must keep your foot on the accelerator, or progress will slow—and perhaps even stop.

GOOD COMES FIRST LESSONS LEARNED

You get the idea. This is not easy. Leading change is a huge commitment. You may wonder if your company is ready for all this—if *you* are ready. You are not alone. Many leaders before you have felt the same way. One of them is Robert Pasin, Chief Wagon Officer at Radio Flyer, who you met in Chapter 3 of this book.

Robert's story—and his company's culture change journey—is inspiring. It provides valuable lessons. As you read his story, consider these questions:

- What was the issue or event—the organizational "heart attack"—that prompted Robert to change the organization's work culture?
- How did Radio Flyer's senior leaders engage employees in developing the company's vision and values?
- In what ways did Radio Flyer's culture evolve to celebrate values and behaviors in the workplace?
- How did Radio Flyer change its performance review process to equally value respect and results?

Radio Flyer began in 1917 as the Liberty Coaster Wagon Company. For seventy years, the factory was the core of the business. They stamped metal into products—primarily those little red wagons for which they have become known. In the '30s, founder Antonio Pasin—Robert's grandfather—renamed the company Radio Steel and Manufacturing. During WWII, the factory shifted to making the five-gallon steel containers that rode the backs of jeeps, trucks, and tanks carrying fuel and water to troops.

Robert said, "Even in this era, my grandad and my dad were very much about treating people right. Yet, the culture was paternalistic. Empowering people was not the norm during their tenures. Information was not widely shared."

That paternalism inspired a culture of entitlement. Many people had been doing the same jobs for many years, so they grew complacent. Robert described his first summer job at the factory at eighteen years old: "It was my first day on the job, and I was paired with a man who had been at the company for twenty years. We were loading a truck for one of our largest customers. I was going crazy, loading this truck as fast as possible," he remembered. "After an hour, this guy says to me, 'What are you doing, man? Why are you working so hard? Slow down.' The guy knows I'm the boss's kid—but he didn't hesitate to share the general mindset: 'We're going to do the minimum.'"

The reality was—the company was selling a huge number of red metal Radio Flyer wagons. The Town and Country model had been their cash cow for thirty years, so it was easy to be complacent. "The company was kind of stagnant at that point," Pasin said.

In 1992, at age twenty-three, Robert started working full-time in a tiny sales group at the company. Within months of his start date, competitors came out with plastic wagons. Robert saw them and thought, "These are a lot better than our wagons! They're molded and have features ours don't, like comfortable seats."

These new molded wagons quickly took sales away from the Town and Country. "For decades, we were an inwardly focused manufacturer," Robert said. "We were thrown into a complete crisis."

"If Radio Flyer had been talking to consumers, moms and dads and kids, we would have learned those families really liked the features on the molded wagons. Consumers said, 'We can leave the wagon outside in the weather. We can hose it off to clean it. This is great!'" Robert wondered if this was the end of Radio Flyer.

Robert still loved the brand and the product . . . he just did not love the business model. But rather than giving in to his fear that this was the end, he saw this crisis as an incredible opportunity to change. "We didn't really have much choice. It was survival mode. It took years of chipping away at this big challenge to our business," he said. "We had no HR team. No one at the company had turned a business around. There was a lot of trial and error to get resources and experts to help me."

It took ten years to stabilize the business and make it financially healthy. "That was Radio Flyer's chapter one," Pasin said. "Our chapter two was moving from stabilizing the patient to building the healthy culture we have now." Stabilizing the patient required shutting down the metal factory in 2004. "That was huge—a very traumatic, painful thing to do," Pasin explained.

They had to change with the market or they would not survive, so they partnered with a vendor outside their business to make molded plastic wagons. As Pasin said, "We didn't know that manufacturing process. We started to learn what we could be really great at." It turns out that what they could be great at was not manufacturing wagons. Instead, it was designing and developing products that make sense with the brand—that ring true to their heritage—and ring true with moms, dads, and kids.

"That major change began to transform the culture. We did a very intentional culture transformation where we started to articulate our vision, mission, and values," Pasin explained. A mentor of Robert's, Jerry Bell, told him, "It's time to articulate how you're going to go forward. You have to include everybody and have an iterative process to define what Radio Flyer means, what your values are, etc." So that is exactly what they did.

"We plastered the cafeteria walls with huge posters and wrote answers to these questions," letting every employee participate by writing their thoughts. "This is when the behaviors we want were articulated. We thought about how our best employees show up, support each other, solve problems, and more," Pasin said.

And it worked. As Robert shared, "I'm a big believer that you get better at what you measure and become what you celebrate as a team. We started to develop a lot of awards and recognition for people who demonstrated our values. We enabled teammates to recognize their peers. Organically, it just took off."

As the company articulated and celebrated its values and behaviors, Pasin said, "We had to have zero tolerance for bad behavior." One big no-no in their culture is sarcasm. Robert admitted, "That's a hard one for me! I can be really sarcastic [but] we found sarcasm killed creativity and the safety that people need to throw out a creative idea." So, against all odds perhaps, Radio Flyer was able to squelch sarcasm.

Pasin said, "One of the things people say after they've been here for a while is 'everywhere I've worked there are jerks. That person doesn't exist here.'" He thinks it boils down to the fact that "people are so grateful to not have the distractions, the politics, etc., here because we have no tolerance for drama."

Once they articulated their desired values and behaviors, they started changing the team. "We started letting people go. We upgraded the team constantly at every position. The culture was built one person, one new hire, at a time."

As incredible as that is, it is not even the best part. The best part? The ultimate sign that Radio Flyer equally values respect and results?

Radio Flyer has incorporated its values and behaviors into its performance review process and compensation model. "One half of the review is about goals, your business results. The other half is the values. If you're a sales guy and kick butt on revenues but are missing integrity, you're not going to get your full bonus. You're not going to get promoted."

"If you're not meeting the standards for values and performance expectations, eventually you're not going to be here anymore," Robert said. "That is the foundation of our culture. There is no compromise."

Radio Flyer's journey—and Pasin's evolution as a culture champion—was a marathon. Once the company was financially stable again, it took a few more years to reboot the company culture.

The result? Pasin and his team turned Radio Flyer into a vibrant, healthy, fun work culture.

As Chief Wagon Officer Robert learned, creating a Good Comes First culture is not easy. There is no quick fix. It takes courage to reboot your company. Then it takes clarity (defining your desired culture) and consequences (aligning your desired culture) to initiate change. It requires discipline, tenacity, and commitment to the ideal work environment (refining your culture) to enable traction.

To sustain your uncompromising—and purposeful, positive, productive—work culture, you need more than a proven culture change process, as we have outlined here in *Good Comes First*.

You need good people, doing good work, in a good company.

But first . . . *you* need to push "Go."

CONCLUSION

Next Steps for Good Comes First Leaders and Teams

Within the pages of this book, our servant purpose was—and is . . .

> . . . *to take you, our reader, beyond a simple understanding of the elements that lead to an effective work culture . . . to present proven and actionable strategies that . . . create a work culture that ensures good comes first.*

We trust we have served you well.

You invested time and energy to learn all you can about Good Comes First work cultures. You defined the initial elements of your company's Organizational Constitution. When it comes to creating and sustaining a purposeful, positive, productive work culture, you are likely the most informed player in your organization. Now, the time has come to act on your new insights about company culture. But before you do, you must find the right pace and the right tone.

If you act too slowly or without firm commitment, you will fail to create the sense of urgency needed for this change to happen. If your actions show that your announced culture change is not a high priority (by, for example, missing key culture deadlines), you send a clear message that everything else is a higher priority. If you speak too softly or too infrequently, you will miss the opportunity to create momentum and foster contagious pockets of excellence.

On the other hand, if you act and speak too boldly, you run the risk of inhibiting others from self-discovering what you already learned about culture change. That means they might not come to the same conclusions you have. They might disagree that you and your senior leaders must act quickly to create a work culture that values respect as well as results.

Remember: Until now, those senior leaders (and all other team members) have been doing exactly what they have been asked, trained, and incentivized to do. Each member of your existing team has done the best they can with the information available. So be thoughtful and strategic about how to engage your fellow leaders in this process.

To help you set the right pace within your organization or team, consider these "The Power of Do" items:

THE GOOD COMES FIRST DO LIST

Every project starts with a to-do list. Here's yours:

- Do engage your fellow leaders in your reasoning. Explain why you believe the time is right to create a Good Comes First culture in your workplace.
- Do invite your fellow leaders to share their perspectives of the work culture today. Ask if they see some of the same issues that you do. Listen to their perceptions of what is working—and what is not.
- Do be open with fellow leaders about your "newbie" standing as a culture change champion. Ask for their help—and for their frank perspective through the change. Be vulnerable. Be ready to learn side by side with fellow change champions.
- Do resist the temptation to *announce* any decision to change the work culture; instead, let your actions and intentions speak for you (no "Managing by Announcement").
- Do enlist each leadership team member in this process. Their full commitment will be vital to the success of your company's culture evolution.

- Do share your knowledge:
  — Share this book with your entire leadership team.
  — Share the Culture Cornerstones Model to help them understand that a proven framework exists to enable vital changes to your company's operation.
  — Share the Performance-Values Matrix to gain perspective on the direction you are going.
  — Share the concept of "Define, Align, and Refine."
  — Share and thoroughly discuss the three components of an Organizational Constitution: servant purpose, declared values and defined behaviors, and strategies and goals.
  — Share the GCF Accountability Model and the three primary methods of collecting objective data (Values and Behaviors Survey, Executive Team Effectiveness Survey, and the Workplace Intelligence Assessment), so leaders and team members understand how your company will achieve its culture change goals.
  — Through your actions and behaviors, share how every leader must demonstrate the values and behaviors in the Organizational Constitution.
  — Most importantly, share with them your passion for making this change . . . for creating a Good Comes First company.
- Do follow the process:
  — **Define** | With your senior leader peers and key personnel, co-create the definition of your desired culture by crafting your Organizational Constitution.
  — **Align** | Set expectations that every leader and team member will live by the company's servant purpose, model the declared values and defined behaviors, and work toward the stated company strategies and goals.
  — **Refine** | Leverage the five practices of the GCF Accountability Model to Model, Coach, Measure, Celebrate, and Mentor; know that tolerating any unproductive behaviors will cost your company time, money, and momentum.

- Do continue learning:
  — As a change champion, the learning never ends. There are always new challenges, so we as leaders are always in constant need of further information.
  — Find new content, examples, and resources on GoodComes First.com.
  — Join the Good Comes First groups on LinkedIn and Facebook—and be sure to follow @GoodComesFirst on Twitter.
- Do let us know how we, your authors, can help. We are here because, together, we can do better.

You're ready. Go ahead . . . start your culture change journey.

Do good. Inspire good. And at every opportunity, make sure good comes first.

ACKNOWLEDGMENTS

S. Chris Edmonds

I'm indebted to a number of people who have paved the way for this book.

My clients have given me access to their most precious resource: the hearts and minds of leaders and team members in their organizations. I appreciate their willingness to let me be a disruptive force and their willingness to consider these ideas as they refine their organizational cultures.

Venus Williams is a remarkable and delightful human, athlete, and entrepreneur. I'm grateful for the opportunity to guide the culture refinement initiatives in both her businesses—and for her willingness to share her culture journey in this book's foreword.

Matt Holt at BenBella Books—and his new imprint, Matt Holt Books— has been our biggest supporter and champion. I'm grateful for Matt's enthusiasm, professionalism, calm, and humor throughout this project.

Our editor at BenBella, Rachel Phares, dug in, line by line, to help our words have the clarity and impact we were hoping for. This book is far better due to her dedication.

Mark Levy has been a vital member of my branding brain trust since 2012. I appreciate Mark's humor, clarity, and wide knowledge base of publishing, branding, and the New York Mets. Mark helped clarify our servant purpose for *Good Comes First*, which set the path for this book to become a reality.

Last but not least, I'm grateful for the love and support of my lovely bride (of forty years), Diane. She has blessed this crazy dream of mine to publish these concepts and build a career helping organizations be better places to hang out.

Mark S. Babbitt

First, I want to acknowledge the dedication and support of the editors of not just this book, but my last book—*A World Gone Social*—for which they never got the credit they deserved. Dave Ellis and Mom, we could not have done this again without you—and couldn't imagine doing it last time without you.

The team members at BenBella and Matt Holt Books, including Matt Holt and Rachel Phares, have made this experience a challenge-filled joy. With each conversation and email, I grew smarter, and the words got better. I thank you. I'd also like to thank Mark Levy for not just his clarity as the book was coming together, but for the introduction to Matt.

I'd also like to thank our many clients, friends, and colleagues, and our social and digital media friends for supporting this work. *Good Comes First* was conceived during the best of times—and then was carried and born during the COVID-19 pandemic, where face-to-face meetings and interviews weren't possible. And yet, you steadfastly served as the best possible sounding board for our work, and this book. (I guess that means I should also thank Zoom and Slack for contributing in their own ways.)

Lastly, I must acknowledge the patience and love shown to me by Deb and my youngest, JW. Living with someone writing a book isn't easy, period. Living with someone so anal that every word must be just right is a challenge on a much different level. You two have watched from the front row as this book came alive over the past couple of years. And you've spent a lifetime watching the concept be proven over and over again, from the workplace to the baseball diamond. Thank you for believing in the vision—and in me.

NOTES

CHAPTER 1

1. DDI, "New DDI Research: 57 Percent of Employees Quit Because of Their Boss," Cision PR Newswire, December 9, 2019, https://www.pr newswire.com/news-releases/new-ddi-research-57-percent-of-employees -quit-because-of-their-boss-300971506.html.

2. Christine Porath, "Make Civility the Norm on Your Team," *Harvard Business Review*, January 2, 2018, https://hbr.org/2018/01/make-civility -the-norm-on-your-team.

3. Jim Harter, "Dismal Employee Engagement Is a Sign of Global Mismanagement," Gallup, accessed March 12, 2021, http://news.gallup.com /opinion/gallup/224012/dismal-employee-engagement-sign-global -mismanagement.aspx.

4. "2017 Employee Job Satisfaction and Engagement: The Doors of Opportunity Are Open," *SHRM*, April 24, 2017, https://www.shrm.org/hr -today/trends-and-forecasting/research-and-surveys/pages/2017-job -satisfaction-and-engagement-doors-of-opportunity-are-open.aspx.

5. TINYPulse, "The Broken Bridges of the Workplace," accessed March 12, 2021, https://cdn2.hubspot.net/hubfs/443262/pdf/TINYpulse-2017 -Employee-Engagement-Report-Broken-Bridges-of-the-Workplace.pdf.

6. S. Chris Edmonds, "Positive Proof That Culture Works," *The Purposeful Culture Group*, accessed March 12, 2021, https://www.drivingresults throughculture.com/2014/10/20/positive-proof-that-culture-works.

7. Business Roundtable, "Our Commitment," *Business Roundtable*, accessed March 12, 2021, https://opportunity.businessroundtable.org/our commitment.

CHAPTER 2

1. Merriam-Webster, *"Good,"* accessed March 12, 2021, https://www
   .merriam-webster.com/dictionary/good.
2. AFL CIO, Executive Paywatch, accessed March 21, 2021, https://aflcio
   .org/paywatch.
3. Payscale, The State of the Gender Pay Gap 2020, accessed March 21, 2021,
   https://www.payscale.com/data/gender-pay-gap.

CHAPTER 3

1. Glassdoor, Radio Flyer Overview, accessed March 12, 2021, https://www
   .glassdoor.com/Overview/Working-at-Radio-Flyer-EI_IE6864.11,22
   .htm
2. Great Place to Work, Radio Flyer Company Overview, accessed March 12,
   2021, https://www.greatplacetowork.com/certified-company/1100464.
3. Crain's Chicago Business, Great Place to Work No. 13: Radio Flyer Inc.,
   accessed March 21, 2021, https://www.chicagobusiness.com/node/729091.
4. Gallup, The 2020 Exceptional Workplace Award Recipients, accessed
   March 12, 2021, https://www.gallup.com/workplace/290909/2020-gallup
   -exceptional-workplace-award-recipients.aspx.
5. Glassdoor, Stryker Reviews, accessed March 12, 2021, https://www
   .glassdoor.com/Reviews/Stryker-Reviews-E1918.htm.
6. Stryker, Culture Book Interactive, accessed March 12, 2021, https://
   www.stryker.com/content/dam/stryker/about/about_landing/pdfs/2019
   _Stryker_Culture_Book_Interactive.pdf.
7. Stryker, Culture Book Interactive, accessed March 12, 2021, https://
   www.stryker.com/content/dam/stryker/about/about_landing/pdfs/2019
   _Stryker_Culture_Book_Interactive.pdf.
8. Great Place to Work, Stryker Overview, accessed March 12, 2021, https://
   www.greatplacetowork.com/certified-company/1001307.
9. Glassdoor, ABC Supply Company Reviews, accessed March 12, 2021,
   https://www.glassdoor.com/Reviews/ABC-Supply-Co-Reviews-E65
   7069.htm.
10. Our culture: Great Workplace Award WINNER 2019: ABC Supply®
    Careers (2021, March 17). Retrieved March 30, 2021, from https://careers
    .abcsupply.com/our-culture.
11. Gallup, I. (2021, March 24). 2021 Gallup EXCEPTIONAL Workplace
    award winners. Retrieved March 30, 2021, from https://www.gallup.com
    /workplace/287672/gallup-exceptional-workplace-award-winners-2020
    .aspx.

12. Glassdoor, In-N-Out Burger Overview, accessed March 29, 2021, https://www.glassdoor.com/Overview/Working-at-In-N-Out-Burger-EI_IE 14276.11,26.htm.

13. In. (n.d.). Retrieved March 30, 2021, from https://www.in-n-out.com/menu /not-so-secret-menu.

14. Emily Moore, *Glassdoor* blog, "Recipe for Success: Why Employees Made In-N-Out a Best Place to Work," December 14, 2017, https://www .glassdoor.com/blog/in-n-out-ceo/.

15. Glassdoor, In-N-Out Overview, accessed March 12, 2021, https://www.glassdoor.com/Overview/Working-at-In-N-Out-Burger-EI_IE 14276.11,26.htm.

16. Glassdoor, St. Jude's Children's Research Hospital Reviews, accessed March 12, 2021, https://www.glassdoor.com/Reviews/St-Jude-Children -s-Research-Hospital-Reviews-E28315.htm.

17. Ibid.

18. Glassdoor, Awards & Lists, accessed March 12, 2021, https://www .glassdoor.com/Award/index.htm.

19. Jim Harter, "The 38 Most Engaged Workplaces in the World Put People First," Gallup, March 18, 2020, https://www.gallup.com/workplace /290573/engaged-workplaces-world-put-people-first.aspx.

20. Great Place to Work, Recent List Publications, accessed March 12, 2021, https://www.greatplacetowork.com/best-workplaces.

CHAPTER 4

1. Merriam-Webster, "Ugly," accessed March 13, 2021, https://www.merriam -webster.com/dictionary/ugly.

2. Rebecca White and Andrew Stevens, CNN, "'Fear is spreading.' Employees expose culture of fear at Hong Kong's flagship airline," https://www .cnn.com/2019/09/30/asia/hong-kong-cathay-pacific-fear-intl-hnk/index .html.

3. Boeing. (n.d.). Retrieved March 30, 2021, from http://www.boeing.com /principles/values.page.

4. Will E. Young, "Inside Liberty University's 'culture of fear,'" *Washington Post*, July 24, 2019, https://www.washingtonpost.com/outlook/2019/07/24 /inside-liberty-universitys-culture-fear-how-jerry-falwell-jr-silences -students-professors-who-reject-his-pro-trump-politics/.

5. Matt Donnelly, *Variety*, July 27, 2020, "'Ellen DeGeneres Show' Workplace Under Investigation by WarnerMedia," https://variety.com/2020/tv /news/ellen-degeneres-workplace-investigation-1234717494/.

6. Keveney, B. (2020, August 05). "'I am sorry': Ellen DeGeneres apologizes to talk-show staff after complaints of mistreatment." Retrieved March 30, 2021, from https://www.usatoday.com/story /entertainment/tv/2020/07/30/ellen-degeneres-apologizes-show-staff -after-mistreatment-complaints/5550464002/.

7. Kim, A. & Fung, B. (2020, July 02). "Facebook boycott: View the list of companies pulling ads." Retrieved March 30, 2021, from https://www.cnn .com/2020/06/28/business/facebook-ad-boycott-list/index.html.

8. Elizabeth Dwoskin, T. (2020, July 04). "Facebook is working to persuade advertisers to abandon their boycott. So far, it hasn't worked." *Washington Post*. Retrieved March 30, 2021, from https://www.washingtonpost.com /technology/2020/07/03/facebook-advertiser-boycott-hate/.

CHAPTER 5

1. Chamberlain, A. & Munyikwa, Z. "What's Culture Worth? Stock Performance of Glassdoor's Best Places to Work 2009 to 2019," Glassdoor, https://www.glassdoor.com/research/stock-returns-bptw-2020/.

2. Dr. Andrew Chamberlain, Glassdoor, December 6, 2017, "6 Studies Showing Satisfied Employees Drive Business Results," https://www.glassdoor .com/research/satisfied-employees-drive-business-results/.

3. Mario Nuñez, Glassdoor, June 18, 2015, "Does Money Buy Happiness? The Link Between Salary and Employee Satisfaction," https://www .glassdoor.com/research/does-money-buy-happiness-the-link-between -salary-and-employee-satisfaction/.

4. Ruth Chapman, "Report: Employee Engagement and Retention in the UK, Ireland, Belgium, and Netherlands 2020," HRD Connect, June 11, 2020, https://www.hrdconnect.com/2020/06/11/report-employee-engagement -and-retention-in-the-uk-ireland-belgium-and-netherlands-2020/.

5. S. Chris Edmonds, "Positive Proof That Culture Works," *The Purposeful Culture Group* (2018, February 26). Retrieved March 30, 2021, from https://www.drivingresultsthroughculture.com/2014/10/20/positive -proof-that-culture-works/.

6. Harter, J. (2020, November 19). "Historic Drop in Employee Engagement Follows Record Rise," Gallup. Retrieved March 30, 2021, from https://www.gallup.com/workplace/313313/historic-drop-employee -engagement-follows-record-rise.aspx.

7. Chapman, R. (2020, June 11). "New Research Examines Employee Engagement and Retention in Europe," HRD Connect. Retrieved March 30, 2021, from https://www.hrdconnect.com/2020/06/11/report -employee-engagement-and-retention-in-the-uk-ireland-belgium-and -netherlands-2020/.

8. Tony Simons, "The High Cost of Lost Trust," *Harvard Business Review*, September 2002, https://hbr.org/2002/09/the-high-cost-of-lost-trust.

CHAPTER 7

1. Nature.com, accessed March 19, 2021, About Nature Publishing Group, http://www.nature.com/npg_/company_info/mission.html.
2. Cambridge University Press, "Effectiveness of mission statements in organizations—A review," February 2, 2015, https://www.cambridge .org/core/journals/journal-of-management-and-organization/article/abs /effectiveness-of-mission-statements-in-organizations-a-review/DB54 DF7C451F1488BA8BEEF06A721E54.
3. Kaiser Tire, Cooper Tires, accessed March 19, 2021, https://kaisertire .com/cooper-tires-2/
4. Darden Restaurants, Julio Suárez, "Nourishing and Delighting," accessed March 19, 2021, https://www.darden.com/blog/nourishing-and-delighting.
5. Reliable Plant, "Flour power plant project for Newmont Mining earns honor," accessed March 19, 2021, https://www.reliableplant.com/Read /20559/fluor-power-plant-project-for-newmont-mining-earns-honor.
6. Starbucks, Our Mission, accessed March 19, 2021, http://www.starbucks .com/about-us/company-information/mission-statement.
7. Bristol Myers Squibb, http://www.bms.com/ourcompany/mission/Pages /default.aspx.
8. "Interview with Sherron Watkins," *Fraud Magazine*, January/February 2007, http://www.fraud-magazine.com/article.aspx?id=583.
9. AccountingDegree.org, "The 10 Worst Corporate Accounting Scandals of All Time," http://www.accounting-degree.org/scandals/.
10. Pink, Daniel H. *Drive*. Riverhead Publishing, 2011.
11. SuperSoul Conversations Podcast By Oprah, "Howard Schultz: Pouring Your Heart into Your Business," https://www.youtube.com/watch ?v=ltkJ5mGHd1I.
12. Ibid.

CHAPTER 10

1. TINYPulse, "The 2019 Employee Engagement Report: The End of Employee Loyalty," accessed March 23, 2021, https://www.tinypulse. com/hubfs/EE%20Report%202019.pdf.
2. Cambridge Dictionary, "Mentor," accessed March 23, 2021, https:// dictionary.cambridge.org/us/dictionary/english/mentor.
3. S. Chris Edmonds, "Culture Leadership Charge: Insights into a Healthy Work Culture," *The Purposeful Culture Group*, accessed March 23, 2021,

https://www.drivingresultsthroughculture.com/2019/04/15/culture
-leadership-charge-insights-into-a-healthy-work-culture/.

CHAPTER 11

1. Lexico, "Emotional Intelligence," accessed March 23, 2021, https://www
   .lexico.com/en/definition/emotional_intelligence.
2. Daniel Goleman, *Emotional Intelligence: Why It Can Matter More
   Than IQ*, Amazon, accessed March 23, 2021, https://www.amazon.com
   /Emotional-Intelligence-10th-Anniversary-Matter/dp/055380491X/.

CHAPTER 13

1. Marika Gerken, CNN Heroes Salutes, September 19, 2020, https://www
   .cnn.com/2020/09/19/us/farmers-finish-neighbors-harvest-trnd/index
   .html.
2. LeadershipIQ, "Why New Hires Fail (The Landmark "'Hiring For Attitude' Study Updated With New Data)," accessed March 23, 2021, https://
   www.leadershipiq.com/blogs/leadershipiq/35354241-why-new-hires-fail
   -emotional-intelligence-vs-skills.
3. Erin Technologies, Inc., "Employee Referral Statistics You Need to Know
   for 2020 (Infographic)," accessed March 3, 2021, https://erinapp.com
   /recruitment/employee-referral-statistics-you-need-to-know-for-2020.
4. Karen Martic, "8 Most Important Employee Referral Statistics," *The
   HR Tech Weekly*, accessed March 23, 2021, https://hrtechweekly.com
   /2018/07/06/8-most-important-employee-referral-statistics/.

INDEX

ABOUT THE AUTHORS

S. Chris Edmonds

S. Chris Edmonds is the founder and CEO of The Purposeful Culture Group. Chris and his colleagues help executives create and sustain purposeful, positive, productive work cultures.

After a fifteen-year career leading and managing teams, Chris began his consulting company in 1990. He also served as an author and senior consultant with The Ken Blanchard Companies from 1995-2019.

Over the years, Chris has helped senior leaders in industries including automotive, financial services, government, hospitality, insurance, manufacturing, nonprofit, retail, sales, pharmaceutical, software, and technology.

Chris has helped clients consistently boost employee engagement by 40 percent, customer service by 40 percent, and results and profits by 35 percent, all within twenty-four months of starting their culture refinement initiatives.

Chris is the author or coauthor of eight books, including the book you hold in your hands and two Amazon best-sellers—*The Culture Engine* and *Leading at a Higher Level* with Ken Blanchard.

Chris has delivered more than five thousand presentations to rave reviews from audiences as large as five thousand.

Chris is one of *Inc.* magazine's "Top 100 Leadership Speakers," Recruiter.com's "10 Corporate Culture Experts You Need to Pay Attention To," and Richtopia's "Top 200 Influential Authors."

He received his master's degree from the University of San Francisco in Human Resource and Organizational Development. He is a professional member of the National Speakers Association.

Chris is an accomplished musician and performer. He provides guitar, banjo, mandolin, and vocals for Graystone Records' recording artist the Brian Raine band. Two singles from the band's 2009 debut album made the Billboard country charts.

Mark S. Babbitt

Mark Babbitt is the president and a senior partner at WorqIQ, where Workplace Intelligence (WQ) comes front and center as today's business leaders attempt to understand and improve their leadership style and company culture. Mark has worked with companies from IBM to faith-based nonprofits and Puget Sound Energy to Silicon Valley start-ups.

Mark also serves as CEO and Founder of YouTern, a community that enables young talent to become highly employable by connecting them to high-impact internships, mentors, and contemporary career advice. Mashable calls YouTern a "Top 5 Online Community for Starting Your Career," and Forbes has repeatedly named YouTern a "Top Website for Your Career."

Mark is coauthor of the Amazon best-seller *A World Gone Social: How Companies Must Adapt to Survive.* You can also find his written work in *Harvard Business Review, Entrepreneur, Forbes,* and many other publications. In addition, the *Wall Street Journal, The Economist, Investors' Business Daily, Men's Journal,* and other top-tier outlets have featured Mark's thought leadership.

Mark has been named a Top 100 leadership speaker by *Inc.* magazine. Tens of thousands of followers benefit from Mark's guidance on the future of work, company culture, workplace, leadership, career, and social intelligence on Twitter as @MarkSBabbitt.

A recovering engineer from Silicon Valley, Mark has also served as a law enforcement officer, a sales and marketing executive, and has been a highly respected youth sports coach for over thirty years.

Mark is a father of five, a grandfather of five more, and dog-dad to two lab-mutts. He and the woman who tolerates him (barely) make Monument, Colorado, their home.